Eternity's Sunrise

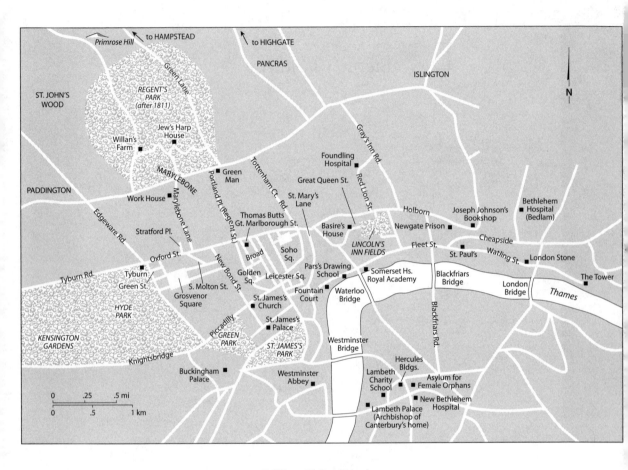

to HAMPSTEAD

Primrose Hill

to HIGHGATE

PANCRAS

ISLINGTON

N

ST. JOHN'S WOOD

REGENT'S PARK (after 1811)

Green Lane

Jew's Harp House

Willan's Farm

MARYLEBONE

Foundling Hospital

Gray's Inn Rd.

PADDINGTON

Work House

Green Man

Portland Pl. (Regent St.)

Marylebone Lane

Tottenham Ct. Rd.

Great Queen St.

Red Lion St.

St. Mary's Lane

Holborn

Joseph Johnson's Bookshop

Bethlehem Hospital (Bedlam)

Edgeware Rd.

Stratford Pl.

Thomas Butts
Gt. Marlborough St.

Basire's House

Newgate Prison

Oxford St.

Broad

Soho Sq.

LINCOLN'S INN FIELDS

Fleet St.

Cheapside

Watling St.

Tyburn Rd.

Tyburn

Green St.

New Bond St.

Golden Sq.

Leicester Sq.

Pars's Drawing School

St. Paul's

London Stone

S. Molton St.

Fountain Court

Somerset Hs. Royal Academy

Blackfriars Bridge

The Tower

HYDE PARK

Grosvenor Square

St. James's Church

Waterloo Bridge

London Bridge

Thames

KENSINGTON GARDENS

Piccadilly

GREEN PARK

St. James's Palace

ST. JAMES'S PARK

Westminster Bridge

Blackfriars Rd.

Knightsbridge

Buckingham Palace

Westminster Abbey

Hercules Bldgs.

Lambeth Charity School

Asylum for Female Orphans

0   .25   .5 mi

New Bethlehem Hospital

0   .5   1 km

Lambeth Palace (Archbishop of Canterbury's home)

William Blake's London

ETERNITY'S SUNRISE

The Imaginative World of William Blake

❖ ❖ ❖

Leo Damrosch

Yale UNIVERSITY PRESS
New Haven & London

Published with assistance from the Annie Burr Lewis Fund and
the Louis Stern Memorial Fund. The acquisition of images was supported
in part by a grant from the Paul Mellon Centre for Studies in British Art.

Yale University Press books may be purchased in quantity for educational, business,
or promotional use. For information, please e-mail sales.press@yale.edu (US office)
or sales@yaleup.co.uk (UK office).

Designed by James J. Johnson.
Set in Dante type by Tseng Information Systems, Inc.
Printed in the United States of America.

Library of Congress Control Number: 2015942776
ISBN 978-0-300-20067-6

A catalogue record for this book is available from the British Library.

This paper meets the requirements of ANSI/NISO Z39.48–1992
(Permanence of Paper).

10 9 8 7 6 5 4 3 2 1

To

Harold Bloom *and* E. D. Hirsch

and in memory of

Charles Ryskamp

three great teachers who first inspired my love of Blake

CONTENTS

ACKNOWLEDGMENTS

I want to express my gratitude to my agent, Tina Bennett, for her unfailing loyalty over many years; to Jennifer Banks, my marvelously encouraging and intuitive editor; to Laura Jones Dooley, who ably guided the manuscript through all the stages of production; and above all to my wife, Joyce Van Dyke, whose imaginative yet rigorous critique of successive drafts improved this book immeasurably.

Eternity's Sunrise

INTRODUCTION

WILLIAM BLAKE was a creative genius, one of the most original artists and poets who ever lived. Some of his works are widely known: the image of a majestic creator tracing the orb of the sun with a pair of compasses; the hypnotically powerful lyric "Tyger tyger burning bright"; the poem known as *Jerusalem* that was later set to music and became a popular hymn. But many years had to pass after Blake's death before he had any reputation at all. His poems were virtually unknown in his lifetime, and even as a visual artist he was considered a minor figure, known mainly for engraving designs—usually by other artists—to illustrate books. These jobs dwindled as the years went by, and his contemporaries would have been incredulous if they could have known that one day he would be recognized as a major figure in not just one art but two, and that the greatest museums and libraries would treasure works that he sold for absurdly low prices when he could sell them at all. The disappointments of Blake's worldly career illustrate Schopenhauer's saying that talent hits a target no one else can hit, while genius hits a target no one else can see.[1]

Blake was not only a superb painter and poet, one of the very few equally distinguished in both arts, but a profound thinker as well. Trenchantly critical of received values, he was a counterculture prophet whose art still challenges us to think afresh about almost every aspect of experience—social, political, philosophical, religious, erotic, and aesthetic. As he developed his ideas, he evolved a complex personal mythology that incorporated elements of Christian belief and drew upon many other strands of symbolism as well. The resulting myth can seem daunting in its complexity, and Blake specialists, focusing on its more esoteric aspects, have naturally tended to talk mainly to one another. This book draws constantly on their insights but is intended for everyone who is attracted to Blake and would like to know more about his art and ideas. It is not just a book about Blake but a book *with* Blake, who urges us again and again to open our imaginations to "thunder of thought, and flames of fierce desire."[2]

It is important to recognize that Blake was a troubled spirit, subject to deep psychic stresses, with what we would now call paranoid and schizoid tendencies that were sometimes overwhelming. During his life he was often accused of madness, but the artist Samuel Palmer, who knew him well, remembered him as "one of the sanest, if not the most thoroughly sane man I have ever known." And a Baptist minister replied, when asked if he thought Blake was cracked, "Yes, but his is a crack that lets in the light."[3]

Throughout his life Blake was bitterly aware that he was an outsider, not just with respect to society as a whole, but even in his chosen profession of graphic art. It was from a wounding sense of alienation and dividedness that his great myth emerged, in response to what Algernon Charles Swinburne called "the incredible fever of spirit, under the sting and stress of which he thought and labored all his life through."[4] In some sense we are all outsiders, and his imaginative words and pictures speak to us with undiminished power.

Although Blake is never pious or doctrinal, his thinking is religious in the sense that it addresses the fundamental dilemmas of human existence—our place in the universe, our dread of mortality, our yearning for some ultimate source of meaning. His goal, he said, was to "rouse the faculties to act," and he hoped that we would use his images and symbols to provoke a spiritual breakthrough. "If the spectator could enter into these images in his imagination, approaching them on the fiery chariot of his contemplative thought; if he could enter into Noah's rainbow or into his bosom, or could make a friend and companion of one of these images of wonder which always entreats him to leave mortal things, as he must know; then would he arise from his grave, then would he meet the Lord in the air, and then he would be happy."[5] The aspiration is both ambitious and touching: to change our lives and to make us happy. But it is a poignant fact that Blake's most powerful writing, as the years went by, was haunted by intractable barriers to happiness.

A little poem that Blake never published, entitled *Eternity,* condenses an important part of his message into four eloquent lines:

> He who binds to himself a joy
> Does the wingèd life destroy,
> But he who kisses the joy as it flies
> Lives in Eternity's sunrise.[6]

Blake believed that we live in the midst of Eternity right here and now and that if we could open our consciousness to the fullness of being, it would be like experiencing a sunrise that never ends. That would not be a mystical escape *from* reality — he was never a mystic in that sense — but a fuller and deeper engagement *with* reality. Yet he also knew how hard it is to relinquish the self-centered possessiveness that kills joy instead of kissing it, and much of his work focuses on that struggle.

This book has a strongly biographical focus, but it is not a systematic biography. Two excellent ones already exist, by Peter Ackroyd and G. E. Bentley, each with its own strengths, and in any case Blake's life was relatively uneventful.[7] Nor is it a comprehensive guide to Blake's work. Rather, it is an invitation to understanding and enjoyment. Its goal is to help nonspecialists appreciate Blake's profoundly original vision and to open "the doors of perception" to the symbols in which he conveyed it. In the words of Plotinus, one of his favorite philosophers, "There are parts of what it most concerns you to know which I cannot describe to you; you must come with me and see for yourselves. The vision is for him who will see it."[8]

A Note on Images

Throughout his life Blake made pictures and paintings that stand alone, with no text at all. Sometimes these illustrated other people's work, though he tended to insinuate implications of his own, and sometimes they were original works that he hoped to sell. One commentator rightly says that all of his pictures are "riddled with ideas" and need to be "read" just as much as his texts do.[9]

In addition to these stand-alone pictures, Blake created an extraordinary series of books in which images and texts are embedded in each other, etched on copper plates and hand-colored after printing. Following a hint of his own, these are known as the illuminated books, on the analogy of medieval illuminated manuscripts. It is certainly not wrong to read poems like *The Tyger* in conventionally printed form, but they will always be richer and more thought-provoking in the format Blake intended.

The publisher of this book has permitted a generous representation of Blake's visual art, but if it were not prohibitively expensive, every plate of his illuminated books would deserve to be seen as he intended, in graphic format and in color. Fortunately, admirable facsimiles are readily available. The William Blake Trust, in collaboration with Princeton University Press, has issued six splendid volumes that reproduce copies of all of the illuminated books, together with excellent commentaries. And multiple copies of most of the books may be seen online at the superb Blake Archive website, blakearchive.org. This resource is maintained to the highest scholarly standard and at the same time is accessible and welcoming to everyone who loves Blake.

Thanks to this archive, we are able to do something that Blake himself never could. Unless he borrowed back copies of his works from friends and patrons with whom he remained in touch, there was no way he could ponder choices he had made long before: for example, looking at a 1789 printing of *Songs of Innocence* before coloring a new version in 1818. But with the archive, it is a simple matter to use a "compare" feature to see multiple versions of a given plate. As for the dates of the various copies, those have been convincingly established by one of the archive editors, Joseph Viscomi, in his indispensable *Blake and the Idea of the Book*.[10]

No matter how scrupulously prepared, even the best reproductions cannot capture the full effect of the originals, with their nuances of coloring, thickness and texture of paper, and width of margins. In early copies of the illuminated books, Blake (sometimes assisted by his wife, Catherine) used pale watercolor washes. These have a delicate glow, and as the printmaker and scholar Michael Phillips observes, "A transparent pigment on white paper will assume its hue more from the color of the light transmitted *through* it, reflecting off the white paper and back to the eye, than from the light reflected *off* of it."[11]

Conversely, Blake's later works were richly colored with dense, opaque paint, with a view to selling them as expensive art objects. These can sometimes appear garish in reproduction, while certain effects, such as the use of gold leaf highlights, don't come through at all. The Blake Archive editors have given scrupulous attention to color correction, but in website reproduction there is another problem: backlit images on a computer monitor glow like stained glass windows. For all we know Blake might have loved that effect, but it is very different from the original. Tristanne Connolly compares looking at a reproduction to reading a translation — "like kissing through a handkerchief."[12]

A Note on Texts

Blake's spelling and punctuation were eccentric. For the purposes of this book, nothing is gained by preserving "recieve" and "opressors" and "rabbet" (for "rabbit"), though some spellings, such as "tyger," have become too familiar to alter. Likewise, Blake's extensive use of capital letters is generally not followed here, except in instances like "Man" and "Eternity" where the context seems to call for capitalization.

Punctuation is also a problem. David Erdman, whose edition has been standard for many years and includes valuable commentary by Harold Bloom, sought to reproduce every idiosyncratic mark in the originals, although the result often gets in the way of understanding the meaning. Commentators used to make much of the supposed significance of periods where commas might be expected, but careful study of multiple copies shows that often the difference was nothing more than an accidental result of the printing process, in which a comma could easily lose its tail. Surely the editor is right who concludes that Blake "was relatively indifferent about punctuation."[13]

So I have not hesitated to alter punctuation in places where it clearly confuses the sense, often adding it in Blake's headlong prose, and I have also eliminated his customary ampersands in place of "and." It is possible that he preferred them simply to save space in a congested line, and they do create unnecessary oddity in such expressions as "every pot & vessel & garment & utensil." Occasionally, in fact, he did write out "and." Also, he seldom used quotation marks, and arguably he sometimes wanted different voices to merge into each other, but I have added them when it seems clear who is speaking. In this I generally follow G. E. Bentley's choices in his edition of *William Blake's Writings*.[14]

References to the illuminated books are by plate and line number, followed by page numbers in the Erdman edition, identified by the letter "E."[15] Since Blake often reshuffled the sequence of plates from one copy of a work to the next, plate numbers will sometimes be different in an edition based on a different copy. And because the Erdman edition is uncompromisingly faithful to the original format, readers who want a more user-friendly text may prefer those of Alicia Ostriker and W. H. Stevenson, both of which have very helpful annotation.[16] They do not, however, include Blake's letters and other prose.

1. THE WORKING ARTIST

Youth

WILLIAM BLAKE was born in London on November 28, 1757. His father, James, was a hosier or haberdasher, selling gloves and stockings, and the family lived above the shop at 28 Broad Street, just south of Oxford Street. Catherine, his mother, had previously been married to a haberdasher named Thomas Armitage, who died in 1751, leaving her a young widow of twenty-eight. The following year she married James Blake, a year younger than herself. As a haberdasher, he was well suited to merging his business with hers, and may indeed have been a friend of her late husband.

The house, at the corner of Broad and Marshall Streets, was joined to its neighbors on the other two sides. Each of the four floors had three large windows (one window in each row on the Marshall Street side was bricked up to avoid an onerous window tax), and the shop occupied the ground floor. That building no longer exists, nor do most of William's other residences over the years.[1]

The Blakes' first child was named James after his father, and in due course he would take over the shop. William was born four years later, and John two years after that. William could never stand John, whom he once referred to as "the evil one" and who seems to have died as a soldier abroad. The youngest brother was Robert, four and a half years younger than William, who became his closest friend but died of tuberculosis at the age of nineteen. Last of all came Catherine, named for their mother. Little is known of William's siblings, but apart from John he seems to have been on good terms with them throughout his life.[2]

Alexander Gilchrist, who wrote an excellent biography thirty-six years after Blake's death, heard from surviving friends that he hardly ever talked about his parents. In his poems, with the exception of *Songs of Innocence,* parents tend to be possessive or even harsh. Nevertheless, one friend recalled that he described his father as "lenient and affectionate, always more ready to encourage than to chide." He also said that because he "despised restraints and rules," his parents thought it best not to send him to school, where beatings were a regular practice. It is quite possible, though, that his siblings didn't go to school either, since the children of tradesmen were often taught to read and write at home.[3]

Blake never regretted his lack of formal education:

> Thank God I never was sent to school
> To be flogged into following the style of a fool.

But he was always a voracious reader. A dozen or so of his books have survived, and their margins are crammed with annotations that show him pondering deeply and often arguing back. As has been well said, he was unschooled but not unlearned.[4]

Some lines of verse in a letter written when Blake was forty-three suggest the wide range of his interests:

> Now my lot in the heavens is this: Milton loved me in childhood and
> showed me his face,
> Ezra came with Isaiah the Prophet, but Shakespeare in riper years gave
> me his hand;
> Paracelsus and Behmen appeared to me . . . .[5]

Blake may be speaking metaphorically when he says that these inspiring figures showed their faces and appeared to him, or he may be recalling actual visions of a kind to be described shortly. "Ezra" is the prophet Esdras, in the Apocrypha. Paracelsus was a Swiss alchemist and occultist, and Jacob Boehme a German mystic; their ideas interested Blake greatly. Self-taught and fiercely independent, he saw the culture of his day from an outsider's perspective, far more so than the other poets we remember as Romantics, who were educated more conventionally. Wordsworth, Coleridge, and Byron all went to Cambridge; Shelley was at Oxford until expelled for political radicalism; and Keats, though never at a university, went to an excellent school and then studied medicine.

The reference to "my lot in the heavens" reflects Blake's lifelong engagement with religious ideas, albeit in a highly oppositional way. His family were probably Dissenters, Protestants but not members of the established Church of England; there is some evidence, however, that Catherine Blake may have been a Moravian. That sect emphasized interior spirituality but regarded itself as in communion with the Church of England, in which William was indeed baptized (at Saint James's, Westminster, on December 11).[6]

As a child, young William alarmed his parents by reporting that he experienced visions. In later life he told his friends that he had seen angels among the haymakers in the fields, which still lay in easy walking distance from Broad Street. When he got home and reported the vision, he barely escaped a thrashing for telling a lie. More disturbingly, his wife once remarked, "You know, dear, the first time you saw God was when you were four years old and he put his head to the window and set you ascreaming."[7] The anecdote surely suggests remarkable anxiety in a small boy.

Since William showed artistic talent from an early age, his parents decided to have him trained as an artist, and were remarkably generous in paying for an extensive collection of prints that he began to acquire. For a boy without much money, however, there was no thought of aiming at a prestigious career in the fine arts. At ten he entered a vocational school in the Strand run by Henry Pars, whose purpose was to produce commercial artists. The school had been founded as part of a campaign to improve British textiles, ceramics, and other luxury goods, and the boys were trained to be "masters of the several arts and manufactures, in which elegance of taste and correctness of drawing are required."[8]

Apprentice Engraver

The next step was a formal apprenticeship. At the customary age of thirteen Blake was apprenticed to an engraver named James Basire in Great Queen Street near Covent Garden, less than a mile from home. The apprenticeship lasted for the usual seven years, during which he lived in Basire's house, usually with one or more other boys. The youths put in thirteen-hour days for a work week of seventy-eight hours, with only Sunday off, and that was usual too.

Basire's specialty was a humble genre, producing detailed depictions of "antiquities," medieval churches and monuments. As it turned out, the work appealed to Blake. One of his tasks, which he loved, was to spend long days in Westminster Abbey making accurate drawings of the tombs and monuments there. That experience inspired him with a love of Gothic style that would continue throughout his life. According to one report, he experienced a memorable vision at the abbey: "The aisles and galleries of the old building (or sanctuary) suddenly filled with a great procession of monks and priests, choristers and censer-bearers, and his entranced ear heard the chant of plainsong and chorale, while the vaulted roof trembled to the sound of organ music."[9]

Engraving was extremely demanding work, requiring great control of the sharp tools with which lines were incised into copper plates. Robert Essick, an experienced printmaker as well as Blake expert, says that since the graver has to be pushed through the metal "like a plow," extreme care must be taken to control the width of the groove. "Engraving is the most exacting of all the graphic techniques, requiring considerable physical strength in anyone who works at it for hours on end. But this energy must always be controlled by a well-disciplined hand, eye, and mind." When the plate was ready for printing, it would be heated over a brazier and dabbed with ink, after which it would be wiped so that ink remained only in the incised lines.[10]

The illustration reproduced here (figure 1), from an eighteenth-century French manual, shows the process in elegant detail. In the rectangles that are labeled Fig. 1 and Fig. 2, the design is transferred from a sheet of paper to the copper plate, which has previously been coated with varnish hardened over a flame. The reverse side of

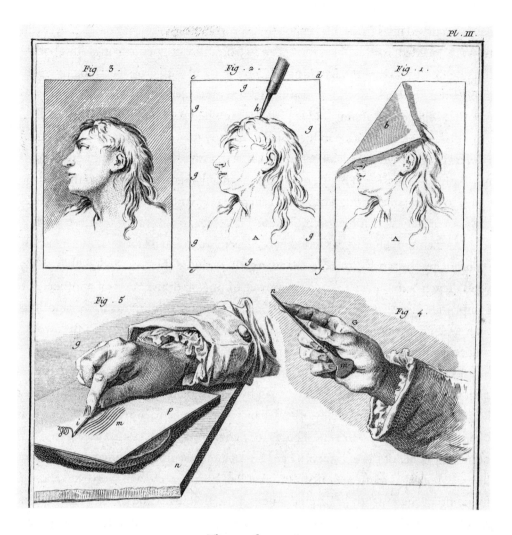

1. The art of engraving

❖ ❖ ❖

the paper has a layer of coloring that, as with carbon paper in later times, will dupli-
cate the image as it is traced or (if the design is to be discarded) pricked through with
a series of tiny dots. In Fig. 3 the design has been incised into the metal with a burin.
Fig. 4 shows the correct way to hold the burin, which in Fig. 5 is being pushed firmly
forward in the manner described by Essick. Since it would be extremely difficult to

engrave curved lines smoothly, the plate rests on a cushion so that the engraver can turn it as needed. As the burin moves away from him, copper shavings spiral off to the side. In this picture the hands have been rendered with cross-hatching to create a three-dimensional effect, and some lines are more deeply incised than others so that they will hold more ink and appear darker when printed.

Blake took great pride in his skill: "I defy any man to cut cleaner strokes than I do, or rougher when I please." But he also acknowledged that "engraving is eternal work. . . . I curse and bless engraving alternately because it takes so much time and is so intractable, though capable of such beauty and perfection." His eyeglasses still exist and show that he was moderately myopic, an advantage for close work.[11]

At the time, engravers were regarded as mere manual laborers, mechanically reproducing the work of others. Blake greatly resented the "pretended philosophy which teaches that execution is the power of one, and invention of another." He complained also that "to engrave after another painter is infinitely more laborious than to engrave one's own inventions."[12] It was his own original works that would preoccupy him all his life.

For a brief time after the apprenticeship ended, Blake was a student at the distinguished Royal Academy, presided over by Sir Joshua Reynolds. He seems to have left after less than a year, deeply offended by what seemed to him the condescension of Sir Joshua and the teachers. There, too, engravers were treated as inferior. Up until the middle of the eighteenth century, painters, sculptors, and architects were likewise regarded as mere craftsmen. That had begun to change, however, and the founding of the academy reflected a new sense that artists deserved higher social standing. But when engravers petitioned to be granted equal status, they were told that the "relative preeminence of the arts has ever been estimated accordingly as they more or less abound in those intellectual qualities of invention and composition, which painting, sculpture and architecture so eminently possess, but of which engraving is wholly devoid." A century would pass before engravers were finally given full privileges by the Royal Academy.[13]

During this period Blake formed a number of close friendships with other artists that would prove to be enduring. These included George Cumberland, an insurance clerk, and John Flaxman, whom Blake would later call his "dearest friend."

2. An artists' picnic: Blake and friends

Thomas Stothard, two years older, was beginning a highly successful career as a designer of book illustrations and when possible would get Blake commissions to engrave them. An etching by Stothard (figure 2) commemorates a remarkable adventure when he, Blake, and a third friend whose identity is uncertain rented a small boat for a sketching expedition on the River Medway southeast of London. This happened in 1780, at the height of Britain's war with the American colonies and France, and the young artists were oblivious enough to pull up on shore across from the immense naval arsenal at Chatham, where forty gigantic men-of-war were being refitted. The three were promptly arrested under suspicion of spying for France, and detained under arrest while their captors sent to the Royal Academy to verify that they were who they claimed to be. While they waited, Stothard's daughter-in-law heard, "their provisions were brought on shore, and a tent formed for them of their sails, suspended over the boat hook and oars, placed as uprights in the ground." Bentley comments that for Blake "the incident must have confirmed what he had always suspected about the arbitrariness of civil and military power."[14]

The Engraver's Work

By the time his apprenticeship ended, Blake was expert in the complex techniques of cross-hatching, dots, and stippling that were used to create the illusion of three-dimensional depth. He continued to employ these skills whenever a publisher commissioned illustrations; a good example is his portrait of Democritus after a painting by Rubens (figure 3), done when he was thirty-two. As Essick observes, the carefully incised patterns "have no similarity to a real face, and only when we 'read' them properly do they give the illusion of a face." Sufficiently magnified they would cease to do even that, just as a computer image becomes a mosaic of pixels.[15]

Blake had virtually no opportunity to see actual paintings by the great masters. The National Gallery did not yet exist, and most of the masterpieces in England were hidden away in private mansions. At one point a would-be patron undertook to raise funds to send him to Italy, but that project fell through. So his impression of Rubens, or for that matter of Michelangelo, who would become his artistic hero, was based entirely on black-and-white prints, a totally different medium from the originals.

The original Rubens painting of Democritus, now in the Prado in Madrid, shows a relaxed philosopher with a genial smile; in ancient times he was known as the laughing philosopher. Blake's engraving is very different, since it was made to illustrate a book about physiognomy by Johann Caspar Lavater, a Swiss pastor whose aphorisms he knew and annotated. The intention of that pseudoscience was to deduce character from the shape of the head and face. In Lavater's opinion Democritus must have been a sarcastic mocker: "Mockery contracts the eyes, and

Rubens delin.   Blake sculp.

DEMOCRITUS.

3. Democritus

gathers the skin round the eye into wrinkles. . . . Mockery puffs up the cheeks, and gives them a globular form. . . . No one can consider the mouth of our Democritus as beautiful; it is observable that its deformity is chiefly owing to a sneering humour, and that it would be still ugly though it were not opened so wide."[16] Blake undoubtedly remembered this analysis when he mentioned Democritus in his notebook lyric *Mock on Mock on Voltaire Rousseau,* to be considered later on.

When he did commercial jobs, Blake was willing to work in a wide variety of styles, many of which don't look "Blakean" in the least.[17] At least four hundred plates by him are known, and many more may exist that have not been identified. But his graphic style was increasingly regarded as dry and old-fashioned, much as his master Basire's had been, which explains why he got fewer and fewer commissions.

One of them, though, was widely noticed: a 1797 illustrated edition of *Night Thoughts on Life, Death, and Immortality,* originally published in installments in the 1740s by the clergyman Edward Young. Young was one of a number of sententious blank-verse poets who have been described as the larger eighteenth-century ruminants. He himself thought of imagination as escapist fantasy: "In the fairyland of Fancy, Genius may wander wild; there it has a creative power, and may reign arbitrarily over its own empire of chimeras."[18] For Blake they weren't chimeras, they were images of truth.

If the project had been carried through as originally planned, it would have been massive and lucrative. Blake made no fewer than 537 watercolor designs in preparation for the engravings. For these he was paid a total of £21, at the extremely modest rate of 9½ pence apiece.[19] The finished engravings would have provided the real payoff, but the first volume didn't sell well and there were no others to follow. So only 43 engravings were published, but these give fascinating glimpses of Blake's implicit criticism of Young's conventional moralizing. The one reproduced here (figure 4) illustrates the lines in the printed poem that are marked with an asterisk: "Where sense runs savage broke from reason's chain, / And sings false peace, till smothered by the pall."

Young took it for granted that it was very wrong to break loose from reason's chain and that indulgence in pleasure invites the "pall" of death. Blake believed just the opposite. In his picture "sense" is naked and lovely, arms joyously raised and

46

Or if we wish a fourth, it is a friend——
But friends how mortal! dangerous the desire.
    Take Phœbus to yourselves, ye basking bards!
Inebriate at fair fortune's fountain-head;
And reeling through the wilderness of joy;
* Where sense runs savage broke from reason's chain,
And sings false peace, till smother'd by the pall.
My fortune is unlike; unlike my song;
Unlike the DEITY my song invokes.
I to day's soft-eyed sister pay my court,
Endymion's rival! and her aid implore;
Now first implored in succour to the muse.
    Thou who didst lately borrow Cynthia's form,
And modestly forego thine own! O thou
Who didst thyself, at midnight hours, inspire!
Say, why not Cynthia patroness of song?
As thou her crescent, she thy character
Assumes; still more a goddess by the change.
    Are there demurring wits, who dare dispute
This revolution in the world inspired?
Ye train pierian! to the lunar sphere,
In silent hour address your ardent call
For aid immortal——less her brother's right.
She, with the spheres harmonious, nightly leads
The mazy dance, and hears their matchless strain;
A strain for gods, denied to mortal ear.
Transmit it heard, thou silver queen of heaven!
What title or what name endears thee most?
Cynthia! Cyllene! Phœbe!—or dost hear
With higher gust fair P——d of the skies?

London. Pub.d Jan.y 1. 1797. by R. Edwards, 142 New Bond St.

4. *Sense Runs Wild*

long tresses tossing freely. A small fetter on her right ankle—hardly more than an ankle bracelet—is the sole trace of Young's chain, and she is walking easily toward the viewer over gently rolling sunlit hills, not running "savage." What she doesn't know is that a gigantic figure, hands clenched with effort, is about to drop his enormous black cloak over her, smothering her in darkness. Most viewers would have assumed that this looming threat was a personification of death, but more likely Blake thought of it as reason, from whom sense has all too briefly escaped.[20]

In the original watercolor the woman's vaginal cleft is discreetly but clearly visible. No doubt the publisher required Blake to conceal it. Even so, this and his other *Night Thoughts* designs caused something of a scandal. "The serious and the pious," a friend commented, "were not prepared to admit shapes trembling in nudity round the verses of the grave divine."[21]

Marriage and Four Portraits

In 1782 a major event in Blake's life occurred: he married Catherine Boucher, the daughter of a market gardener, whose surname was probably pronounced "Butcher." He was twenty-five and she was twenty, a servant and essentially illiterate, though he later taught her to read and write. An early biographer heard that he was taken with "the whiteness of her hand, the brightness of her eyes, and a slim and handsome shape, corresponding with his own notions of sylphs and naiads." Another said, "'A brunette' and 'very pretty' are terms I have picked up as conveying something regarding her appearance in more youthful days. Blake himself would boast what a pretty wife he had."[22]

William was on the rebound when he met Catherine, and according to one account he told her "the lamentable story of Polly Wood, his implacable lass, upon which Catherine expressed her deep sympathy, it is supposed in such a tender and affectionate manner that it quite won him. He immediately said, with the suddenness peculiar to him, 'Do you pity me?' 'Yes indeed I do,' answered she. 'Then I love you,' said he again. Such was their courtship." The echo of *Othello* is curious—"She loved me for the dangers I had passed / And I loved her that she did pity them"— and episodes of jealousy would provoke serious tension over the years. But late in life, at any rate, they struck all who knew them as an exceptionally devoted couple. Catherine became a skilled collaborator in the printing process, as well as sustaining her husband during periods of depression, and Peter Ackroyd suggests convincingly that without her none of his greatest works would have appeared.[23]

The biographer Gilchrist gives a good sense of what Catherine's support entailed. "She would get up in the night, when he was under his very fierce inspirations, which were as if they would tear him asunder, while he was yielding himself to the muse, or whatever else it could be called, sketching and writing. And so terrible a task did this seem to be that she had to sit motionless and silent, only to stay him mentally, without moving hand or foot; this for hours, and night after night." Gilchrist also reports that Catherine learned to see visions of her own. "Not only was she wont to echo what he said, to talk as he talked on religion and other matters—this may be accounted for by the fact that he had educated her—but she too learned to have visions: to see processions of figures wending along the river, in broad daylight, and would give a start when they disappeared in the water."[24]

When Catherine was in her early forties, Blake made an appealing sketch of her (figure 5) on the reverse side of a printed text that partly shows through. Her eyes, with striking eyelashes, look downward—she seems to be drawing or painting—and curls of hair escape from her cap.

A number of portraits of William Blake also exist. The most impressive (figure 6) was the work of a rival engraver, and appeared as the frontispiece to an edition of another gloomy poem, *The Grave* by Robert Blair. It was included there because Blake had designed (but not engraved) the images, and was copied from a portrait in oils by Thomas Phillips that now hangs in the National Gallery, made when Blake was fifty.

Another portrait (figure 7), rediscovered in 1974, was at first thought to have been by Blake's friend John Linnell, but Linnell knew him only at the end of Blake's life, and his own style was much more naturalistic. This shows Blake in his mid-forties, and its present owner, Robert Essick, argues persuasively that it is a self-portrait, with the fixity of gaze characteristic of an artist studying himself in a mirror. Bentley observes that it resembles miniatures Blake was painting at the time and that many of the features correspond closely to the Phillips portrait: "the high-

5. Catherine Blake

collared coat with its odd lapels, the white stock, the domed forehead, piercing eyes, arched eyebrows, and hair receding from the peak."[25]

That the eyes are compelling is appropriate, for everyone who knew Blake was struck by their power. "His eye was the finest I ever saw," his young disciple Samuel Palmer told Gilchrist, "brilliant, but not roving, clear and intent, yet susceptible. It

6. William Blake, engraved after Thomas Phillips

❖ ❖ ❖

flashed with genius, or melted in tenderness; it could also be terrible. Cunning and falsehood quailed under it, but it was never busy with them. It pierced them, and turned away." Another close friend, Frederick Tatham, called Blake's eyes "most unusually large and glassy, with which he appeared to look into some other world."[26]

Another possible self-portrait is altogether uncanny (figure 8). Toward the

7. Probable self-portrait by Blake

8. The Man Who Taught Blake Painting

end of his life Blake began to draw "visionary heads" of historical characters for a painter, astrologer, and phrenologist named John Varley, who was convinced that Blake enjoyed direct contact with the spirit world. Linnell inscribed this picture "The Portrait of a Man who instructed Mr. Blake in Painting etc. in his Dreams." The unwavering gaze of the enormous eyes is filled with calm expectation, like that of a being from another universe, and the slight smile might make one think of a bodhisattva. As for the mysterious branching shape on the forehead, it has been variously identified as flames of inspiration, as the tree of knowledge, and as the bulges from which phrenologists claimed to deduce specific mental faculties. Many commentators have thought that this is indeed an idealized avatar of Blake himself, and Gilchrist's description of Blake's appearance can easily be applied to it: "There was great volume of brain in that square, massive head, that piled-up brow, very full and rounded at the temples, where, according to phrenologists, ideality or imagination resides."[27]

Inventing a New Way of Etching

The process of etching, as opposed to engraving, was valued by printmakers because it was much simpler than the laborious incision of lines into metal. The copper plate would be coated with a layer of wax and the design drawn into it with a needle. Next, the plate was bathed in a weak solution of nitric acid, held in place by a wax dike around the edges. The acid would bite into the metal wherever the needle had cut into the wax, leaving unchanged the areas still protected by wax. The length of time during which the plate was bathed in acid would determine how deeply the lines were bitten.

It needs to be emphasized that in Blake's day engraving and etching were regarded not as mutually exclusive art forms but simply as practical techniques to be used in whatever way would facilitate reproduction. Often both were employed in a single image, engraved lines adding detail to an initial etching. Many works that are now described as etchings in fact contain a good deal of engraving, and many so-called engravings were almost entirely etched.[28] Blake often combined the two techniques, and used pen and ink as well to emphasize lines on individual printed copies.

In his early thirties, Blake adopted a method of etching that was the reverse of the normal process. He believed that it was his own invention—inspired, he said, by the spirit of his dead brother, Robert—and although researchers have located some predecessors, the process was certainly unfamiliar to London printmakers at the time. Instead of drawing lines into the wax-coated surface of the plate, Blake raised his outlines above the surface, in what is known as relief etching. He would draw the design directly onto the bare copper using a quill or brush dipped in an acid-resistant varnish. The plate would then be bathed in acid, which would eat away everything except the drawing, so that the design would stand out from the plate. This practice allowed a freedom of execution that was very like freehand drawing. "Painting is drawing on canvas," Blake said, "and engraving is drawing on copper." The resulting images, the scholar-printmaker Joseph Viscomi says, have the freshness of original compositions, "free of the visual distortion that characteristically occurs when one set of codes is translated into another."[29]

But if execution was freer in this respect, in another it was more demanding. In normal etching, ink is applied with a roller to the entire plate, which is then wiped clean. When paper is afterward forced down on the plate in a press, it picks up the ink that remains in the etched grooves. In Blake's procedure, however, ink had to be dabbed very gently onto the raised lines with a leather printer's ball. Whenever ink got on parts of the plate where it wasn't wanted, as would often happen, it had to be carefully wiped off.

Ordinary illustrated books, such as *Night Thoughts,* combined conventionally printed typeface with a pictorial border. Blake's novel practice allowed him to combine words and images in a single design. When he inscribed his text, the lettering of course needed to be written backwards, in order to appear correctly when printed. He learned to do that fluently; his friend Cumberland said that "he alone excels in that art."[30]

Relief etching gave Blake complete control of the entire process from start to finish, and that was one of the chief reasons he adopted it. In commercial publishing a series of individuals were involved in making each page of an illustrated book: the writer, the compositor who set the text in type, the designer of the images, the engraver who reproduced the designs on the plates, and finally the printer who would pass each page twice through the press, once for text (in raised type) and once for images (incised into the metal). For expensive editions—Audubon's are a familiar example—still another specialist would color the images. Blake acted as sole writer, designer, engraver, printer, and colorist.

At various times Blake insinuated sly references to the way he created his books. This is how he introduced the startling Proverbs of Hell in *The Marriage of Heaven and Hell:*

> When I came home, on the abyss of the five senses, where a flat sided steep frowns over the present world, I saw a mighty Devil folded in black clouds, hovering on the sides of the rock. With corroding fires he wrote the following sentence, now perceived by the minds of men and read by them on earth:
> How do you know but ev'ry bird that cuts the airy way
> Is an immense world of delight, closed by your senses five?

The "mighty Devil" is Blake himself, seeing his own reflection in the bath of acid on the plate. Corrosives, he adds, "in Hell are salutary and medicinal, melting apparent surfaces away, and displaying the infinite which was hid. If the doors of perception were cleansed, everything would appear to man as it is, infinite."[31] Long afterward, this passage would take on a new life in the mid-twentieth-century counterculture. Describing experiences with mescaline, Aldous Huxley entitled his book *The Doors of Perception,* and from either Huxley or Blake Jim Morrison got the name of the Doors.

Blake etched hundreds of copper plates during his life, sometimes on both sides since copper was expensive. These he kept for reprinting when new customers would appear, but after his death they were apparently melted down for reuse. One single fragment has survived. Now at the Library of Congress, it is the broken-off corner of a plate originally intended for the 1793 poem *America: A Prophecy* (figure 9). After deciding for some unknown reason not to use this plate (the gouges at the right are not thought to have been made by him), Blake cut it up and gave this piece to the son of a friend, who kept it in a cabinet, where it was eventually rediscovered in 1937. To save expense the plates were thin and therefore had to be etched very shallowly. On this one he stopped the acid from biting when it reached a depth of .005 inches (0.12 mm)—less than the thickness of a postcard.[32]

As is apparent in a print made from the now-lost complete plate (figure 10), Blake's script is more like calligraphy than like conventional typeface. He himself referred to "illuminating the manuscript," by analogy with medieval manuscripts he had seen, and he would have appreciated E. H. Gombrich's comment, "The Egyptians had largely drawn what they *knew* to exist, the Greeks what they *saw*; in the Middle Ages the artist also learned to express in his picture what he *felt*."[33]

The huge word "PROPHECY" swirls with vitality, vines and tendrils sprouting from the letters. In many of Blake's plates, what would otherwise be blank spaces in the text swarm with living forms — tiny people, birds in flight, leafy growths. Their practical function may have been to ensure that the lines to be printed were not spaced too far apart, but they also serve as a constant reminder of the difference between Blake's handmade lettering and an ordinary printed text.

The words italicized below are the ones that can still be seen on the fragment:

> The Guardian Prince of Albion *burns in his nightly tent;*
> Sullen fires across the Atlantic *glow to America's shore:*
> Piercing the souls of warlike men, *who rise in silent night,*
> Washington, Franklin, Paine & Warren, *Gates, Franklin, & Green;*
> Meet on the coast glowing with blood *from Albions fiery Prince.*

When Blake reengraved this plate he altered the fourth line slightly, so that in the final version it ends "Gates, Hancock & Green."[34]

How Blake Made His Prints

Though never well to do, Blake owned a press, which he and another former apprentice, James Parker, had acquired when they briefly managed a print shop together. When they parted ways, amicably it seems, Parker kept the shop and its stock of prints, and Blake kept the press. Whenever he and Catherine moved, which they did several times, the press went with them. That was no simple matter since it stood five feet high and weighed seven hundred pounds. It could be disassembled for transport, but only with the help of four strong men.[35]

This impressive device (figure 11) was called a rolling press, to distinguish it

9. Fragment of etched plate by Blake

from the kind in which pressure is applied from above by a screw mechanism. Considerable strength was needed to turn the big "star wheel" that the printer is grasping with both hands, pushing hard with his foot as well. The inked plate lies face up on the flat bed *R*, with a dampened sheet of paper on top of it, protected by thin layers of cloth. After the upper wooden roller (*I*) has been lowered so as to apply

10. *America: A Prophecy,* copy E, plate 3

moderate pressure, the bed is moved smoothly along between rollers *I* and *H;* the star wheel that the printer is turning is connected to the upper roller, which is joined by cogwheels to the lower. Near the ceiling, previously printed sheets can be seen hanging up to dry.[36]

Like other artists, Blake preferred high-quality "Whatman paper," a consider-

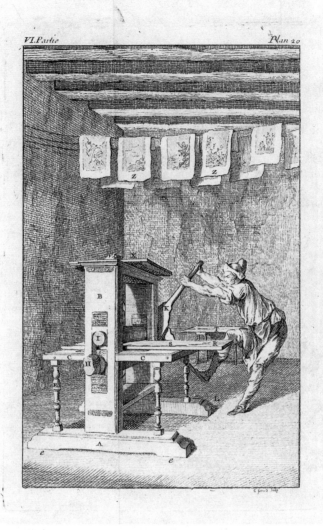

11. A rolling press

able expense, since it was handmade from cotton or rags. As is never apparent in reproductions of his plates, which show only the images themselves, the size of the printed sheets can vary greatly in the multiple copies that exist. In copy Z of the *Songs of Innocence and of Experience,* seven plates from which are reproduced in this book, the images average three inches by four in size, while the pages that contain them are nearly twice as large.

Once the sheets were dry, the final step was to apply watercolors and to touch up with ink any lines that had failed to print well. Frederick Tatham, who knew the Blakes well in later life, said that Catherine had "an excellent idea of colouring" and that she worked on the images "to a much greater extent than is usually credited." Like other artists at the time, the Blakes ground and mixed their watercolors from powder. Their preferred colors were Prussian blue, gamboge (from the French name for Cambodia—the color in Buddhist monks' saffron robes), yellow ocher, Indian red, various umbers, black, vermilion, rose madder, raw sienna, and alizarin crimson.[37]

From start to finish, this was extremely time-consuming work. Two or at most three sheets, progressively lighter in appearance, could be printed from a single inking. It would then be necessary to wipe the plate clean and ink it all over again. Michael Phillips, after much practical experimentation, estimates that it took three to four hours to print ten impressions and a full week to print ten complete copies of the eighteen-plate poem *America.* His conclusion has more than practical interest: "The length of time taken to build up an even and sufficiently dense layer of ink on the often tiny network of relief on the facsimile plates came as a genuine surprise [to me]; but it seems perfectly in accord with Blake's character and creative aspiration that the arduousness of the process was of little concern to him."[38]

Blake valued profoundly the uniqueness of each copy produced in this way. In conventional printmaking the goal was a completely standardized product. A few years after Blake's death, the efficiency expert Charles Babbage cited copper engraving as an example of perfect reproduction: "The impressions from the same copperplate have a similarity which no labour could produce by hand. The minutest traces are transferred to all the impressions, and no omission can arise from the inattention or unskillfulness of the operator."[39] That was exactly what Blake disliked.

To be sure, when Blake produced multiple copies of a work from a single printing session, they would resemble one another closely, but even then there was variation in coloring; copies from different periods of his career often vary drastically. And even when the copies are similar, they have a forceful energy very different from the pedantic accuracy of standardized illustration. A modern expert on prints observes, "The more complex and artificial the technique of a print, especially in the way its lines are laid, the more certain one may be that its maker was a craftsman translator and not a creative artist."[40]

Blake hoped that his unique process would enable him to produce his works cheaply, bypassing publishing-house middlemen in order to reach a wide audience. The opposite happened. Not only was the process laborious, but a reading public eager for conventional books would have been baffled by his, if they had ever seen them. Blake's books were apparently seldom on view in shops or advertised in catalogs. Nearly all the copies that were ever bought were probably sold by Blake himself from his house.

Between 1789 and 1795 Blake made approximately £40 from 125 copies of his works in illuminated printing, as contrasted with more than £500 from plates he engraved for commercial booksellers. Not counting the investment of his time and labor, he would have needed to sell at least a dozen copies of each book just to recover the cost of copper, paper, and other materials. If he did sometimes turn a profit, it was never much.[41]

Outline and Ideal Forms

Blake had a fierce belief in his individuality of vision that struck some people as pigheaded, and he soon developed the style that we recognize as Blakean. But for many years, as he later acknowledged, he found it hard to free himself from the influence of earlier painters, which was "like walking in another man's style, or speaking or looking in another man's style and manner, unappropriate and repugnant to your own individual character." Rubens, he said, "is a most outrageous demon, and by infusing the remembrances of his pictures, and style of execution, hinders all power of individual thought." The meaning is explained by Morris Eaves:

"Demons (in their New Testament form) are external forces that take up internal residence—a kind of mental parasite that causes the host to be unlike itself."[42]

This is not to say that Blake's style was totally unique. His close friend John Flaxman, who designed some Wedgwood catalog illustrations that Blake engraved, was a leading figure in what has been called romantic classicism, or alternatively the international linear style. This featured heroic figures drawn from classical sculptures, Greek vase paintings, and Michelangelo's frescoes; they were usually nude or wearing clinging draperies, and placed in timeless, nonillusionistic settings.[43]

Another friend, George Cumberland, published a book called *Thoughts on Outline* in which he said that outline should be like "a wire that surrounds the design," and should always be "fine, firm, flowing and faint." Blake would agree with all of that—except for "faint." He even asserted that clarity of outline had a moral dimension: "What is it that distinguishes honesty from knavery, but the hard and wiry line of rectitude and certainty in the actions and intentions? Leave out this line and you leave out life itself; all is chaos again."[44]

Blake disliked the engraving techniques that produced the illusion of three dimensions, which he regarded as a slavish imitation of nature instead of a vision of its inner meaning, and he despised equivalent effects even in painting. One writer described Correggio's style as "passing by almost imperceptible degrees through pellucid demi-tints and warm reflections into broad, deep, and transparent shade," producing "the greatest possible *effect* with the sweetest and softest *repose* imaginable." In Blake's opinion it was disastrous for an artist to succumb to Correggio's "soft and even tints without boundaries." A comment by Gombrich on Correggio is especially helpful here, relating his technique to "Leonardo's famous invention which the Italians call *sfumato*—the blurred outline and mellowed colours that allow one form to merge with another and always leave something to our imagination." Blake too wanted to inspire the viewer's imagination, but with distinct outlines, not sfumato.[45]

On Rubens, Blake was downright abusive: "To my eye Rubens's colouring is most contemptible. His shadows are of a filthy brown, somewhat of the colour of excrement; these are filled with tints and messes of yellow and red. His lights are all the colours of the rainbow, laid on indiscriminately and broken one into another."

The Venetian school was just as bad: "The Venetian and Flemish practice is broken lines, broken masses, and broken colours. Mr. Blake's [that is, his own] practice is unbroken lines, unbroken masses, and unbroken colours. Their art is to lose form, his art is to find form, and to keep it."[46]

Blake seldom used oils, preferring tempera or watercolor, and in either medium he usually emphasized outline (a set of superb color prints in the mid-1790s are a major exception). Most watercolorists at the time used washes to make tints blend into each other, as in the evocative landscapes that were immensely popular. Blake never painted landscapes, except as sketchy backgrounds for human figures, and his outlines were drawn carefully with ink before being filled in with colors.

It may be surprising to learn that Blake insisted on "minute particulars," since his artistic style is heavily stylized and nonnaturalistic; he writes in *Jerusalem* that the Divine Humanity "protects minute particulars, every one in their own identity." An important statement explains what that means:

> General knowledge is remote knowledge; it is in particulars that wisdom consists, and happiness too. Both in art and in life, general masses are as much art as a pasteboard man is human. Every man has eyes, nose, and mouth; this every idiot knows. But he who enters into and discriminates most minutely the manners and intentions, the characters in all their branches, is the alone wise or sensible man, and on this discrimination all art is founded. I entreat then that the spectator will attend to the hands and feet, to the lineaments of the countenances. They are all descriptive of character, and not a line is drawn without intention, and that most discriminate and particular. As poetry admits not a letter that is insignificant, so painting admits not a grain of sand or a blade of grass insignificant, much less an insignificant blur or mark.

Blake's art is iconic and symbolic, using conventional gestures and poses that were known as "pathos formulae," and everything in it is intended to convey meaning. Thus, paradoxically, what he means by "particulars" is not the external characteristics that make a specific individual unique, but universal truths that are somehow uniquely embodied in every individual.[47] It is fair to say that for most people, lacking Blake's Platonic belief in such truths, his art doesn't seem "particular" at all. To put it another way, his theoretical commitment to individuality leads him, paradoxically, to an artistic style based on highly conventional gestures.

For the commercially successful productions of his time, Blake coined a phrase, "the contemptible counter arts." He was fond of sarcastic puns like "the cunning sures and the aim at yours" — "connoisseurs" and "amateurs." When he read Sir Joshua Reynolds's much-admired *Discourses on Art* he filled the margins with furious commentary, starting with the title page: "This man was hired to depress art." And on the next page: "Having spent the vigour of my youth and genius under the oppression of Sir Joshua and his gang of cunning hired knaves, without employment and as much as could possibly be without bread, the reader must expect to read in all my remarks on these books nothing but indignation and resentment." An account of Reynolds's death provoked a deft dismissal in verse:

> When Sir Joshua Reynolds died
> All Nature was degraded;
> The King dropped a tear into the Queen's ear,
> And all his pictures faded.[48]

Blake says that "the reader" must be prepared for indignation because he does, in fact, expect these marginal notes to be read by others. He and his friends used to circulate books among themselves, sharing their written reactions.

Personal resentment aside, Blake's antagonism to Reynolds was at bottom a profound philosophical difference, and understanding what that meant is crucial to appreciating his personal vision. "The disposition to abstractions," Reynolds wrote, "to generalizing and classification, is the great glory of the human mind." Blake retorted, "To generalize is to be an idiot; to particularize is the alone distinction of merit. General knowledges are those knowledges that idiots possess."[49]

Actually Reynolds believed, just as Blake did, that artists should depict ideal forms, and he too disparaged the circumstantial details in Dutch paintings. But Reynolds accepted the empiricist view that the mind is a blank slate until inscribed with sense data. Ideal forms, therefore, are artificially constructed by collecting actual examples in order to determine what they all have in common. In Reynolds's words, the artist learns "to distinguish the accidental deficiencies, excrescences, and deformities of things from their general figures; he makes out an abstract idea of their forms more perfect than any one original."[50]

Blake too believed in ideal forms, but in an entirely different, Platonic way. "All forms," he wrote in his copy of Reynolds's *Discourses*, "are perfect in the poet's mind, but these are not abstracted nor compounded from nature, but are from imagination." And he had only contempt for the Lockean metaphor of the tabula rasa. "Reynolds thinks that man learns all that he knows. I say on the contrary that man brings all that he has or can have into the world with him. Man is born like a garden ready planted and sown; this world is too poor to produce one seed."[51]

At bottom Blake's disagreement with Reynolds was more theoretical than practical, and it might be argued that the two kinds of idealized images can look pretty much the same. But it was also true that Reynolds got rich painting portraits of the wealthy and powerful, which was something Blake would never have done even if he had had the chance. And in intellectual terms, he regarded as hopelessly muddled Reynolds's struggle to reconcile Platonic universals with the empiricist particulars. "The contradictions in Reynolds's *Discourses*," he wrote acerbically, "are strong presumptions that they are the work of several hands, but this is no proof that Reynolds did not write them. The man, either painter or philosopher, who learns or acquires all he knows from others must be full of contradictions."[52]

A Career of Disappointments

Since Blake increasingly refused to work in the styles that were then popular, his failure to reach an audience was probably inevitable. Mere illustration bored him profoundly; he called it the "sordid drudgery of facsimile representations of merely mortal and perishing substances." The kindly publisher Joseph Johnson, Gilchrist says, tried in vain to "help so unmarketable a talent." Blake expressed contempt for contemporaries who achieved success by pandering to fashion. Their attention was fixed, he commented wittily, "on the many, or rather on the money." Meanwhile his friends shook their heads at his improvidence. "On the subject of engravers," one of them wrote in 1805, "you will be glad to hear that Blake has his hands full of work for a considerable time to come, and if he will only condescend to give that attention to his worldly concerns which everyone does that prefers living to starving, he is now in a way to do well."[53] The reverse turned out to be true. After 1806 there were no commissions at all for a decade.

In 1809, in his early fifties and utterly frustrated by lack of recognition, Blake decided to mount a public exhibition of his own. Held in the family haberdashery shop, now owned by his brother James, it was modest in the extreme, and his highly idiosyncratic paintings must have made a startling contrast with the everyday inventory of stockings and gloves. As Gilchrist says, "An exhibition set going under such auspices was likely to remain a profound secret to the world at large." On view were not the works that we admire today but large paintings on public themes. Blake called them frescoes, in homage to Michelangelo and Raphael. Two were symbolic representations of Britain's naval hero Lord Nelson and prime minister William Pitt: *The Spiritual Form of Nelson Guiding Leviathan* and *The Spiritual Form of Pitt Guiding Behemoth*. These were covert attacks on Britain's counterrevolutionary war policies, but they were so obscure that the few viewers who showed up were very unlikely to have understood them. We know that Blake dreamed of creating actual public frescoes, and there is a poignant allusion to that ambition in Kingsley Amis's novel *The Alteration*. Amis's premise is that Martin Luther became pope instead of launching the Reformation. As a result, the Catholic Church still rules supreme, and its great English cathedral now displays "Blake's brilliant frescoes depicting St. Augustine's progress through England."[54]

There was one extended review of the exhibition, and it was crushing. The reviewer, Robert Hunt, coeditor of the *Examiner* with his brother Leigh, declared that it was his duty to speak out "when the ebullitions of a distempered brain are mistaken for the sallies of genius. . . . Such is the case with the productions and admirers of William Blake, an unfortunate lunatic, whose personal inoffensiveness secures him from confinement." As for the *Descriptive Catalogue* that Blake had prepared, it was "a farrago of nonsense, unintelligibleness, and egregious vanity, the wild effusions of a distempered brain."[55] The Hunt brothers would subsequently appear as villains in Blake's poems.

After the failure of his exhibition, Blake gave up hope of reaching a wide public. In one way that was a handicap, since it allowed him to produce work that was increasingly self-absorbed and obscure. But it was also immensely empowering. He was now free to follow his vision wherever it might lead, making a modest living by selling his productions to a small number of sympathetic collectors. And he resumed the mode of creation that he had virtually invented in the 1790s, to which we now turn: images and words combined in "illuminated books." "He had found the form of his life's work," one commentator says; "he had confronted and triumphantly solved one difficulty that most people never overcome — how to use their creative abilities to their fullest purpose."[56]

2. HOW SHOULD WE UNDERSTAND BLAKE'S SYMBOLS?

Visions

A T TIMES, especially in his later works, Blake may seem to be using a language that has only one speaker. But it is important to recognize that his imagination was fundamentally visual and that by learning to "read" the images that accompany his words, we can gain access to the heart of his vision.

And vision it literally was. Blake continued to see actual visions throughout his life and to draw inspiration from them. They were not hallucinations—he understood that other people couldn't see them when he did—but he definitely perceived them as vividly as if they were physically present. This phenomenon is known as eidetic vision, thought to be common in children and often persisting in artistic adults. It generally entails the mental revival of images that were once actually seen, and many images in Blake's art, though he thought of them as visionary, can indeed be traced to prints and paintings with which he was familiar. They share the aesthetic code of romantic classicism: feelings are personified in human form, either naked or clothed in diaphanous garments through which the body is clearly visible, and they stand out from a loosely sketched background that suggests timelessness. As in medieval art, which always interested Blake, these figures may differ greatly in size, reflecting their symbolic significance rather than any naturalistic scale.

Whatever the source of his visions, Blake was convinced that he was not recycling ordinary sense impressions—which is how eighteenth-century psychology understood "imagination"—but perceiving reality with exceptional fullness and depth. In the catalog for the failed exhibition of his paintings he declared, "A spirit and a vision are not, as the modern philosophy supposes, a cloudy vapour or a nothing. They are organized and minutely articulated beyond all that mortal and perishing nature can produce. He who does not imagine in stronger and better lineaments, and in stronger and better light than his perishing mortal eye can see, does not imagine at all." Elsewhere he said, borrowing a thought from Plato, "I question not my corporeal or vegetative eye any more than I would question a window concerning a sight; I look through it and not with it."[1]

A quarrel with a dissatisfied customer provoked from Blake a clear statement about visionary art. A very conventional clergyman named John Trusler, author of a work entitled *The Way to Be Rich and Respectable,* commissioned a drawing entitled *Malevolence,* which if satisfactory would be followed by *Benevolence, Pride,* and *Humility.* Trusler seems to have furnished very specific directions, and when Blake sent him the picture he said that he had tried his best to show "a father taking leave of his wife and child, [who] is watched by two fiends incarnate, with intention that when his back is turned they will murder the mother and her infant." In the end, however, he had felt "compelled by my Genius or Angel to follow where he led." Trusler replied indignantly, "Your fancy, from what I have seen of it . . . seems to be in the other world or the world of spirits, which accords not with my intentions, which whilst living in this world, wish to follow the nature of it." Blake retorted, "I know that this world is a world of imagination and vision. I see everything I paint in this world, but everybody does not see alike. To the eyes of a miser, a guinea is more beautiful than the sun, and a bag worn with the use of money has more beautiful proportions than a vine filled with grapes. The tree which moves some to tears of joy is in the eyes of others only a green thing that stands in the way."[2]

Personification

Before we explore the symbolic images in Blake's own work, it will be helpful to look at some illustrations he made for poems by other writers (he never

illustrated novels). It was his custom to give visual embodiment to metaphors—
Yeats called him "a literal realist of the imagination"—and that was common among
artists at the time, following the practice of eighteenth-century poets to personify
abstract ideas.[3] But far more than other artists, Blake added conceptions of his own
in a kind of dialogue with the text, or even a critique of it. At times his visual images
differ so strikingly from their verbal sources that we need to go to his own symbolic
mythology in order to understand them. He considered it entirely appropriate to
import his personal symbols in this way, for he saw them as reflecting the ultimate
reality that we all inhabit.

A relatively simple example of personification is a picture illustrating a passage
in Thomas Gray's *Ode on a Distant Prospect of Eton College* (figure 12), one of a set of
watercolors that Blake made for a friend in 1797–98. Pasting texts from a standard
edition of Gray's poems onto the middle of each page, he surrounded them with
images. In this poem Gray imagines that he is looking down from Windsor Castle
at the famous school from which he had graduated, yearning for a lost paradise of
"careless childhood." The Thames flows between Eton and Windsor, and Gray asks
the river to describe the schoolboys of the present day:

> Say, Father Thames, for thou hast seen
> Full many a sprightly race
> Disporting on thy margent green
> The paths of pleasure trace,
> Who foremost now delight to cleave
> With pliant arm thy glassy wave?
> The captive linnet which enthrall?
> What idle progeny succeed
> To chase the rolling circle's speed,
> Or urge the flying ball?[4]

Samuel Johnson, who detested poetic personification, commented sternly, "His sup-
plication to Father Thames, to tell him who drives the hoop or tosses the ball, is
useless and puerile. Father Thames has no better means of knowing than himself."
But for Blake personification was no mere rhetorical device; it expressed his belief
that nature is fundamentally human. That is to say, we inhabit a universe that is per-

56 ODE ON A DISTANT PROSPECT

Ah happy hills! ah pleasing shade!
Ah fields belov'd in vain!
Where once my careless childhood stray'd,
A stranger yet to pain!
I feel, the gales that from ye blow,
A momentary bliss bestow,
As waving fresh their gladsome wing,
My weary soul they seem to sooth,
And, redolent of joy and youth,
To breathe a second spring.

Say, Father THAMES, for thou hast seen
Full many a sprightly race
Disporting on thy margent green
The paths of pleasure trace;
Who foremost now delight to cleave,
With pliant arms, thy glassy wave?

The

12. Father Thames

vaded by spirit, altogether different from the soulless machine postulated by empiricist science and by materialist philosophy. Since our imaginations are human, we find human meaning and value in the world. And it is thus that nature can move us to tears — or to intuitions that are even deeper, as Wordsworth said in a poem that Blake admired, *Ode: Intimations of Immortality:*

> Thanks to the human heart by which we live,
> Thanks to its tenderness, its joys, and fears,
> To me the meanest flower that blows can give
> Thoughts that do often lie too deep for tears.[5]

River gods were conventionally depicted with urns from which their waters flow, and Blake's Father Thames leans on just such an urn. But nothing in Gray's poem suggests that this god should be a massive giant, dwarfing the youths at play. In part, perhaps, his size reflects the significance of the Thames in British national consciousness. But even more striking than his bulk is his brooding expression, with furrowed brow (crowned, for some reason, with vine leaves). His mood seems to reflect that of the two youths just below him who are looking downward, while a tiny figure on his urn gazes into the distance. The swimmers may be blithely oblivious of the disappointments and suffering that await them, but their happiness can only be momentary, and the seated pair seem to know it. They are pensive and withdrawn, already experiencing the melancholy that suffuses Gray's poem — "Ah fields belov'd in vain!" Perhaps the little figure on the urn is already gazing into the unknown but ominous future. Seventy lines later, the poem will end with an aphorism that has become proverbial: "Where ignorance is bliss, / 'Tis folly to be wise." Nostalgia came early to Gray, as did a sense of his life as one long defeat. He was just twenty-six when he wrote the *Ode on a Distant Prospect of Eton College.*

More startlingly imaginative is a color print with watercolor that illustrates a speech in *Macbeth* (color plate 1). Paintings based on Shakespeare's plays were popular, but they normally illustrated one or another dramatic episode. If a different artist had chosen this speech, the resulting picture would probably have shown Macbeth lost in thought or pacing uneasily. Blake's picture does nothing of the kind.

What it does do is give visual embodiment to Macbeth's *words* as he contemplates murdering the king and foresees the dreadful consequences:

> Besides, this Duncan
> Hath borne his faculties so meek, hath been
> So clear in his great office, that his virtues
> Will plead like angels, trumpet-tongued, against
> The deep damnation of his taking-off;
> And pity, like a naked newborn babe
> Striding the blast, or heaven's cherubin horsed
> Upon the sightless couriers of the air,
> Shall blow the horrid deed in every eye,
> That tears shall drown the wind.

These are not easy metaphors to find visual equivalents for. The literary critic Cleanth Brooks complained long ago that a newborn baby "could not of course even toddle, much less stride the blast," whereas if it could indeed stride the blast, it would hardly be pitiable.[6]

Blake never gave this picture a title; it was his friend Frederick Tatham who called it *Pity*. It could just as well have been *Heaven's Cherubin* or *The Sightless Couriers of the Air* or *The Naked Babe*.[7] For he has actually managed to combine the two very different metaphors that Shakespeare separates with the word "or." We usually think of cherubs as infantile putti, but that is not the original meaning of the word. In his 1755 *Dictionary* Samuel Johnson, quoting Shakespeare's lines, defines a cherub as "a celestial spirit which, in the hierarchy, is placed next in order to the seraphim." These are mighty angels ("cherubin" is plural) and were usually depicted as male. In Blake's picture, however, a pitying female cherub bends down and opens her hands protectively to receive a tiny infant from a mysterious woman reclining below. The babe—with adult proportions, not a realistic newborn—is not so much "striding" as joyously flinging open its arms, perhaps to be received into eternal life.

The sightless couriers are there too, in equine form as suggested by the word "horsed." Their eyes are closed to indicate sightlessness, though what Shakespeare probably meant—as Johnson suggested in his edition of the play—was that wind is invisible. A second cherub, with arms outstretched, looks off into the distance, half-hidden in shadow so as not to detract from the luminous central image. The celestial horses hurtle forward with immense energy, making the female cherub's tender intervention all the more moving. Lashing rain suggests the tears that drown the wind.

The poet and painter Dante Gabriel Rossetti, an early admirer of Blake (and owner of his precious manuscript notebook), is an admirable guide to this picture:

> Upon a green sward, wonderful in detail of form and colour, a beautiful woman lies, her stiffened body covered with a drapery of greyish white. Above her leaden clouds break in a storm of wind and rain, through which, in furious flight, rush the white "couriers of the air." Gaunt and blind, with flying manes and tails, they sweep across the sky, while from the nearer horse a Spirit leans and snatches up the "naked newborn babe" from beside the dying mother. The more distant rider, with widespread arms and streaming hair, seems a part of the storm. . . . The flying vision is tremendously vivid in effect, seeming almost like a pale lightning flash cleaving the darkness.[8]

Father Thames was a more or less literal equivalent for Gray's lines, but even there Blake was able to express not just the immediate address to the river but the mood of the poem as a whole. In *Pity* he goes much further. Who, after all, *is* the woman on the ground? There is no mother in Shakespeare's lines. She may be dying in childbirth, as Rossetti thought; a later commentator suggests that she may represent the virtues of the doomed Duncan: "It is implicitly Duncan's pleading virtues that give birth to the babe of Pity, and the mother in the print is indeed pleading."[9] Quite possibly Blake means the cherub's face to resemble that of the woman below, as if a projection of her spirit; it is notable that they share the same conical hairdo. In *Pity*—if that is indeed the correct title—we are presented with extraordinarily complex imagery, taking off from Macbeth's speech to create a conceptual universe that is altogether Blake's own. As always, his goal is not to convey an explicit message but to rouse the faculties to act.

A Sunshine Holiday

With both Father Thames and Pity, Blake may have thought that he was simply bringing out the essential meaning of the words. In other illustrations he goes well beyond them, subjecting the poet's conception to a critique that draws on his own mythical thinking. *A Sunshine Holiday* (color plate 2) is based on two passages in Milton's poem *L'Allegro*:

> Mountains on whose barren breast
> The labouring clouds do often rest. . . .

> Sometimes with secure delight
> The upland hamlets will invite,
> When the merry bells ring round
> And the jocund rebecks sound
> To many a youth and many a maid,
> Dancing in the chequered shade;
> And young and old come forth to play
> On a sunshine holiday.

Blake wrote a description of his picture, in which he emphasized his conception of a humanized nature: "Mountains clouds rivers trees appear humanized on the sunshine holiday. The church steeple with its merry bells; the clouds arise from the bosoms of mountains, while two angels sound their trumpets in the heavens to announce the sunshine holiday."[10]

The scene is predominantly cheerful, as it should be, for *L'Allegro* is explicitly opposed to its melancholy companion poem *Il Penseroso*. The church among the trees at far left must be the source of the bell-ringing mentioned by Milton, and a musician with a rebeck—a kind of violin—accompanies the youthful dancers. But Blake has added the visionary trumpeters on high. The dancers are tripping around a maypole, traditional emblem of courtship and fertility, and the figures at the right represent the community as a whole from childhood to old age. Since the dancers are in sunlight, it must be the woods that represent the "chequered shade." Johnson quotes Milton's lines to illustrate "to chequer": "to diversify, in the manner of a chessboard, with alternate colours or with darker and brighter parts."

Everything else in the picture is entirely original with Blake, apart from adopting Milton's rather casual reference to mountains with clouds on them, and showing an "upland hamlet" at their foot. Here his mountain is fully humanized, just as the Thames had been, and she has a city in her loins. She holds one nipple in the classical pose of Rhea producing the Milky Way, which hardly suggests a "barren breast," and her hair turns into a waterfall.[11] This becomes the source of a river that flows below, poured out of an urn by a river goddess. She is apparently drinking some of it from an upturned goblet.

What, exactly, is the vision of nature implied by these Blakean personifications? His mountain spirit looks strangely wistful or disconsolate, in no holiday mood at all, and so does her male consort, who is not mentioned by Milton. In Blake's personal symbolism, nature as we ordinarily experience it is a trap or prison, the scene of an endless cycle of mortality from birth to death. He often depicts nature in this sense as the Mediterranean Magna Mater with a spiky or battlemented crown, and the mountain spirit in *A Sunshine Holiday* does indeed wear such a crown.[12] Far from barren, she is fertile, but not necessarily in a positive sense. And another mountain, just above the church at the left, has the form of a pyramid. In Blake's symbolism pyramids represent repressive geometrical order, and also the cruel bondage of the Israelites in Egypt.

The six-winged figure just above the group in the right foreground may suggest the cycle of mortality too, a humanized moth or butterfly that has emerged from its chrysalis but will soon enough die in its turn. There are other figures in the trees, and perhaps they are trapped there; in his long poem *The Four Zoas* Blake adapts an image from Dante's *Inferno* that describes suicides who have been transformed into trees and are unable to speak. Strikingly, a solemn face in the midst of the trees looks distinctly like common representations of Christ. Is this the "man of sorrows, acquainted with grief"?[13] And what gesture is implied by his dendritic hand? Is he beckoning to the dancers—who all seem to be female except for one complacent male at whom they gaze—to encourage them to break away from the celebration of fertility?

These are questions, not answers, and questioning is what Blake encourages us to do. Although he has by no means debunked Milton's cheerful vision, he has complicated it profoundly with resonances of his own. In terms of his personal symbolism, this could be a vision of what he calls Beulah: a temporary resting place from suffering and strife, but one from which it is necessary to move either up or down. Below Beulah lies Generation, the mortal cycle that threatens to entrap us, as this picture seems to warn. But above it is Eden, a condition of dynamic activity that participates in the fullness of Eternity. In *A Sunshine Holiday,* that must be the destination of the diaphanous figures in the rosy sky, a realm altogether different from the scene below whose mortal inhabitants pair off, give birth, grow old, and die. One of the soaring figures seems to be bearing a basket of food on its head, destined perhaps for the communal banquet of eternity.

The skeptical philosopher David Hume thought that all religions had their origin in animist superstition, in which "trees, mountains, and streams are personified . . . while each grove or field is represented as possessed of a particular genius or invisible power which inhabits or protects it."[14] Blake describes much the same thing in *The Marriage of Heaven and Hell,* but for him it is visionary insight, not superstition, that finds human value in nature.

> The ancient poets animated all sensible objects with gods or geniuses, calling them by the names and adorning them with the properties of woods, rivers, mountains, lakes, cities, nations, and whatever their enlarged and numerous senses could perceive. And particularly they studied the genius of each city and country, placing it under its mental deity, till a system was formed which some took advantage of, and enslaved the vulgar by attempting to realize or abstract the mental deities from their objects: thus began priesthood, choosing forms of worship from poetic tales. And at length they pronounced that the gods had ordered such things. Thus men forgot that all deities reside in the human breast.[15]

Blake was just as fierce a critic of institutional religion as Hume and the other Enlightenment thinkers were, but at the same time he believed in a nature that was not mechanistic but human. Hume thought that polytheism, followed by monotheism, were positive improvements over primitive animism, and that the logical end result should be his own kind of agnostic skepticism. Blake runs the sequence the other way. In his opinion people in early cultures were quite right to perceive "gods and geniuses" in every river and mountain, expressing their experience of belonging in the world. The transition to worshipping deities far off in the heavens was a false step, and still worse was worship of a single God. That progression could indeed terminate in skepticism, and for Blake skepticism was destructive blindness to imaginative reality.

3. INNOCENCE

Visionary Songs

THE most accessible of Blake's poems are the *Songs of Innocence*, intended to be read aloud by adults to small children, and embedded in images that enrich the texts. Some of these are simple illustrations, but others differ suggestively from the words, hinting at perspectives that adult readers may ponder while the children receive a simpler message. More than in his illustrations for other poets, Blake was developing symbolic ideas that were very much his own, but the same techniques of "reading" the images are called into play.

Containing just twenty-three short lyrics, *Songs of Innocence* was first printed in 1789, five years before being reissued with a set of companion poems as *Songs of Innocence and of Experience*. The combined volume, in which four of the earlier poems were moved to Experience, is subtitled *Showing the Two Contrary States of the Human Soul*. Experience complements Innocence rather than supplanting or refuting it, for Innocence has a hopefulness and sense of trust that it is crucial not to lose. "Innocence dwells with wisdom," Blake later wrote, "but never with ignorance."[1]

The early biographer Alan Cunningham said that "the original genius of Blake was always confined through poverty to small dimensions." Copper was indeed expensive, and the plates were just three inches by five, but that was not necessarily a drawback. The format suited the engraving style in which he had been trained, and large plates might have diminished his intensity of focus. An art historian comments, "Blake was a miniaturist, a jeweler in his colouring, always preferring the small-scale. The movement in his art always comes from the wrist, never from the shoulder."[2]

The jewel-like effect is vividly apparent in the title page, reproduced here from the late copy Z, printed in 1826 for Blake's friend Henry Crabb Robinson and now in the Library of Congress (color plate 3). At the knee of their mother or nurse, a little boy and girl are gazing at the pictures that accompany the words. Behind them a tree laden with apples supports a climbing vine, a traditional symbol for children sustained by adults. The word "Innocence" flows in a graceful cursive script, and "SONGS" bursts out in leaves.

For a parent, aware of the bleak truths of Experience, the situation is poignant. "Reassuring gestures and words experienced in early childhood," the sociologist Peter Berger says, "build in the child a fundamental trust in the world. Yet speaking empirically, this trust is misplaced, is an illusion. The world is not at all trustworthy. It is a world in which the child will experience every sort of pain, and it is a world that in the end will kill him." The apples hanging above the mother and children may hint at the tree of knowledge — knowledge that will be acquired all too soon.[3]

William and Catherine Blake never had a child, and we don't know how much unhappiness that may have caused. In any event, the *Songs of Innocence* were clearly written by someone deeply sympathetic to children, and in this they differ greatly from the publications for children that were widely consumed at the time. Some of those took a stern line on childish wickedness, as in a hymn by Isaac Watts:

> O Father, I am but a child,
>   My body is made of the earth,
> My nature, alas! is defiled,
>   And a sinner I was from my birth.

John Wesley, cofounder of Methodism, instructed parents, "Whatever pains it costs, break the will if you would not damn the child. Let a child from a year old be taught to fear the rod and to cry softly; from that age make him do as he is bid, if you whip

13. *Songs of Innocence,* frontispiece, copy L, plate 1

him ten times running."[4] The child should cry softly because loud cries would provoke further thrashing.

Progressive books for children did exist, but although no longer obsessed with
hellfire, they were just as didactic in their own way. A typical title was *The History of
Tommy Playlove and Jacky Lovebook: Wherein Is Shown the Superiority of Virtue over Vice;*

another was *Fables in Monosyllables, by Mrs. Teachwell, to Which Are Added Morals, in Dialogues, between a Mother and Children.*[5] Blake wants to challenge and inspire children, not preach, and his world of Innocence is filled with beauty, tenderness, sympathy, and joy.

The title page of *Songs of Innocence* is not the actual first plate. Preceding it comes a remarkable frontispiece (figure 13) in which a musician gazes up at a soaring child, framed by trees and with sheep grazing in the background. The mother and children on the title page were clothed, but Blake's more overtly symbolic figures are usually naked or wear diaphanous garments, in accordance with his conviction that in a good painting "the drapery is formed alone by the shape of the naked body."[6]

Since there are no words in this frontispiece, it invites us to ponder whatever the image may suggest. The poem entitled *Introduction* on the third plate (not reproduced here) clarifies what we were seeing in the frontispiece:

> Piping down the valleys wild,
> Piping songs of pleasant glee,
> On a cloud I saw a child,
> And he laughing said to me:
>
> "Pipe a song about a lamb;"
> So I piped with merry cheer;
> "Piper pipe that song again,"
> So I piped, he wept to hear.
>
> "Drop thy pipe, thy happy pipe,
> Sing thy songs of happy cheer."
> So I sung the same again
> While he wept with joy to hear.
>
> "Piper sit thee down and write
> In a book that all may read — "
> So he vanished from my sight,
> And I plucked a hollow reed.

> And I made a rural pen,
> And I stained the water clear,
> And I wrote my happy songs
> Every child may joy to hear.

Judging from references in poems further on, the lamb is suggestive of the Lamb of God. Weeping here expresses joy, not grief, as in one of the Proverbs of Hell in *The Marriage of Heaven and Hell*: "Excess of sorrow laughs, excess of joy weeps."[7]

Floating above the piper's head in the frontispiece, the visionary child tells him what his song should be. First comes melody alone, then melody with words, and finally words that are written down, using natural materials. And then the airborne child vanishes, leaving the poem on the page as his gift. It is the gift of the musician-poet too. On the title page a miniature piper is shown leaning against the sloping "I" of the word "Innocence."

When Blake called these lyrics songs, he meant it literally. Someone who knew him recalled that he used to compose his own tunes, "and though, according to his confession, he was entirely unacquainted with the science of music, his ear was so good that his tunes were sometimes most singularly beautiful, and were noted down by musical professors." Alas, none of their transcriptions have survived, but in all likelihood Blake's melodies would have resembled the hymns and folk songs that he loved. Another writer reported that he liked to compose in all three arts simultaneously: "As he drew the figure he meditated the song which was to accompany it, and the music to which the verse was to be sung was the offspring too of the same moment."[8]

Infant Joy

An expression of Innocence at its simplest is a rhapsodic little lyric entitled *Infant Joy*:

> "I have no name;
> I am but two days old."
> What shall I call thee?

"I happy am,
Joy is my name."
Sweet joy befall thee!

Pretty joy!
Sweet joy but two days old,
Sweet joy I call thee;
Thou dost smile;
I sing the while,
Sweet joy befall thee.[9]

Unobtrusively, Blake varies the stresses from the regular underlying beat:

Thóu dost smíle.
I síng the while,
Swéet jóy befáll thee.

The language has the extreme simplicity of childish speech or of traditional nursery rhymes, which Dylan Thomas says that he loved before he was old enough to understand them: "I had come to love just the words of them, the words alone. . . . And as I read more and more, my love for the real life of words increased until I knew that I must live *with* them and *in* them, always."[10]

In any effective lyric, rhythm is as important as verbal meaning. Blake occasionally uses anapests, in which an accented syllable is preceded by two unaccented ones. If used without variation, it can sometimes sound too bouncy for serious verse, as in a poem Blake knew, William Cowper's *The Poplar Field:*

Twelve years have elapsed since I last took a view
Of my favourite field and the bank where they grew,
And now in the grass behold they are laid,
And the tree is my seat that once lent me a shade.

By shortening the line length in another poem, *The Ecchoing Green,* Blake gives anapests an elegiac resonance:

Old John with white hair
Does laugh away care,

Sitting under the oak
Among the old folk.
They laugh at our play,
And soon they all say,
"Such such were the joys
When we all girls and boys
In our youth time were seen
On the echoing green."[11]

That rosy impression of community is proper to the mood of Innocence, although in hindsight it will look different. George Orwell entitled his searing memoir of life in an abusive boarding school "Such, Such Were the Joys."

Simple as *Infant Joy* is, the ecstatic baby talk departs from fact, for as Coleridge reprovingly noted, a two-day-old baby doesn't smile. The age is symbolic. It was customary to baptize an infant on the third day after birth, at which moment the parents would confer its name. So at this point the infant is absolutely innocent and gets to name herself—Joy is a girl's name—in the immediacy of her happiness, while her mother foresees the future and can only hope that sweet joy will continue to befall her.[12]

The ravishing picture (color plate 4) is self-evidently symbolic. Copy Z, reproduced here, is the very one that Coleridge saw and admired in the last year of Blake's life. Seated in a huge open blossom are a mother and child with a winged figure facing them, unmistakably recalling paintings of the Virgin Mary adoring the Christ child. But Blake despised the theological doctrine that Mary was a virgin, and liked to suggest that if Joseph didn't get her pregnant, somebody else must have.

And what flowers are these? They are anemones, sacred in classical lore to Venus, supposedly stained red by the blood of the dying Adonis. It was a recent revelation in botany that plants have sex, and Erasmus Darwin (grandfather of Charles) published an immensely popular poem called *Loves of the Plants*. Darwin's language is unabashedly erotic:

With honeyed lips enamoured woodbines meet,
Clasp with fond arms, and mix their kisses sweet.

In Darwin's poem the anemone, recalling the association with Venus's grief, is a victim of autumnal frost:

> All wan and shivering in the leafless glade
> The sad Anemone reclined her head;
> Grief on her cheeks had paled the roseate hue,
> And her sweet eyelids dropped with pearly dew.[13]

Blake was interested in *Loves of the Plants,* and in *Songs of Innocence* flowers participate in a sexual energy that human beings share with the rest of nature. Commentators have suggested that the maternal blossom in *Infant Joy* is meant to look womblike and the drooping bud below it phallic. Throughout *Innocence* there are further hints of sexuality, along with references to stroking, playing, licking, kissing, and touching. In *Visions of the Daughters of Albion* a few years later, the feminist character Oothoon exclaims, "Infancy, fearless, lustful, happy! nestling for delight / In laps of pleasure." As for the winged figure in the *Infant Joy* picture—the dotted wings seem more insectlike than angelic—that is probably Psyche, symbol of the immortal spirit, as in *A Sunshine Holiday.*[14]

The Blossom

Since the poems express multiple facets of Innocence, there is no correct order in which to read them. Twenty copies of *Songs of Innocence* still exist for which the original sequence is known (Blake and his wife sewed the pages together with simple paper covers, to be rebound by purchasers later on). Remarkably, the sequence is uniquely different in each.[15] *Infant Joy* sometimes appears near the beginning of the book, sometimes almost at the end. Another poem, *The Blossom* (color plate 5), usually appears at some distance from it, but visually they have much in common. Again we see a mother and infant, but this time she has wings, and little winged beings are dancing and soaring around. The mother and child are seated on what is evidently some form of vegetation, but it surges with extraordinary energy and resembles no actual plant. David Erdman's description has caught on: it is a flame-flower. One may think of Dylan Thomas's line, "The force that through the green fuse drives the flower."[16]

The text is like a riddle.

> Merry merry sparrow
> Under leaves so green
> A happy blossom
> Sees you swift as arrow
> Seek your cradle narrow
> Near my bosom.
>
> Pretty pretty robin
> Under leaves so green
> A happy blossom
> Hears you sobbing sobbing
> Pretty pretty robin
> Near my bosom.

What is going on, spoken by the blossom itself? A merry sparrow flies down to a nest that is described, in terms a small child can understand, as its cradle. As for the pretty robin, it is not merry at all, for it sobs. Very likely an allegory of birth is implied, and the sobs express the pains of childbirth—pain even in joy. One of Blake's made-up proverbs is "Joys impregnate. Sorrows bring forth."[17] The sparrow and robin might also represent two aspects of a small child's mood, sometimes nestling and content, at other times sobbing. It may seem surprising that neither bird actually appears in the picture, but it is characteristic of Blake to emphasize symbolic significance, not literal imagery. The focus is on the speaking blossom.

If the figures surrounding the mother and child can be seen as a sequence moving clockwise from left to right, then the ones embracing above her head might symbolize the sexual union that will lead to birth, while the final figure, holding up wingless arms as it drops from the air, is a cherub about to be born. Such an interpretation makes sense, but others do too. "We may think of the five winged joys," Erdman suggests, "as the aroused senses, capable of soaring, and the wingless but actually soaring boy as the imagination or genius." We may also be reminded of the infant Jesus and his mother. In a few late copies, a white sun shines out from behind the mother's head, surrounding it like a halo.[18]

Might the sobbing of the robin make the listener think also of a familiar nursery rhyme?

> Who killed Cock Robin?
> "I, said the sparrow,
> With my little bow and arrow,
> I killed Cock Robin."

Innocence is trusting, but it is not ignorant of death, which was all too frequent for the very young in Blake's day.

Blake is sometimes referred to as a Cockney, but there is no evidence that he had a specifically Cockney pronunciation ("hartist" for "artist," and so on). By looking at his rhymes, however, it is possible to get some notion of how he did pronounce words, and he often heard exact rhymes where we no longer do. "Poor" rhymes with "more," "devil" with "civil," and "creature" with "later" (like the American "critter"). Since he left off the final "g" in words that ended in "-ing," "sobbing" did indeed rhyme with "robin."[19]

The Lamb

Still another sweetly simple lyric, *The Lamb,* explicitly invokes a religious theme:

> Little lamb who made thee?
> Dost thou know who made thee?
> Gave thee life and bid thee feed
> By the stream and o'er the mead;
> Gave thee clothing of delight,
> Softest clothing wooly bright;
> Gave thee such a tender voice,
> Making all the vales rejoice!
> Little lamb who made thee?
> Dost thou know who made thee?

> Little lamb I'll tell thee,
> Little lamb I'll tell thee:
> He is callèd by thy name,
> For he calls himself a lamb:
> He is meek and he is mild,
> He became a little child:
> I a child and thou a lamb,
> We are callèd by his name.
>   Little lamb God bless thee.
>   Little lamb God bless thee.[20]

It is the child who speaks, catechizing the lamb — "Little lamb I'll *tell* thee." The God who protects the world of Innocence is the Jesus who was born a little child, not a patriarch far off in heaven.

The picture accompanying *The Lamb* (figure 14) has a comfortable realism very different from the symbolic intensity of *Infant Joy* and *The Blossom*. The text nestles within an arch formed by sinuous trees, wreathed in vines and tendrils. A flock of sheep has gathered at the door of the thatched cottage, and a naked boy holds out his hand for a lamb to lick. A pair of white birds, lovebirds perhaps, perch at the far end of the roof. In some copies a green lawn fills the bottom of the picture; in others a stream of blue water is flowing there. It is sometimes suggested that the trees look fragile, implying that their protection may not last, but at any rate the immediate impression is of security and trust, which is certainly reinforced by the massive shade tree in the background.

This is not to say that Innocence possesses an adequate understanding of existence. In a much later poem Blake asks,

> Why is the sheep given to the knife? the lamb plays in the sun;
> He starts! he hears the foot of man! he says, "Take thou my wool,
> But spare my life;" but he knows not that winter cometh fast.[21]

In winter the lamb will lament the loss of its wool, transformed into garments to keep humans warm. And lambs as well as sheep often end up as dinner.

At various places in *Songs of Innocence* there are intimations of the threaten-

The Lamb

Little Lamb who made thee
Dost thou know who made thee
Gave thee life & bid thee feed.
By the stream & oer the mead;
Gave thee clothing of delight,
Softest clothing wooly bright;
Gave thee such a tender voice,
Making all the vales rejoice;
Little Lamb who made thee
Dost thou know who made thee

Little Lamb I'll tell thee,
Little Lamb I'll tell thee;
He is called by thy name,
For he calls himself a Lamb:
He is meek & he is mild,
He became a little child:
I a child & thou a lamb,
We are called by his name.
Little Lamb God bless thee.
Little Lamb God bless thee.

14. *The Lamb, Songs of Innocence,* copy L, plate 24

ing aspects of life. *On Another's Sorrow* hints at the Crucifixion when it explains why Jesus is able to empathize with human suffering:

> He doth give his joy to all;
> He becomes an infant small.
> He becomes a man of woe;
> He doth feel the sorrow too.[22]

He feels the sorrow because he is a man of sorrows himself.

The Chimney Sweeper

In most of these poems any ambiguities are deeply buried, but a few embody a double message very clearly: the consoling one that small children need to hear, and another that reflects adult perspective. In one such poem, a little black boy hopes that an English boy can learn to love him despite his dark skin, but imagines having to wait for a heaven in which his skin too will be white. In another, poor children who were being educated in charity schools file into Saint Paul's Cathedral for an annual service of thanksgiving:

> Now like a mighty wind they raise to heaven the voice of song,
> Or like harmonious thunderings the seats of heaven among.
> Beneath them sit the aged men, wise guardians of the poor;
> Then cherish pity, lest you drive an angel from your door.

There is an echo of the Book of Revelation: "I heard as it were the voice of the great multitude, and as the voice of many waters, and as the voice of mighty thunderings." And perhaps there is an echo as well of the Epistle to the Hebrews: "Be not forgetful to entertain strangers: for thereby some have entertained angels unawares."[23]

This may sound positive, but as Blake well knew, conditions in charity schools were truly dreadful, and the last line can therefore be read as grimly ironic. Far from cherishing pity, these "wise guardians" will send their wards right back to labor in exploitative workhouses. A small child, listening to the poem, will take in the positive message, but an adult will notice what has been described as the "latent presence of Experience within Innocence."[24]

One poem especially, *The Chimney Sweeper,* brings this double perspective into the open.

> When my mother died I was very young,
> And my father sold me while yet my tongue
> Could scarcely cry "weep weep weep weep,"
> So your chimneys I sweep and in soot I sleep.
>
> There's little Tom Dacre, who cried when his head
> That curled like a lamb's back was shaved, so I said,
> "Hush Tom never mind it, for when your head's bare,
> You know that the soot cannot spoil your white hair."
>
> And so he was quiet, and that very night,
> As Tom was a sleeping he had such a sight,
> That thousands of sweepers, Dick, Joe, Ned and Jack,
> Were all of them locked up in coffins of black,
>
> And by came an angel who had a bright key,
> And he opened the coffins and set them all free.
> Then down a green plain leaping laughing they run
> And wash in a river and shine in the sun.
>
> Then naked and white, all their bags left behind,
> They rise upon clouds, and sport in the wind.
> And the angel told Tom if he'd be a good boy,
> He'd have God for his father and never want joy.
>
> And so Tom awoke and we rose in the dark
> And got with our bags and our brushes to work.
> Though the morning was cold, Tom was happy and warm,
> So if all do their duty, they need not fear harm.[25]

The condition of chimney sweeps was horrendous, and a campaign to do something about it produced a stream of books and pamphlets that make harrowing reading. The usual age to start an apprenticeship, as in Blake's own case, was thirteen, but by then a boy would be too large to squeeze into narrow, crooked chimneys. He—very occasionally she—would therefore begin work by the age of seven, and sometimes as young as four. "My father sold me" is literally correct. Parents normally paid a master a premium in return for the skills he would teach, as Blake's parents did with the engraver Basire, but in this horrible trade it was the master who paid the parents. The children suffered injuries of all kinds, such as twisted joints and spines, and since there were no facilities for washing off soot, cancer of the scrotum was common. They were often required to be naked while they worked, lest clothing catch on the rough plaster with which chimneys were lined.[26]

A bill was passed in Parliament in 1788, one year before *Songs of Innocence,* to prohibit apprenticeship of boys younger than eight, and it required that they bathe once a week, though without specifying how facilities for that were to be provided. Just how callously young sweeps were treated is indicated by another provision: that they should no longer be forced to go up ignited chimneys. Even that modest attempt at reform was never enforced, and employing small children as chimney sweeps did not become illegal until 1875.[27]

Yet Blake's poem is remarkable, as Heather Glen observes, for avoiding any explicit note of protest. The speaker accepts it as simply inevitable that *because* his mother died, his father sold him when he was still too little to pronounce the cry of "Sweep!" in search of work. "Weep weep weep weep" is a poignant lamentation. And there is a casual but telling challenge to the reader: "So *your* chimneys I sweep and in soot I sleep." The children did indeed sleep on bags they had filled with soot.[28]

The plight of injured innocence is evoked by a hint of rural imagery in Tom's hair "that curled like a lamb's back," recalling the loving trust in *The Lamb.* The older boy clearly knows that he's offering a consoling rationalization when he says that shaving Tom's blond curls will make it easier to keep his head clean. But the last line of the poem is a much more insidious rationalization that the older boy himself has internalized: "So if all do their duty, they need not fear harm." The implication is that if they ever slack off for a moment, punishment will promptly follow. And the still more chilling implication is that they *are* doing their appalling duty, yet even so they experience harm every day of their lives—with the further threat that if they should ever fail to do that duty, God will refuse to be their father.

The picture that accompanies this poem (color plate 6) is strangely minimal. The text fills up nearly the whole page, and the boys running toward the river are tiny stick figures at the very bottom, where an angelic figure stoops to help the smallest one out of a coffin—a dream version of the claustrophobic chimneys. Blake was perfectly capable of using two plates for a poem when he wanted to; evidently the congested effect here was deliberate. Zachary Leader offers a persuasive interpretation: "The scene lacks the very qualities the sweeps most long for: open spaces, sun, warmth, clear bright colors. The great block of text presses down upon Tom's dream like a weight, stunting and crushing it, much as Innocence itself is ground down by a life of poverty and oppression."[29] In a few copies, however, the effect is startlingly different. As in the one reproduced here, the sky is suffused with golden light, and the stooping figure has a bright halo around his head. That is the Jesus of Innocence, fully human as well as divine.

Institutional religion serves here as ideology, inculcating a coercive message about obedience and duty. Still, it is not "false consciousness" in the negative Marxist sense. The consolation that the boys feel is very real, and their lives would be even more miserable if it were taken away from them. Little Tom's dream is likewise a desperately needed refuge from too much reality. By day the boys may cry "Weep weep weep weep"; in dreams they can wash themselves clean and leap in the sun.[30]

To illustrate Blake's wide range of reference, Kathleen Raine points to a passage in Emanuel Swedenborg, the self-styled prophet whose works Blake read and annotated:

> There are also spirits amongst those from Jupiter, whom they call Sweepers of Chimneys, because they appear in like garments, and likewise with sooty faces. . . . One of these spirits came to me, and anxiously requested that I would intercede for him to be admitted into heaven. . . . At that instant the angel called to him to cast off his raiment, which he did immediately with inconceivable quickness from the vehemence of his desire. . . . I was informed that such, when they are prepared for Heaven, are stripped of their own garments and are closed with new shining raiment, and become angels.[31]

This is the Neoplatonic concept of the body as a temporary covering for the immortal spirit, which Swedenborg thought of as a wholly positive symbolism. In Blake's poem it is grimly ironic, since he does not believe in waiting for an afterlife to compensate for the sufferings of this one.

Rationalization of what cannot be avoided is not the same thing as willing acceptance, and some aphoristic verses in Blake's notebook, collected under the title *Auguries of Innocence,* are keenly expressive of cruelty and injustice.

> A robin red breast in a cage
> Puts all Heaven in a rage;
> A dove house filled with doves and pigeons
> Shudders Hell through all its regions.
> A dog starved at his master's gate
> Predicts the ruin of the state;
> A horse misused upon the road
> Calls to Heaven for human blood.[32]

The plain meaning of the first lines is that robins fly free and ought not to be caged, whereas domesticated doves come home willingly to their dovecotes. But the reason Hell shudders may be that the harmonious friendship of humans and doves is only apparent—people kept doves in order to eat them. There are religious echoes as well. In folk tradition, the robin got its red breast—much redder in the little British robin than in the American thrush also called by that name—for having done a kindness to Jesus on the cross. And Hell shuddered with earthquake when Jesus harrowed it to redeem the souls of the just.[33]

Innocence, as Blake imagines it, is trusting but not naïve, inexperienced but already anticipating immersion in Experience. He was apparently willing to sell separate copies of *Songs of Innocence* to purchasers who didn't want *Songs of Experience,* but in the combined *Songs* he achieves an extraordinary extension of imaginative insight. And with few exceptions, the poems in the second set are ones that nobody would want to read to small children.

4. EXPERIENCE

Contrary States

WITH *Songs of Experience*—clearly aimed at adults, not children—we enter an altogether different imaginative world, one
haunted by loneliness, frustration, and cruelty. Sometimes a
poem in the second series corresponds directly to one in the
first; there is a *Chimney Sweeper* in both sets, and *The Tyger* makes a direct allusion to
The Lamb. For other poems, the brilliant *London* for example, there is no corresponding poem in *Innocence,* whose imagery is usually rural rather than urban.

Songs of Experience has a separate title page of its own (figure 15) that shows
leaves and tendrils sprouting from "SONGS," but the stiff block letters of "EXPERI-
ENCE" might be chiseled on a tombstone, and indeed, two mourners bend over
bodies or funerary effigies that probably belong to their parents. Experience may
believe that death is final, but Innocence is more hopeful, and the little figures in
the air suggest that the spirit does not perish with the mortal body. That is not to
say, though, that Innocence is entirely right. Blake did believe that the human spirit
lives on, but not in the orthodox sense of reanimation in an otherworldly heaven
altogether different from the life we know. In *Europe,* published in the same year
as *Songs of Experience,* he contemptuously called that heaven "an allegorical abode
where existence hath never come."[1]

The frontispiece for *Songs of Experience* (figure 16) echoes, but also contrasts

15. *Songs of Experience,* title page, copy L, plate 30

❖ ❖ ❖

16. *Songs of Experience*, frontispiece, copy L, plate 29

with, the one in *Innocence*. In this one the man no longer carries a musical instrument, the sheltering bower has been replaced by a thick trunk close by and another tree far away, and the winged child is seated oddly on the man's head. Are the child's hands being held to help him balance there or to prevent his escape? Both man and child stare directly at us, with expressions that are hard to read—questioning? coolly challenging? In some copies the sky glows golden, in others red, suggesting that the sun has set. The landscape in this frontispiece seems barren, and the flock of sheep has been replaced by two, or possibly three, grazing in a single shadowy mass.

There is also a new title page for the combined volume (color plate 7), and in this one Experience is dominant. Fig leaves conceal the genitals of a couple who are prostrating themselves and are unmistakably Adam and Eve just after eating the forbidden fruit. Sex, which was innocent before the Fall, now provokes shame, and flames of divine wrath blaze above. But since Blake rejected the concept of original sin, the guilt must be their own projection, and so are the punitive flames. In Blake's view, the story in Genesis that an angel was stationed to bar the reentry of Adam and Eve into Paradise is likewise false. In *The Marriage of Heaven and Hell*, probably printed in 1793, a year before *Songs of Experience,* he proclaims, "The cherub with his flaming sword is hereby commanded to leave his guard at the tree of life."[2] If Adam and Eve have been expelled from Paradise, it is because they mistakenly expelled themselves.

Patriarchy and Repression

There is an explicit counterpart to *Infant Joy* in *Songs of Experience,* entitled *Infant Sorrow.*

> My mother groaned! my father wept.
> Into the dangerous world I leapt:
> Helpless, naked, piping loud,
> Like a fiend hid in a cloud.
>
> Struggling in my father's hands,
> Striving against my swaddling bands,

> Bound and weary I thought best
> To sulk upon my mother's breast.

All of the sounds are distressing: a mother groaning in childbirth, a father weeping (at her anguish?), and a newborn infant squalling like an alarming fiend. In the earlier poem "joy" was an emotion and also a name. "Sorrow" here is not an identity, just a condition of sadness and pain, and the infant might be either male or female. After its spirited leap into the dangerous world, it finds itself frustrated by helplessness and confined in swaddling clothes. The only choice open to it is "to sulk upon my mother's breast."[3]

The picture (figure 17) is ambiguous. Does it suggest maternal love or maternal control? Beneath heavy curtains, the child—bigger and more robust than an actual newborn—seems to be recoiling from the mother rather than reaching out. Her expression is sternly determined, perhaps irritated. Though the room is well furnished and comfortable, this is indeed going to be a dangerous world, and from the very outset the child is conscious of threatening emotions that are very different from the mood of *Infant Joy*.

Fathers were barely visible in Innocence. In Experience they are patriarchs who impose repression even when they mean well. *A Little Girl Lost* begins with a vehement declaration:

> Children of the future age,
> Reading this indignant page,
> Know that in a former time
> Love! sweet love! was thought a crime.

Then comes a frank celebration of nakedness:

> In the age of gold,
> Free from winters cold,
> Youth and maiden bright
> To the holy light
> Naked in the sunny beams delight.

They dally innocently in a garden, like an unfallen Adam and Eve, and agree to meet again at nightfall. But the patriarch intervenes:

INFANT SORROW

My mother groand! my father wept.
Into the dangerous world I leapt:
Helpless, naked, piping loud:
Like a fiend hid in a cloud.

Struggling in my fathers hands:
Striving against my swadling bands:
Bound and weary I thought best
To sulk upon my mothers breast.

17. *Infant Sorrow, Songs of Experience*, copy L, plate 39

To her father white
Came the maiden bright;
But his loving look,
Like the holy book,
All her tender limbs with terror shook.

"Ona! pale and weak!
To thy father speak:
O the trembling fear!
O the dismal care!
That shakes the blossoms of my hoary hair."

It is a loving father who creates guilt, blaming the daughter for provoking his own fear, and recalling the "holy book" that teaches guilt for sin. According to Saint Paul that is precisely what the Bible is for: "I had not known sin, but by the law: for I had not known lust, except the law had said, Thou shalt not covet."[4]

Institutional religion, Blake thought, had a wicked commitment to promoting sexual repression. Innocence exists in a world of nurturing gardens; Experience is haunted by memories of the lost garden from which Adam and Eve were ejected—or ejected themselves.

I went to the garden of love,
And saw what I never had seen:
A chapel was built in the midst,
Where I used to play on the green.

And the gates of this chapel were shut,
And "thou shalt not" writ over the door;
So I turned to the garden of love
That so many sweet flowers bore.

And I saw it was filled with graves,
And tombstones where flowers should be,
And priests in black gowns were walking their rounds,
And binding with briars my joys and desires.[5]

The picture (not reproduced here) shows an open grave and a boy and girl kneeling nearby in prayer while a monk reads from a black book.

Another garden poem suggests how deeply repression can be internalized.

> Ah sunflower! weary of time,
> Who countest the steps of the sun:
> Seeking after that sweet golden clime
> Where the traveler's journey is done;
>
> Where the youth pined away with desire
> And the pale virgin shrouded in snow
> Arise from their graves and aspire
> Where my sunflower wishes to go.[6]

Sunflowers are heliotropes, turning to follow the moving sun across the sky, and therefore weary of time in a cycle that never ends. The frustrated youth and the pale virgin are wasting their lives in needless self-denial, waiting for eventual reward in an unreal heaven instead of seizing pleasure here and now.

The Sick Rose

These poems may suggest that a hopeful resolution could still be possible, but a central theme throughout Blake's work is the persistent conflicts that seem inseparable from sexuality. One of the most memorable *Songs of Experience,* just eight lines long, is filled with disturbing implications. It has, Harold Bloom says, the "ruthless economy of thirty-four words."

> O rose, thou art sick.
> The invisible worm
> That flies in the night,
> In the howling storm,
>
> Has found out thy bed
> Of crimson joy,
> And his dark secret love
> Does thy life destroy.

The picture (color plate 8) shows a crimson blossom bent down to the ground, with a worm wriggling into it while a terrified female figure tries to escape. Above, a caterpillar is feeding, and two more females—withered blossoms, perhaps—huddle on bare stems. The big thorns are no help in protecting the rose from blight. A critic comments, "Attack is a worm's form of 'love.'"[7]

However one chooses to interpret this enigmatic poem, it is clearly concerned with corrosive sexual guilt, and also with the excitement that taboo and secrecy provoke. Roses were an age-old symbol for the transitory nature of beauty, as in Robert Herrick's "Gather ye rosebuds while ye may." In addition Blake is likely to have had two recent texts in mind. One is scribbled by the heroine of Samuel Richardson's popular novel *Clarissa,* after realizing that her frustrated seducer had raped her while she was drugged unconscious: "Thou pernicious caterpillar, that preyest upon the fair leaf of virgin fame, and poisonest those leaves which thou canst not devour! . . . Thou eating canker-worm that preyest upon the opening bud, and turnest the damask rose into livid yellowness!"[8] Convinced that she has been defiled, even though against her will, Clarissa wastes away and dies as a saint who is too good for this world.

The other text is a jeu d'esprit by Matthew Prior entitled *A True Maid* ("maid" meaning "virgin"):

> "No, no; for my virginity,
>   When I lose that," says Rose, "I'll die."
> "Behind the elms last night," cried Dick,
>   "Rose, were you not extremely sick?"[9]

This is a girl who is literally named Rose, and she has escaped the fate worse than death, but just barely—the poem is a knowing dirty joke, with an aptly named Dick. Blake evidently had the inspiration of taking Prior's last line and making it his first: "O Rose, thou *art* sick." The implication is that there is something very wrong with a culture that chuckles at Prior's sly innuendo.

In Blake's poem, who is saying, "O Rose, thou art sick"? Unlike the other Romantics, he rarely uses a confessional first-person style. His lyrics reflect what Susanne Langer calls "impersonal subjectivity," as in hymns, where a whole congregation can sing, "Jesu, lover of *my* soul."[10] Richardson's Clarissa is a character in a realistic narrative; Prior's Rose and Dick are protagonists in a joke. Blake's poem is about universal experience.

Goethe does something similar in the remarkably "Blakean" *Heidenröslein* (*Little Heath Rose*), which was set superbly to music by Schubert. It needs to be read in the original, because the lyric beauty evaporates in translation. A boy reaches down to pluck a rose, it warns that it will prick, and he plucks it all the same:

> Und der wilde Knabe brach
> 's Röslein auf der Heiden;
> Röslein wehrte sich und stach,
> Half ihm doch kein Weh und Ach,
> Mußt es eben leiden.
> Röslein, Röslein, Röslein rot,
> Röslein auf der Heiden.
>
> And the rough boy picked the rose,
> Little rose on the heath;
> Little rose defended itself and pricked,
> No "woe" or "alas" was any use,
> It simply had to bear it.
> Little rose, little rose, little red rose,
> Little rose on the heath.

But Goethe's poem is tender and sad, acknowledging the way things always are. Blake's is indignant, indicting the way things are.

The Sick Rose has often been interpreted as a call for sexual liberation. If priests would stop enforcing "thou shalt not," and if naked love were indulged instead of prohibited, wouldn't erotic liberation ensue? Blake does sometimes talk that way: "This will come to pass by an improvement of sensual enjoyment."[11] But since the worm is just as much part of nature as the rose, the problem seems deeper than an effect of repressive ideology. And some of the songs of Experience suggest a much darker possibility: that inhibition and frustration are so deeply bound up with sexuality that they are impossible to transcend. That will form a major, even an obsessive, theme in the later poems beyond the *Songs*.

The Clod and the Pebble

In another song of Experience the speakers are inanimate objects, presenting contrasting philosophies of life in a symmetrical format.

> Love seeketh not itself to please,
> Nor for itself hath any care,
> But for another gives its ease,
> And builds a Heaven in Hell's despair.
>
> So sang a little clod of clay,
> Trodden with the cattle's feet;
> But a pebble of the brook
> Warbled out these metres meet:
>
> Love seeketh only self to please,
> To bind another to its delight:
> Joys in another's loss of ease,
> And builds a Hell in Heaven's despite.[12]

Not only are Innocence and Experience contrary states of the soul, but from the perspective of Experience they are irreconcilable. The pebble here is obviously selfish and sadistic, but critics disagree about the clod. Some have argued that it is noble in its self-sacrifice. It is true that selfless love is praised in the first Epistle to the Corinthians, and that according to one of Blake's Proverbs of Hell, "The most sublime act is to set another before you." However, a consciously chosen action on someone else's behalf is very different from continuous self-abnegation, and Blake never approved of turning the other cheek:

> Was Jesus humble or did he
> Give any proofs of humility?[13]

It is often assumed that the clod is female and the pebble male, but they could perfectly well be the same sex, if indeed we should see them as gendered at all. And what kind of relationship do they have, if any? Are their two songs going right past each other, or are we overhearing a dialogue? If we do imagine them together, then their relationship would be profoundly sadomasochistic, and Blake can hardly be recommending that. The poem is like a miniature diagram of *Les Liaisons Dangereuses,* in which a pious woman suffers tragically for giving herself to a narcissistic Don Juan. Bloom says succinctly, "The clod joys in its own loss of ease, the pebble in another's loss, but there is loss in either case."[14] And if one does imagine a relationship, the clod's self-abasement might just stimulate the pebble's selfish desire.

In the picture, once again, Blake neglects to illustrate, inasmuch as the clod and pebble aren't shown at all (figure 18). We see sheep drinking from a stream, together with two impressively horned bovines. All of them are oblivious of both the clod and the pebble, who are presumably conducting their little psychodrama below. So the hard pebble, just as much as the soft clod, is "trodden with the cattle's feet." Meanwhile a duck drifts placidly on the stream, and a frog reposes while another frog jumps into the air with an earthworm beneath. These are creatures at home in their world, as if visitors from pastoral Innocence. But then, the clod and the pebble are at home here too.

The Tyger

Two of the *Songs of Experience* are masterpieces. The best known, and deservedly so, is *The Tyger.*

> Tyger Tyger, burning bright,
> In the forests of the night:
> What immortal hand or eye
> Could frame thy fearful symmetry?
>
> In what distant deeps or skies
> Burnt the fire of thine eyes?
> On what wings dare he aspire?
> What the hand dare seize the fire?
>
> And what shoulder, and what art,
> Could twist the sinews of thy heart?
> And when thy heart began to beat,
> What dread hand? and what dread feet?

The CLOD & the PEBBLE

Love seeketh not Itself to please.
Nor for itself hath any care;
But for another gives its ease,
And builds a Heaven in Hells despair

So sang a little Clod of Clay.
Trodden with the cattles feet:
But a Pebble of the brook,
Warbled out these metres meet.

Love seeketh only Self to please.
To bind another to its delight:
Joys in anothers loss of ease,
And builds a Hell in Heavens despite.

18. *The Clod and the Pebble, Songs of Experience*, copy Z, plate 32

What the hammer? what the chain,
In what furnace was thy brain?
What the anvil? what dread grasp
Dare its deadly terrors clasp!

When the stars threw down their spears
And watered heaven with their tears,
Did he smile his work to see?
Did he who made the Lamb make thee?

Tyger Tyger, burning bright,
In the forests of the night:
What immortal hand or eye,
Dare frame thy fearful symmetry?[15]

The final stanza is a verbatim reprise of the first—except that contemplating this formidable being has led the speaker to replace "could frame" with "*dare* frame."

Alexander Welsh, noting the similar metrical pattern in "Rain, rain, go away, come again another day," says that Blake has managed to combine "the rhythms of innocent nursery rhymes and game-songs and the rhythms of magical incantation, epiphanic invocation, and prophetic hymn." The standard poetic meter in English is iambic, stressing every second syllable, as in Milton's "I may assert eternal Providence / And justify the ways of God to men." Throwing the accent on the first syllable instead of the second, in trochaic meter, accentuates the stresses as Blake does here. If the phrase "in the forests of the night" appeared in a piece of prose, one would probably hear just two stresses: "in the fórests of the níght." But cast into pounding trochees, there are four powerful stresses in each line:

Týger Týger búrning bríght
Īn the fórests óf the níght. . . .[16]

Blake was an exacting reviser. Multiple drafts of *The Tyger* can be discerned in the notebook known as the Rossetti Manuscript. He once wrote, "Ideas cannot be given but in their minutely appropriate words," and the pains he took with *The Tyger* reflect that conviction. In preliminary versions the tiger was conventionally scary.

Near the bottom right-hand side of the notebook page reproduced here (figure 19), some almost obliterated lines suggest a really horrible beast:

> Could fetch it from the furnace deep
> And in thy horrid ribs dare steep
> In the well of sanguine woe
> In what clay and in what mould
> Were thy eyes of fury rolled

Englishmen who had lived in India regularly described man-eating tigers as remorseless. According to the first edition of the *Encyclopaedia Britannica,* "The tiger is more ferocious, cruel, and savage than the lion. Although gorged with carnage, his thirst for blood is not appeased; he seizes and tears to pieces a new prey with equal fury and rapacity, the very moment after devouring a former one." But the tiger in Blake's poem is no naturalistic beast, and whatever the forests of the night may be, they are not an ordinary Indian jungle. Blake's tiger dwells in mysterious distant deeps or skies, not on earth at all.[17]

The companion poem to *The Tyger* is *The Lamb,* as is implied in the question, "Did he who made the Lamb make thee?" *The Lamb* asks a single question that yields a single answer: "Little Lamb, I'll tell thee." *The Tyger* is all questions and no answer, with a driving, accelerating tempo. In *The Lamb* creation is imagined as a loving gift of life to children and lambs by a God who is himself a shepherd and a lamb. In *The Tyger* creation gives form to a majestic tiger, a labor that requires titanic daring and strength.

In Genesis, "God said, Let there be light, and there was light." For creators in Blake's poems—and he has many versions of them—it is not so effortless as that. Often, as here, they are blacksmiths heating resistant material to be hammered into shape. The chain probably refers to the vertebrae, and the product is organic as well as metallic, with twisted sinews for the beating heart.

Critics who look for irony in Blake's poems sometimes claim that the speaker of this one is deluded, foolishly worshipping a phantom of his own imagination. But the awesome power of the tiger's creator simply cannot be dismissed. The questions are challengingly open, for as David Fuller says, "The poem wonders at; it does not explain or expound."[18]

19. Manuscript page from Blake's Notebook

Not only does *The Tyger* question what kind of creator makes predators as well as their prey, it hints as well at other myths that suggest further lines of questioning. Intoxicated by the driving verse, readers may not stop to ask what is meant by "When the stars threw down their spears / And watered heaven with their tears." The spears are presumably rays of starlight, and they also recall the weapons of the fallen angels in *Paradise Lost,* cast down after the Almighty crushed their rebellion; it is their bitter weeping that waters heaven. A clear hint in *The Tyger* does indeed point to Satan as the creator in the poem. "On what wings dare he aspire" recalls his flight through chaos to destroy the newly created Adam and Eve, as narrated by Milton: "Now shaves with level wing the deep, then soars / Up to the fiery concave towering high."[19] Blake knew *Paradise Lost* practically by heart, argued with it throughout his life, and eventually summoned Milton back to earth to unite with him in a poem called *Milton.*

In Blake's wonderfully condensed lyric, yet another rebel is invoked in "What the hand dare seize the fire?" The striking resemblance of Prometheus to Satan was well known to the early Church fathers. Zeus punished Prometheus with eternal torture for disobeying the commandment that no god should give the gift of fire—in effect, civilization—to the human race. Not surprisingly, Christian theologians held that Prometheus was right to rebel whereas Satan was wrong. For Blake, however, both rebellions are equally justified, since in his opinion the God of Genesis is just as tyrannical as Zeus. That is why Blake claims in *The Marriage of Heaven and Hell* that "Milton was a true poet, and of the Devil's party without knowing it."[20] Milton rebelled against the earthly tyrant Charles I, but in Blake's view, he tried in vain in *Paradise Lost* to justify the tyranny of a patriarchal God.

This doesn't mean that Blake was a Satanist. His meaning is that Christian doctrine has confused two very different things, wrongly calling them both by the name of Satan. One is resistance to tyranny, whereas the other is sadistic cruelty. The Satan who revenges himself on God by tempting Adam and Eve to sin has nothing in common with the heroic rebel at the beginning of *Paradise Lost.* Blake thought it outrageous to believe that an omnipotent, all-knowing God could first prohibit the fruit of knowledge and then allow an immensely powerful fallen angel to tempt the just-created Adam and Eve to pluck it and incur damnation.

Finally, what is one to make of the picture of the tiger? Although in the original format it would be seen simultaneously with the text, it strikes most viewers as bizarrely incongruous. In addition, it differs markedly from one copy to another, depending on how it is colored and how the tiger's expression is rendered. In the first of the two copies reproduced here (color plate 9), the scene is dark and rather ominous. In the second (color plate 10), the wide-eyed tiger looks merely anxious or bemused, in a bright daytime scene—hardly forests of the night. Erdman describes the single tree as "scared leafless." This tiger is certainly not burning bright, and there is nothing to suggest fearful symmetry.[21]

Many commentators have complained that the image is miserably inadequate to the poem; one calls this tiger "mild and silly," another "simpering." It has even been suggested that Blake wasn't any good at drawing animals, but that's absurd. He was perfectly capable of drawing fierce tigers, and there are two of them in a page of his notebook.[22]

There is another possibility. From the perspective of Experience, whatever seems overwhelming in existence should arouse fear and awe. Innocence sees it differently. Not only did the same God make tigers and lambs, but both of them inhabit the world we live in. Predators exist that seek to kill us, just as we ourselves kill trusting sheep and lambs. But an animal that can suggest nature as threat may also symbolize nature as our proper home. In a beautiful lyric in *Songs of Innocence* called *Night,* "wolves and tygers howl for prey," but a tender lion stands guard:

> And there the lion's ruddy eyes
> Shall flow with tears of gold,
> And pitying the tender cries,
> And walking round the fold:
> Saying "Wrath by his meekness
> And by his health, sickness,
> Is driven away
> From our immortal day."[23]

The Tyger doesn't answer the questions it poses. The picture reminds us that there can be more than one way of trying to answer them. Experience speaks in the text; Innocence responds in the picture. Thus Innocence and Experience continue to be in dialogue, and although the poem is filled with challenging questions about what a creator might be like, it is also an eloquent celebration of creativity and life.

Social Protest

*T*he *Chimney Sweeper* in *Songs of Innocence* hinted strongly at social protest, both against the exploitation of small children and against the religious ideology that teaches them to accept their lot. A poem in *Songs of Experience* is also entitled *The Chimney Sweeper,* and here the political issues are explicit.

> A little black thing among the snow,
> Crying "weep, weep," in notes of woe!
> Where are thy father and mother, say?
> "They are both gone up to the church to pray.
>
> Because I was happy upon the heath,
> And smiled among the winter's snow,
> They clothed me in the clothes of death,
> And taught me to sing the notes of woe.
>
> And because I am happy and dance and sing,
> They think they have done me no injury,
> And are gone to praise God and his priest and king
> Who make up a heaven of our misery."[24]

The picture (figure 20) presents what for Blake is an unusually three-dimensional, naturalistic scene. The boy, carrying his bag of soot on his back and a wire brush (not easy to see in this copy) in his right hand, looks anxiously up into the pelting snow as he passes houses that are closed against him. He believes that he has been forced to suffer simply *"because* I was happy upon the heath," and his blackened garments are indeed clothes of death.

One might suppose that churches in Blake's day would have seen it as their mission to relieve such suffering, but far from it—they taught that child labor of every kind was a moral obligation. Chimney sweepers, owing to their filthy appear-

THE Chimney Sweeper

A little black thing among the snow:
Crying weep, weep, in notes of woe!
Where are thy father & mother? say?
They are both gone up to the church to pray.

Because I was happy upon the heath,
And smil'd among the winters snow:
They clothed me in the clothes of death,
And taught me to sing the notes of woe.

And because I am happy, & dance & sing,
They think they have done me no injury:
And are gone to praise God & his Priest & King
Who make up a heaven of our misery.

20. *The Chimney Sweeper, Songs of Experience,* copy L, plate 41

ance, were forbidden even to enter a church. If they did try to go in, a reformer said, "They were driven out by the beadle with this taunt, 'What have chimney sweepers to do in a church?'" Even when churches promoted charity, Blake saw it as hypocritical evasion of responsibility for the injustice that makes charity necessary. *The Divine Image* in *Songs of Innocence* declares optimistically:

> Mercy has a human heart,
> Pity, a human face,
> And love, the human form divine,
> And peace, the human dress.

In *Experience* the corresponding poem, *The Human Abstract,* is bitterly disillusioned.

> Pity would be no more
> If we did not make somebody poor,
> And mercy no more could be
> If all were as happy as we.

It may be worth mentioning that "poor" still rhymes with "more" in the speech of many British people, as it does in Mark Twain—"drot your pore broken heart."[25]

Besides *The Tyger,* the other masterpiece in *Songs of Experience* is an overwhelming indictment of social injustice. It is entitled simply *London*.

> I wander through each chartered street,
> Near where the chartered Thames does flow,
> And mark in every face I meet
> Marks of weakness, marks of woe.
>
> In every cry of every man,
> In every infant's cry of fear,
> In every voice, in every ban,
> The mind-forged manacles I hear.
>
> How the chimney sweeper's cry
> Every blackening church appalls,
> And the hapless soldier's sigh
> Runs in blood down palace walls.

> But most through midnight streets I hear
> How the youthful harlot's curse
> Blasts the newborn infant's tear
> And blights with plagues the marriage hearse.[26]

Blake was a lifelong Londoner. As he imagines wandering through his native city—there is nothing to suggest that the poem's speaker is different from himself—he is assaulted on every side by sights and sounds of human suffering. Men and children cry aloud ("bans" are curses); chimney sweeps call, "Sweep! Sweep!" in search of work. Indeed, sounds are heard so intensely that they can become sights, in the synesthesia with which Blake seems to have perceived the world. The sighs of soldiers drip like blood on the palace that orders them abroad to die for the British Empire. The cries of chimney sweeps are likewise made visible, in the soot that covers churches like a funeral pall (there may also be a suggestion that the churches should grow pale with horror or shame). James Joyce put it well: "Looking at St. Paul's cathedral, Blake heard with the ear of the soul the cry of the little chimney sweep. Looking at Buckingham Palace, he sees with the eye of the mind the sigh of the hapless soldier running down the palace wall."[27] It is probably no accident that the initial letters of the third stanza of *London* spell out the word HEAR, just as the "newborn infant's tear" near the end of the poem echoes "every infant's cry of fear" near the beginning.

Like *The Tyger, London* has an urgent, driving rhythm. The underlying meter is iambic, but so passionately indignant that it often surges into a trochaic drumbeat:

> Hów the yóuthful hárlot's cúrse
> Blásts the néwborn ínfant's téar. . . .

The accusation is repeated with hypnotic intensity: "in every—in every—in every—in every—in every." And in the intensity of visionary perception, verbs can become nouns: "*Mark* in every face I meet / *Marks* of weakness, *marks* of woe." Blake is thinking of passages in the Bible such as the Lord's command to Ezekiel: "Go through the midst of the city, through the midst of Jerusalem, and set a mark upon the foreheads of the men that sigh and that cry for all the abominations that be done in the midst thereof."[28]

The streets are "chartered" because charters played an important role in an intense political debate at the time. London radicals, with whom Blake identified, hoped that a revolution like the one in France could establish liberty, equality, and fraternity. Conservatives, Edmund Burke for example, countered that the English people had more than enough liberty already, guaranteed by legal charters that went all the way back to the Great Charter, the thirteenth-century Magna Carta. But the radicals, such as Thomas Paine, saw this legal system as narrowly restrictive, prohibiting whatever it did not specifically permit. In Blake's *London* the very streets are legalistically defined, and even the flowing river is confined between man-made walls.

London is a political protest in a profoundly moral sense, not in a programmatic way. Orwell said, "There is more understanding of the nature of capitalist society in a poem like 'I wander through each chartered street' than in three-quarters of socialist literature." Michael Ferber remarks that near Westminster Bridge today, Blake's *London* can be seen chiseled into the stone pavement. Across the river are the Houses of Parliament and the Ministry of Defense, twin strongholds of the very power structure that the poem was written to expose.[29]

The picture for *London* (figure 21) complements the text. An aged man on a crutch is being led by a small boy, passing a door closed tight against them. It is evidently winter, since another boy is warming his hands at a fire in the street. The old man may well be blind, as he is when a similar image is invoked in the late poem *Jerusalem:*

> I see London blind and age-bent begging through the streets
> Of Babylon, led by a child. His tears run down his beard. . . .
> The corner of Broad Street weeps; Poland Street languishes
> To Great Queen Street and Lincoln's Inn, all is distress and woe.[30]

In his later poems Blake imagined an ideal London as Jerusalem, and the actual London as Babylon. He was born in the family shop in Broad Street, Poland Street was right around the corner, and Great Queen Street is where he spent his seven years' apprenticeship to James Basire. Close by is Lincoln's Inn where lawyers were and are trained. In a number of copies of the *Songs,* the undulating border at the foot of

LONDON

I wander thro' each charter'd street,
Near where the charter'd Thames does flow
And mark in every face I meet
Marks of weakness, marks of woe.

In every cry of every Man,
In every Infants cry of fear,
In every voice; in every ban,
The mind-forg'd manacles I hear

How the Chimney-sweepers cry
Every blackning Church appalls,
And the hapless Soldiers sigh
Runs in blood down Palace walls

But most thro' midnight streets I hear
How the youthful Harlots curse
Blasts the new born Infants tear
And blights with plagues the Marriage hearse

21. *London, Songs of Experience,* copy N, plate 21

the page in *London* resembles an earthworm, emblem of mortality; in the copy reproduced here it is a hissing snake.

All of these victims have internalized a cruel ideology, crystallized in the brilliant expression "the mind-forged manacles." In an earlier draft Blake called them "German forged links," with the Hanoverian monarchy in mind (see figure 19, page 82, above), but that was too reductive. A generation later Shelley too spoke of fetters that bite "with poisonous rust into the soul," but he suggested that they might turn out to be "brittle perchance as straw." Blake's metaphor is suggestive of manacles made of iron or steel, not straw, and in later poems he often acknowledged how hard it would be to shed them: "He could not take their fetters off for they grew from the soul." The South African martyr Steve Biko said memorably, "The most potent weapon of the oppressor is the mind of the oppressed."[31]

Finally, it is in "midnight streets" that the most harrowing sound is heard. The plight of the youthful harlot forms the culmination of this amazing social indictment, for it gathers together all of the themes of the poem. In *Jerusalem* Blake speaks of "a religion of chastity, forming a commerce to sell loves / With moral law." Marriages were regularly arranged between families for financial considerations, wives were encouraged to be chastely asexual, and divorce was virtually unobtainable. So a subculture of prostitution, officially condemned but in practice condoned, grew up for dissatisfied men; women's needs were not considered. In *Jerusalem* Blake poses a telling question:

> What is a wife and what is a harlot? what is a church? and what
> Is a theatre? are they two and not one? can they exist separate?
> Are not religion and politics the same thing?

Conventional marriage was thus institutionalized prostitution, and conventional religion was a theatrical performance for a passive audience. Blake would have heard the voice of Satan in T. S. Eliot's remark, "The only dramatic satisfaction that I find now is in a High Mass well performed."[32] Religion and politics are the same thing because the Church of England is a tool of the repressive state. For Blake the mission of religion should be to inspire change in the world we live in right now, not to preach resignation while awaiting the hereafter.

The most startling thing in the poem is its very last word. In the opinion of the poet and critic John Holloway, "It gives to *London* the most powerful closing line of any poem known to me in any language." "Marriage bed" would be the expected idea: the husband contracts a venereal disease from the harlot and then transmits it to his wife, who in turn infects their child (symptoms of gonorrhea, potentially fatal, could show up in a newborn's tears). In that sense the carriage that bears them away from their wedding is really a hearse in disguise. But society is diseased at a more profound level than just the literal infections that a prostitute might pass on. As with the mind-forged manacles, the implications are all-embracing. "Blake is talking about *every* marriage," Bloom says, "and he means literally that each rides in a hearse" — a kind of living death.[33]

According to a trenchant Proverb of Hell, "Prisons are built with stones of law, brothels with bricks of religion."[34] The distinction is thought-provoking. Stone is a natural substance, hard and durable, shaped with effort and skill into building blocks. Blake unquestionably believed that the criminal justice system in England was corrupt and unjust, but he would not have denied that societies do need laws. Bricks are not stones but mock-stones, soft clay held together with straw and cast in identical molds. And it is religion that builds brothels with them, for the policing of sex by religion is what creates the incentive for brothels to exist.

In the notebook poem known as *Auguries of Innocence,* we hear the harlot's cry again, together with the rhyme on "curse" and "hearse."

> The whore and gambler by the state
> Licensed build that nation's fate;
> The harlot's cry from street to street
> Shall weave old England's winding sheet.
> The winners shout, the losers curse,
> Dance before dead England's hearse.
> Every night and every morn
> Some to misery are born;
> Every morn and every night
> Some are born to sweet delight.
> Some are born to sweet delight,
> Some are born to endless night.

Quoted by themselves, as they often are, "sweet delight" and "endless night" may seem to acknowledge inevitable human differences, but they are not inevitable at all. The key insight is in the phrase "by the state licensed." Without it, David Punter observes, "the extract would be mere lamentation; with it, it becomes already a diagnosis." In *London,* in just sixteen lines, Blake manages to indict the church, the law, the monarchy, property, and marriage. In marriage, as he sees it, nearly all of the others are combined — maybe even all of them, if one thinks of monarchy as the symbolic embodiment of patriarchy.[35]

It might seem that *London* would serve as an appropriate culmination to *Songs of Experience,* and it does usually appear near the end, but not as the final poem. Just as in *Songs of Innocence,* Blake varied the sequence of poems from one copy to another. In copy N, the one reproduced here, *London* is fifth from the end, followed by *The Little Vagabond, Holy Thursday, Nurse's Song,* and finally a rather mild poem called *The Schoolboy. The Tyger,* in the two copies reproduced here, is ninth from the end in copy F and thirteenth in copy Z.

"What Is the Price of Experience?"

In part because his poems were issued in such limited editions, but also because they are undeniably strange, Blake was virtually unknown as a poet during his lifetime. The few people who bought his illuminated books paid little attention to the texts. Even as an artist he was marginalized, known for little else besides the illustrations to *Night Thoughts* and *The Grave.* In his annotations to Reynolds he wrote bitterly, "Fuseli almost hid himself — I am hid."[36] He first wrote, "I was hid," and then changed "was" to "am." Henry Fuseli was a mentor and friend, more successful as an artist than Blake, but likewise regarded as eccentric and outside the mainstream.

A few of the early lyrics did find their way into print, for example, the *Innocence* version of *The Chimney Sweeper* in a reformist treatise entitled *The Chimney Sweeper's Friend and Climbing Boy's Album.* A reviewer commented, "We know not how to characterize the song given from Blake's *Songs of Innocence.* It is wild and strange, like the singing of a 'maid in Bedlam in the spring;' but it is the madness of genius."[37] That this perfectly straightforward poem could be called mad suggests just how conventional most readers' tastes were.

A friend of Blake's named Benjamin Heath Malkin included a number of the poems, including *The Tyger,* in a little volume in 1806, and reviewers were even more dismissive. One said condescendingly that the poems were "not devoid of merit," another that "the poetry of Mr. Blake does not rise above mediocrity." Shortly after his death someone who knew him well had this to say: "The poetry of these songs is wild, irregular, and highly mystical, but of not great degree of elegance or excellence, and their prevailing feature is a tone of complaint of the misery of mankind."[38] "Complaint" is a feeble description of Blake's searing exposure of cruelty, hypocrisy, and exploitation.

Through their mutual friend Henry Crabb Robinson, two great poets, Wordsworth and Coleridge, did hear of Blake near the end of his life. Coleridge actually paid him a visit, and Robinson reported that Coleridge "talks finely about him," though without mentioning what he said. Wordsworth responded favorably to the *Songs;* he and his sister Dorothy copied out several of them, including *The Tyger.* But according to Robinson their admiration was qualified. "There is no doubt that this man is mad," he remembered Wordsworth saying, "but there is something in this madness which I enjoy more than the sense of Walter Scott or Lord Byron." Coleridge too borrowed Robinson's copy of the *Songs* and used a system of markings to indicate the ones he liked best and least, putting *Infant Joy* at the top. He thought *The Sick Rose* was good and *The Tyger* still better, but he ranked *The Chimney Sweeper* (probably the Experience version) and *The Blossom* at the very bottom.[39]

It was a long time before even Wordsworth and Coleridge attained the prestige they now enjoy. When Samuel Johnson's friend Charles Burney reviewed their breakthrough volume, *Lyrical Ballads,* he found the poems entertaining but concluded, "We cannot regard them as *poetry,* of a class to be cultivated at the expense of a higher species of versification." During that era the most admired poets were Sir Walter Scott, Lord Byron, Robert Southey, Samuel Rogers, and Thomas Moore.[40]

An eloquent lament in *The Four Zoas,* begun in the late 1790s, captures all too convincingly the story of Blake's career:

What is the price of experience? do men buy it for a song,
Or wisdom for a dance in the street? No it is bought with the price
Of all that a man hath, his house his wife his children.
Wisdom is sold in the desolate market where none come to buy
And in the withered fields where the farmer ploughs for bread in vain.[41]

5. REVOLUTION

Albion Rose

DURING the early 1790s, inspired by the French Revolution, an organized campaign developed for British political reform. Its focus was on extending the franchise so that more men could vote (not women, of course) and on restructuring parliamentary districts so that the rapidly growing industrial cities would have proper representation. There was also a call to abolish so-called pocket boroughs, in which local magnates would choose members of parliament to suit themselves, as well as rotten boroughs, seats established in the Middle Ages but now with few inhabitants, and in some scandalous instances none whatsoever.

These were important goals, and it took forty years to achieve them if only partially, in the Reform Bill of 1832. Still, the reformers were attempting to work within the political system, not to overthrow it. A small number of radicals saw this program as pitifully inadequate and hoped instead to ignite a vast remaking of the entire social order. Historians have tried hard to identify these people, but that is far from easy, since they were compelled to operate in secrecy. What is clear is that they shared many ideas with the revolutionaries of the 1640s who had executed King Charles I and who proudly appropriated a biblical description of the early Christians as "these that have turned the world upside down." Those seventeenth-century radicals were known as antinomians, meaning "against the law," from the Greek *nomos*. Detesting institutional religion, they believed that the Law of the Old Testament had been abolished, and they anticipated that Puritan victory would ignite a revolution far more profound than mere political change. Jerusalem was to be created anew and an age of brotherhood achieved, as had long been prophesied under the name of the Everlasting Gospel, a phrase from the Book of Revelation.[1] One of Blake's notebook poems is *The Everlasting Gospel.*

After the Puritans gained power in the 1650s, however, they turned conservative, and made it clear that their radical fringe was no longer welcome. As it turned out, their own rule was short-lived, and the English people welcomed back King Charles II in the Restoration of 1660. Thereafter the antinomians were fiercely persecuted and driven underground, all but invisible until they began to surface again in Blake's time, a century and a half later. They were never organized and never had a collective program, but the most extreme among them still hoped to get rid of the monarchy, and even to abolish class distinctions altogether.

What contacts Blake may have had with the radical fringe of his day is unknown. The eminent historian E. P. Thompson was convinced that he must have been connected with a tiny splinter group known as Muggletonians, which had a few dozen members at most, but he was never a joiner, and anyway the Muggletonian writings are conventional and obvious by comparison with his.[2]

Whatever Blake's personal connection with the radical underground may have been, he certainly sympathized with many of its ideas. It is less illuminating to associate him, as is sometimes done, with self-styled prophets such as Richard Brothers, who proclaimed himself Prince of the Hebrews and was institutionalized for insanity. Blake never claimed to be specially appointed, and he stated explicitly that he was not a prophet in any literal sense. "Prophets in the modern sense of the word," he wrote, "have never existed. . . . Every honest man is a prophet; he utters his opinion both of private and public matters. Thus, if you go on so, the result is so. He never says such a thing shall happen, let you do what you will. A prophet is a seer, not an arbitrary dictator." At another time Blake quoted Moses: "Would to God that all the Lord's people were prophets!"[3]

A magnificent color print known as *Albion Rose* (color plate 11) epitomizes Blake's vision of national rebirth. The print exists in several versions made over a period of years, and its meaning probably changed for him during that time. The copy reproduced here, now in the Huntington Library in Pasadena, is the second impression from a printing that was done in 1795 or 1796 (the first impression is in the British Museum). Since paint was not reapplied after each printing, it inevitably got thinner after the first copy was made. In this one, lines show through that reveal that the design was engraved on copper before colors were applied.[4]

At first the print was untitled, and Gilchrist, just guessing, called it *Glad Day,* a name it continued to go by for a long time. But Blake's own title is indicated by an inscription he added to a final copy around 1804:

> Albion rose from where he laboured at the mill with slaves
> Giving himself for the nations he danced the dance of eternal death

"Death" for Blake means what we normally call life — the living death of isolated selfhood in a mechanical universe. In an early work, *There Is No Natural Religion,* he likens that existence to the endless grinding of a mill: "The same dull round even of a universe would soon become a mill with complicated wheels."[5]

Albion was a traditional poetic name for England, and in Blake's early works it refers simply to the land, as it does in Spenser and Milton. But in his poems in the 1800s, when this inscription was added, Albion becomes a full personification, a giant form in whom all the people of England are embodied. "At the mill with slaves" alludes to Milton's blind Samson, forced to labor "eyeless in Gaza, at the mill with slaves." Like Samson, Albion triumphs through death, but in Blake's symbolism that self-sacrifice is actually an ascent into life, "giving himself for the nations." He must have been thinking also of a famous passage in Milton's *Areopagitica:* "Methinks I see in my mind a noble and puissant nation rousing herself like a strong man after sleep, and shaking her invincible locks."[6]

On the final state of the print Blake inscribed "W.B. inv 1780." "Inv" was the printmakers' term for "invenit," referring to the "invention" of the design. But it is not likely that he actually engraved it at that early date, for in that case he would have added "sculp" for "sculpsit," the sculptural process of incising lines into the plate. What he probably meant is that he first conceived the design, perhaps in the form of a sketch, in 1780, even though he didn't produce the print until fifteen years later.[7]

The 1780 date suggests at least two implications. That was the year when Blake completed his apprenticeship and was free at last to develop his own style. And it was also when he found himself unexpectedly swept along in what became known as the Gordon Riots. An enraged mob, inflamed by anti-Catholic feeling but also by general grievances, surged through the streets and broke open Newgate Prison, allowing hundreds of prisoners to escape. After a week of anarchy the army was called out and opened fire indiscriminately, killing nearly three hundred rioters. *Albion Rose* may well have been originally conceived as a symbol of popular insurrection, and when Blake later added the reference to the dance of death he may have been thinking of Edmund Burke's contemptuous phrase, "the death dance of democratic revolution," which implied that calls for reform were really just a cover for mob anarchy.[8]

With a radiant sunrise behind him, Albion's pose is expansive. As W. J. T. Mitchell says, the picture gives an impression of "a human body glowing with vitality, radiating an aura of sensuous light and heat—the image of Albion dancing in liberated ecstasy." Mitchell notes also that while the posture recalls Renaissance diagrams of ideal human proportions, they usually center on the navel, whereas this one is centered on the genitals. There may even be a personal reference in Albion's curly golden hair. Frederick Tatham said that in Blake's youth "his hair was of a yellow brown, and curled with the utmost crispness and luxuriance. His locks, instead of falling down, stood up like a curling flame, and looked at a distance like radiations."[9]

In the late, uncolored 1804 print of *Albion Rose* (figure 22) two creatures have been added. In the original version Albion's feet had rested on stone covered with mottled vegetation. In this revised print the vegetation is gone, the right foot is in the air, and the left foot tramples on what may be an earthworm, or else the larval form of the moth taking wing above it. As already noted, earthworms are a recurring symbol of the cycle of mortality, and moths or butterflies of the soul's liberation from it. But then, why does this weird moth have wings like a bat? Bats are negative

Albion rose from where he labourd at the Mill with Slaves
Giving himself for the Nations he danc'd the dance of Eternal Death

22. *Albion Rose*, second state

symbols for Blake. One possible interpretation is that Albion is indeed liberated and that the bat-moth is an oppressive fiend from which he has joyfully escaped. But it may also be that these additions reflect disillusionment with revolution. Just as the French Revolution, which Blake had eagerly hailed in 1789, degenerated into the horrific Terror, so in the perspective of 1804 Albion's dance may be a true dance of death after all.[10]

Marrying Heaven and Hell

Blake's most overtly antinomian work is *The Marriage of Heaven and Hell,* probably published in 1793. It seems to have begun as a limited satire on the teachings of Emanuel Swedenborg, who struck Blake as a conventional church founder only pretending to be an inspired visionary.[11] Soon, however, it grew into a wide-ranging challenge to orthodox morality, in an extraordinary medley of biblical imitation, prose satire, poetry, and homemade proverbs.

In celebrating what he calls Hell, Blake has in mind something very different from the usual connotations of that word. The fundamental idea in *The Marriage of Heaven and Hell* is that theologians and preachers have wrongly stigmatized energy as diabolical, even though it is absolutely essential to existence. They claim that "good is the passive that obeys reason; evil is the active springing from energy."[12] Blake's counterclaim is that Heaven and Hell must interact as vital contraries, like partners in a marriage who are different yet joined. Both are equally important, though in his enthusiastic polemic Hell gets the better of the argument.

The title page (color plate 12) magnificently embodies these ideas. Gilchrist may not have understood it fully, but he described it well: "The ever-fluctuating colour, the spectral pigmies rolling, flying, leaping among the letters; the ripe bloom of quiet corners, the living light and bursts of flame, the spires and tongues of fire vibrating with the full prism, make the page seem to move and quiver within its boundaries."[13]

In a rather pallid scene at the top, a courting couple strolls demurely and a woman reclines while her suitor reads to her (or perhaps plays a musical instrument). The trees above them are drooping and leafless. But from below, energy surges powerfully up, and a pair of naked figures embrace. An antinomian devil rises from the flames, and an orthodox angel rests upon a cloud; their union is repeated above in the small soaring couples. But the torsion in the embrace is striking: although they are locked in a kiss, their bodies extend and twist in opposing directions. Marriage is not identity, and for that matter, gender is not necessarily its basis. Both figures are female, as is clearly apparent in an uncolored copy, although the one on the left—the devil, presumably—is more voluptuous.[14] Over the years Blake's ideal figures would become increasingly androgynous.

A recurring theme of Blake's work is that his symbols express what goes on in our minds, and it is possible to see in this title page design the shape of a human head. The trees outline its hairy scalp, the courting couples are its eyes, and the circle around the word "and" is its mouth. Our world as we normally perceive it lies above the line that runs, as it were, from ear to ear. Beneath burns the energy that makes life possible. And both worlds, Heaven and Hell, exist within human consciousness.[15]

Flaming energy is one aspect of vital existence, but there are tranquil aspects too. In another image (color plate 13) a naked young man, with genitals frankly exposed, looks up hopefully into the sky. The skull under his knee is a reminder that revolution abolishes bondage to dead ancestors. Horrified by the French Revolution, Burke declared that society is a contract that must not be altered: "As the ends of such a partnership cannot be obtained in many generations, it becomes a partnership not only between those who are living, but between those who are living, those who are dead, and those who are to be born." Thomas Paine retorted, "Mr. Burke is contending for the authority of the dead over the rights and freedom of the living. . . . As government is for the living and not for the dead, it is the living only that has any right in it." Blake put it crisply in one of the Proverbs of Hell: "Drive your cart and your plow over the bones of the dead."[16]

Remarkably, in every copy of this plate except the one reproduced here, there are no pyramids. They were never in the etched design but were added with watercolor on this particular copy. It must have struck Blake as appropriate to introduce a symbol that he often used in his poems, the pyramids of Egypt, recalling the bondage from which the Israelites escaped. In his last poem, *Jerusalem,* London laborers don't just make bricks, they *become* bricks:

> Here they take up
> The articulations of a man's soul, and laughing throw it down
> Into the frame, then knock it out upon the plank, and souls are baked
> In bricks to build the pyramids of Heber and Terah.

(Terah was the father of Abraham, and Heber an earlier patriarch.)[17]

A memorable section of *The Marriage of Heaven and Hell* is entitled "Proverbs of Hell," which are really anti-proverbs. Ordinary proverbs convey conventional truisms, even when they sometimes contradict each other, as in "Absence makes the heart grow fonder" but also "Out of sight, out of mind." Blake's aphorisms are anything but conventional: "Exuberance is beauty"; "The cistern contains, the fountain overflows"; "The tygers of wrath are wiser than the horses of instruction"; "He who desires but acts not, breeds pestilence"; "The road of excess leads to the palace of wisdom." At times these anti-proverbs seem deliberately intended to shock: "Sooner murder an infant in its cradle than nurse unacted desires."[18] Blake can't mean that every possible desire should be acted on, and still less that babies should be murdered, but rather that an unacted desire is *like* an infanticide. Just as we nurse a grudge, so we may nurse a desire that we are unable or too cowardly to gratify. Yet if that is indeed the meaning, it is not an immediately obvious one. The point of Blake's proverbs is not to restate what we already know but to make us think.

Since they are so very open-ended, these proverbs are easily detachable from their context. "What is now proved was once only imagined," says one of the Proverbs of Hell, referring presumably to spiritual insight. But some years ago I encountered it blazoned on the display window of a Paris boutique: what was once only imagined by the designer now dresses the mannequins in the window (figure 23). The library in Donald Trump's extravagant edifice on Central Park in New York reportedly displays another Proverb of Hell, transformed into a self-congratulatory slogan: "The road of excess leads to the palace of wisdom."

23. Paris boutique

America: A Prophecy

In 1793, the same year as *The Marriage of Heaven and Hell,* Blake published his most hopeful account of revolution. *America: A Prophecy* is prophetic in the sense already explained, a commentary on the meaning of events, not a prediction of the future. The illuminated books from this period are known collectively as the Lambeth Books, after the district south of the Thames where the Blakes were then living. It was amusing that a near neighbor was the archbishop of Canterbury, whose official residence is Lambeth Palace.

The "Preludium" of *America* introduces a new character, Orc, a name adapted from a Latin word for the infernal regions (it is also the source of an Old English word from which J. R. R. Tolkien named his orcs). Blake's Orc seems demonic to the established order, for he is the youthful spirit of rebellion, striving to burst his shackles. In *America* he first appears as a sprawling naked youth fettered to a rock (color plate 14). This late copy, made to appeal to an art collector, is stunningly beautiful. The outline is printed in rich blue, and in applying watercolors great care has been taken to keep the blue sky and yellow leaves from blurring into each other.[19] The text is an especially elegant example of Blake's italic lettering, easily legible but obviously inscribed by hand, and at times it flourishes into life in ways that printed typography never could. In the sixth line, for example, the initial "W" trails a tendril downward, and the "d" of the final word "need" spirals upward.

What exactly are we looking at? Many possibilities have been proposed. The youth resembles Prometheus fettered to his cliff in the Caucasus, and there may also be an allusion to the Crucifixion, since Christ too is a god who suffers on behalf of humankind. The adults in the picture resemble Adam and Eve in traditional depictions of the expulsion from Paradise, but instead of repenting for sin as in the title page of *Songs of Innocence and of Experience,* they recoil in shock at what they are seeing. Perhaps the young man is a conflated version of their two sons, the martyred Abel and the murderer Cain.[20]

In the classical myth Prometheus occupies a kind of absolute space, hanging above the world on his rock of agony. In Blake's picture we are gazing down at the rock, which is really just the surface of the ground, with gnarly humanized roots below. At the bottom a naked man sits huddled and brooding, as if awaiting resurrection, and beneath the text is an earthworm, symbolic of mortality once again. It has six coils because, in a phrase Blake used several times, man is "a worm of sixty winters."[21]

In the accompanying text, "red Orc" has reached his fourteenth year, the age of puberty, and yearns to seize "the shadowy daughter of Urthona," who brings him food and drink. She is not otherwise identified, and for that matter neither is Urthona, though the name may suggest "earth owner." Perhaps she is the American continent itself.

In the next plate Orc has somehow broken free and is able to gratify his desire.

> Silent as despairing love, and strong as jealousy,
> The hairy shoulders rend the links; free are the wrists of fire.
> Round the terrific loins he seized the panting struggling womb;
> It joyed: she put aside her clouds and smiled her first-born smile,
> As when a black cloud shows its lightnings to the silent deep.
> Soon as she saw the terrible boy then burst the virgin cry:
> "I know thee, I have found thee, and I will not let thee go."

This is commonly seen as a rape, which is undoubtedly right; similar sexual violence occurs in *Visions of the Daughters of Albion,* which was published in the same year as *America.* Blake's ambiguous and often disturbing view of sexuality will be considered later. Here it has to be acknowledged that the violation is apparently welcomed by the "shadowy daughter." Her womb "joys," and her speech echoes the Song of Solomon, "I found him whom my soul loveth: I held him, and would not let him go."[22]

Perhaps Blake's meaning is that although revolutions are inevitably violent, Orc's energy is libidinal, not destructive. Otherwise it would be inexplicable that it is Orc who is given this eloquent speech later on:

> For every thing that lives is holy, life delights in life;
> Because the soul of sweet delight can never be defiled.

Similarly, the picture that accompanies the lines about Orc's union with the shadowy daughter (figure 24) is not violent at all. No longer chained down, the young man gazes hopefully into the sky while a grapevine spirals upward from underground roots. This monochrome copy shows Blake's firm outlines to advantage, and since ten of the copies in the original 1793 printing are uncolored, he may have hoped to sell them cheaply to a wide audience, not just to collectors of art.[23]

As Blake imagines it, the American Revolution could have been the spark to ignite a universal uprising, in which the French Revolution would be followed by a British revolution yet to come. Though actual events in America are barely mentioned in the poem, we do meet some familiar characters:

> Fury! rage! madness! in a wind swept through America
> And the red flames of Orc that folded roaring fierce around

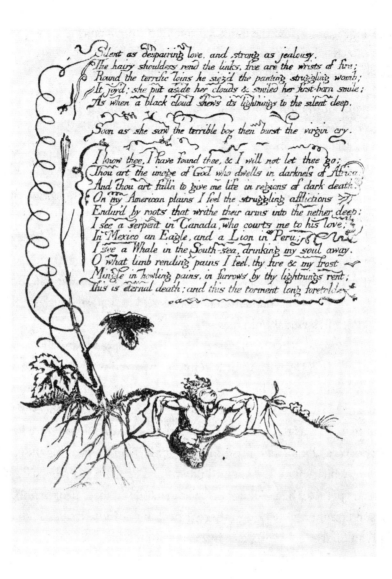

Silent as despairing love, and strong as jealousy.
The hairy shoulders rend the links, free are the wrists of fire;
Round the terrific loins he siezd the panting struggling womb;
It joy'd: she put aside her clouds & smiled her first-born smile;
As when a black cloud shews its lightnings to the silent deep.

Soon as she saw the terrible boy then burst the virgin cry.

I know thee, I have found thee, & I will not let thee go;
Thou art the image of God who dwells in darkness of Africa
And thou art fall'n to give me life in regions of dark death.
On my American plains I feel the struggling afflictions
Endur'd by roots that writhe their arms into the nether deep:
I see a serpent in Canada, who courts me to his love;
In Mexico an Eagle, and a Lion in Peru;
I see a Whale in the South-sea, drinking my soul away.
O what limb rending pains I feel. thy fire & my frost
Mingle in howling pains, in furrows by thy lightnings rent;
This is eternal death; and this the torment long foretold.

24. *America: A Prophecy*, copy E, plate 4

✧   ✧   ✧

> The angry shores, and the fierce rushing of th' inhabitants together.
> The citizens of New York close their books and lock their chests;
> The mariners of Boston drop their anchors and unlade;
> The scribe of Pennsylvania casts his pen upon the earth;
> The builder of Virginia throws his hammer down in fear.
> Then had America been lost, o'erwhelmed by the Atlantic,
> And Earth had lost another portion of the infinite,
> But all rush together in the night in wrath and raging fire.

The mariners are the Sons of Liberty in Boston, Franklin is the scribe of Pennsylvania, and Jefferson is the builder of Virginia. In their own minds those rebels were rejecting the authority of George III but keeping the social order pretty much unchanged. In Blake's vision it is the people united who "rush together," much to the alarm of their self-styled leaders, who drop their pen and hammer and lock up their valuables. It didn't actually happen like that, as he knew perfectly well, but from a prophetic point of view it should have.[24]

In another picture (figure 25) Orc appears in a pose very similar to one that we saw in *The Marriage of Heaven and Hell,* genitals displayed without shame and a skull at his side. In colored copies he has curly yellow hair, reminiscent of *Albion Rose*—and of William Blake. Commentators have noted also the relevance of an ancient Roman statue known as the Barberini Faun, in which a dissolute figure lounges in a suggestive posture, dozing and presumably drunk. There is nothing indecent about Blake's figure, which might be taken to illustrate a Proverb of Hell: "The head sublime, the heart pathos, the genitals beauty, the hands and feet proportion." Christopher Hobson comments, "Though there is nothing homosexual as such about this design, it is an image of intense, and intensely vulnerable, male beauty."[25]

The text in this plate celebrates liberation, in some of the most eloquent lines that Blake ever wrote:

> The morning comes, the night decays, the watchmen leave their stations;
> The grave is burst, the spices shed, the linen wrapped up;
> The bones of death, the covering clay, the sinews shrunk and dried
> Reviving shake, inspiring move, breathing! awakening!
> Spring like redeemed captives when their bonds and bars are burst.

The morning comes, the night decays, the watchmen leave
    their stations;
The grave is burst, the spices shed, the linen wrapped up;
The bones of death, the cov'ring clay, the sinews shrunk & dry'd.
Reviving shake, inspiring move, breathing! awakening!
Spring like redeemed captives when their bonds & bars are burst;
Let the slave grinding at the mill, run out into the field:
Let him look up into the heavens & laugh in the bright air:
Let the inchained soul shut up in darkness and in sighing,
Whose face has never seen a smile in thirty weary years;
Rise and look out, his chains are loose, his dungeon doors are open.
And let his wife and children return from the oppressors scourge;
They look behind at every step & believe it is a dream.
Singing. The Sun has left his blackness, & has found a fresher morning
And the fair Moon rejoices in the clear & cloudless night;
For Empire is no more, and now the Lion & Wolf shall cease.

25. *America: A Prophecy*, copy E, plate 8

Let the slave grinding at the mill run out into the field;
Let him look up into the heavens and laugh in the bright air;
Let the enchained soul shut up in darkness and in sighing,
Whose face has never seen a smile in thirty weary years,
Rise and look out, his chains are loose, his dungeon doors are open,
And let his wife and children return from the oppressor's scourge.
They look behind at every step and believe it is a dream,
Singing: "The sun has left his blackness, and has found a fresher morning,
And the fair moon rejoices in the clear and cloudless night,
For empire is no more, and now the lion and wolf shall cease."

These lines are full of biblical echoes. The slave at the mill and the watchmen come from the Gospel of Matthew, and the linen clothes from Christ's empty tomb in the Gospel of John. Ezekiel saw the dry bones revive: "I prophesied as I was commanded: and as I prophesied, there was a noise, and behold a shaking, and the bones came together . . . and the breath came into them, and they lived, and stood up upon their feet, an exceeding great army."[26]

The language is dynamic—shaking, springing, running—but the seated figure is at rest, pondering the future now that the dungeons have been broken open. The plants and small creatures at the bottom of the picture may be allegorical references of some kind, but if so they are obscure. At any rate they seem to be at home in a healthy natural world, very like the creatures in the picture for *The Clod and the Pebble*.[27]

Revolution is fed by energy, and in another picture (figure 26) Orc is buoyed up by flames that even invade the text. William Michael Rossetti, Dante Gabriel's brother, called Blake "the supreme painter of fire," and Blake himself coined the memorable phrase "fire delights in its form." In another work from this period he speaks of the "thick-flaming, thought-creating fires of Orc" (he knew Shakespeare well and may have been recalling Lear's "sulfurous and thought-executing fires"). As Mitchell says, in this picture the flames "are to be seen as *inside* him, as an externalization or projection of his consciousness."[28]

It could also be said that Orc embodies an aspect of our own consciousness. But he is not the only aspect, and in this picture his expression is uneasy, for he has

Thus wept the Angel voice & as he wept the terrible blasts
Of trumpets, blew a loud alarm across the Atlantic deep.
No trumpets answer; no reply of clarions or of fifes,
Silent the Colonies remain and refuse the loud alarm.

On those vast shady hills between America & Albions shore;
Now barrd out by the Atlantic sea: call'd Atlantean hills:
Because from their bright summits you may pass to the Golden world
An ancient palace, archetype of mighty Emperies.
Rears its immortal pinnacles, built in the forest of God
By Ariston the king of beauty for his stolen bride.

Here on their magic seats the thirteen Angels sat perturb'd
For clouds from the Atlantic hover o'er the solemn roof.

26. *America: A Prophecy*, copy E, plate 12

a mighty antagonist who is equally fundamental to consciousness. That character Blake calls Urizen, a white-bearded patriarch who is associated with God the Father, and with patriarchs of every kind from kings and bishops down to ordinary fathers.

In a visual parallel to the image of Orc in flames, Urizen appears in a similar pose (figure 27), although balanced on the opposite foot, and not naked but robed in a heavy, full-length gown. In the text immediately below,

> The terror answered: "I am Orc, wreathed round the accursèd tree.
> The times are ended; shadows pass, the morning gins to break;
> The fiery joy, that Urizen perverted to ten commands,
> What night he led the starry hosts through the wide wilderness:
> That stony law I stamp to dust, and scatter religion abroad
> To the four winds as a torn book, and none shall gather the leaves."[29]

The accursed tree is the prohibited tree of knowledge, at whose foot the biblical serpent tempted Eve. The implication is that to the forces of reaction, Orc does appear a diabolical serpent, twining around the forbidden tree. Like the activist Satan in *The Marriage of Heaven and Hell,* his mission is to smash the repressive law that Moses brought down from Mount Sinai on tablets of stone.

Urizen is sitting on heavy clouds, embracing them like boulders, while he gazes gloomily down on the world below. His expression is no more hopeful than Orc's in the companion picture, but everything about Urizen expresses heaviness, whereas Orc rises upward in his flames, spreading his fingers to catch the updraft. Urizen's clouds are modeled with elaborate cross-hatching of the kind used in commercial copy engraving, and it has been argued that Blake thought of this laborious technique as a visual sign of repressive control.[30]

Northrop Frye once described the struggle of Urizen and Orc as an "Orc cycle," in which every revolution degenerates into repression and every Orc becomes a Urizen. Frye was so persuasive that generations of critics adopted his idea, but in fact there is no basis for it in the poems themselves. Blake understood very well that revolutions can turn cruel, as was happening in France, but Orc and Urizen are not two names for the same thing. An older commentator, Milton Percival, described Orc more accurately as "a deathless phenomenon, the spirit of revolution that arises when energy is repressed."[31]

The terror answerd: I am Orc, wreath'd round the accursed tree:
The times are ended; shadows pass the morning gins to break;
The fiery joy, that Urizen perverted to ten commands,
What night he led the starry hosts thro' the wide wilderness:
That stony law I stamp to dust: and scatter religion abroad
To the four winds as a torn book, & none shall gather the leaves;
But they shall rot on desart sands, & consume in bottomless deeps,
To make the desarts blossom, & the deeps shrink to their fountains,
And to renew the fiery joy, and burst the stony roof.
That pale religious letchery, seeking Virginity,
May find it in a harlot, and in coarse-clad honesty
The undefil'd tho' ravish'd in her cradle night and morn;
For every thing that lives is holy, life delights in life;
Because the soul of sweet delight can never be defil'd.
Fires inwrap the earthly globe, yet man is not consumd;
Amidst the lustful fires he walks; his feet become like brass,
His knees and thighs like silver, & his breast and head like gold.

27. *America: A Prophecy*, copy E, plate 10

Multiple Serpents

Even in this optimistic early poem, Blake was thinking about revolution from multiple points of view, and his creative deployment of symbols was well suited to expressing that complexity. In conventional art, iconic symbols usually have a stable, consistent meaning; thus a cross signifies Christianity, a pair of scales justice. But Blake's symbols are dynamic, not iconic. We learn what they mean by observing what they do, and their actions change according to context. Another way of saying this is that they play active roles in an ever-evolving myth, and since the myth is being invented by Blake himself, we can't rely on traditional associations, even when he borrows materials from the Bible or Milton or the Bhagavad Gita.[32]

The imagery of the serpent is an excellent example of the range of implications in a single dynamic Blakean symbol. The sequel to *America* is a poem called *Europe: A Prophecy,* with a startling title page (color plate 15). This spectacular reptile is usually thought to symbolize Orc's rebellious energy, as perceived by the forces of repression, and perhaps recalling the snake with three coils in the American "Don't Tread on Me" flag. Erdman sees the image as entirely positive, "embodying energy, desire, phallic power, the fiery tongue," but other interpreters suspect a negative message. Morton Paley asks, "Does the grinning, coiled Orc serpent of the title page suggest that although Energy promises apocalyptic freedom, it actually betrays man to the cycle of history?"[33]

During the course of *Europe,* the serpent does in fact become a symbol of nature-worshipping repression. An "ancient temple serpent-formed" is constructed of huge stones in a winding pattern, like the one at Avebury that in Blake's time was attributed to Druid priests (see figure 38, page 193, below).

> Thought changed the infinite to a serpent; that which pitieth
> To a devouring flame; and man fled from its face and hid
> In forests of night. Then all the eternal forests were divided
> Into earths rolling in circles of space, that like an ocean rushed
> And overwhelmed all except this finite wall of flesh.
> Then was the serpent temple formed, image of infinite
> Shut up in finite revolutions, and man became an angel;
> Heaven a mighty circle turning; God a tyrant crowned.[34]

Planets revolve endlessly in the solar system, which is mimicked by the serpent temple in which priests propitiate their god with human sacrifice. "Forests of night" recalls the ambiguous creator of *The Tyger.*

In *America,* however, there is also an auspicious image of a serpent, on whose back three children ride at their ease (figure 28). The oldest holds the reins lightly, while the middle child reaches back to help the youngest. The serpentine form is repeated higher up in the neck of a soaring swan whose reins are held by a muscular young man. Above his head appear the words "Boston's Angel"—he might be an aerial version of Paul Revere. Both swan and serpent can be seen as phallic, and Blake knew of a sculpture from Herculaneum that showed a child riding on an enormous penis.[35] Here serpent symbolism is clearly positive, though no one has satisfactorily explained why images of night are glimpsed behind the clouds—a crescent moon, and the constellation of the Pleiades.

There are other animals in *America* besides serpents. One lovely picture (color plate 16) presents a total contrast to the furious text on the same plate, in which a wrathful Albion's Angel, the "spiritual form" of George III, denounces Orc as "serpent-formed . . . blasphemous demon, Antichrist, hater of dignities." Under a delicate tree on which birds of paradise perch, a naked young woman lies asleep on the ground, and a curly-headed young man rests on the woolly back of a sleeping ram. Very likely they have been making love. In this late, colored copy a sunrise suffuses the sky. It is a vision of Innocence, more explicitly sexualized than in *Songs of Innocence,* that invokes an alternative reality to rebellion and repression. It also fulfills the declaration that concludes the previous plate, "For empire is now no more, and now the lion and wolf shall cease."[36]

In *The Marriage of Heaven and Hell* sexuality was positive, and in the heyday of the 1960s counterculture Blake was often invoked to that effect. But he was always aware that sex can be a means of exerting control, and at times he was tormented by it. It is probably no accident that most of the naked bodies in Blake's pictures are unerotic, and at times positively repellent. We know that his hero was Michelangelo, about whom an art historian asks, "Why are his Madonnas so unmaternal? Why are his figures of superhuman scale and size?"[37]

Here, in *Europe,* two of the most attractive bodies Blake ever depicted (color

Fiery the Angels rose, & as they rose deep thunder roll'd
Around their shores, indignant burning with the fires of Orc
And Bostons Angel cried aloud as they flew thro' the dark
                                                            night.

He cried, Why trembles honesty and like a murderer,
Why seeks he refuge from the frowns of his immortal station;
Must the generous tremble & leave his joy, to the idle: to
        the pestilence!
That mock him? who commanded this? what God? what Angel!
To keep the genrous from experience till the ungenerous
Are unrestraind performers of the energies of nature;
Till pity is become a trade, and generosity a science,
That men get rich by, & the sandy desart is givn to the strong
What God is he, writes laws of peace, & clothes him in a tempest
What pitying Angel lusts for tears, and fans himself with sighs
What crawling villain preaches abstinence & wraps himself
In fat of lambs? no more I follow, no more obedience pay.

28. *America: A Prophecy*, copy E, plate 13

✧   ✧   ✧

plate 17) turn out to have highly negative implications. "No nude, however abstract," Kenneth Clark says, "should fail to arouse in the spectator some vestige of erotic feeling, even though it be only the faintest shadow — and if it does not do so, it is bad art and false morals." Insofar as that is true, Blake makes ironic use of it, for what his text describes is "Albion's Angel smitten with his own plagues," in consequence of England's counterrevolutionary war against France. These two shapely figures are in fact fairies scattering blight upon the crops through swirling trumpets. In a kind of visual pun, the trumpets emit blasts of sound just as mildew blasts grain. So England is being punished by the very plague it has brought into being, and the context completely undermines the erotic attractiveness of the picture.[38]

A sign of Blake's disillusionment with revolution is that in one of two copies of *America* that he printed in 1795, four lines were added on the plate that shows the young man clambering out of the ground:

> The stern Bard ceased, ashamed of his own song; enraged he swung
> His harp aloft sounding, then dashed its shining frame against
> A ruined pillar in glitt'ring fragments; silent he turned away,
> And wandered down the vales of Kent in sick and drear lamentings.

Smashing a harp was a traditional bardic refusal to perform in slavery.[39]

Retreat from Radical Politics

As early as 1792 a royal proclamation promised "to prosecute with severity all persons guilty of writing and publishing seditious pamphlets tending to alienate the affections of his Majesty's subjects, and to disturb the peace, order, and tranquility of the State, as well as to prohibit all illegal meetings." Prosecutions and imprisonment followed, and it must have been especially concerning for Blake that the Stationers' Company published a "determined resolution utterly to DISCOUNTENANCE and DISCOURAGE all seditious and inflammatory productions whatever." That resolution was signed by numerous publishers on whom he depended for income, as well as by his former master Basire.[40]

Whatever contribution Blake may once have thought of making to the anticipated revolution, by the mid-1790s he was retreating from any active political stance, and the few copies of his early illuminated books that still exist today were all sold or given to trusted friends. Starting with *The Book of Urizen,* which will be considered later, he turned instead to a critical dialogue with the Bible and then stopped creating illuminated books altogether for over a decade. He genuinely believed that if the authorities should become aware of his writings, his life might be in danger. He wrote in his notebook, "I say I shan't live five years, and if I live one it will be a wonder. June 1793." He was talking about legal persecution, not physical health. In 1797, annotating a bishop's attack on Thomas Paine, he declared, "I have been commanded from Hell not to print this; it is what our enemies wish."[41]

Besides fearing prosecution, Blake was becoming apolitical in any activist sense, and commentators who insist that he never retreated from political commitment are using the term in a very broad sense. In the more usual sense, he wrote in 1810, "I am really sorry to see my countrymen trouble themselves about politics. If men were wise the most arbitrary princes could not hurt them. If they are not wise the freest government is compelled to be a tyranny. Princes appear to me to be fools; Houses of Commons and Houses of Lords appear to me to be fools. They seem to me to be something else besides human life."[42]

Blake lived for sixty-nine years, and Britain was at war during half of that time. It fought in vain to hold on to its American colonies, it fought in vain to suppress the French Revolution, and then it fought with success to bring down the Napoleonic empire. Writing about Blake during World War II, Jacob Bronowski commented that "after the eagles and the magnificence, [the age of Napoleon] remains in the memory as Goya savagely pictured it: twenty-two years without conscience, stamping the men and the treasure of Europe into the dirt."[43]

The increasing pessimism of Blake's later poems has perplexed critics who would like to see him as a forerunner of Marxism, or at least of working-class radicalism. But class solidarity was never part of his thinking, and although he resented many aspects of capitalism, his values were those of an independent artisan. Whatever may have been lost when the dream of revolution faded, as he continued to develop his ideas he wrote no more political poems like *America* and *Europe,* and instead explored perennial tensions in human experience in ever-increasing depth. In

The Marriage of Heaven and Hell he had made a declaration that is often quoted as if it were the key to his thought: "Without contraries is no progression. Attraction and repulsion, reason and energy, love and hate, are necessary to human existence."[44] In Blake's later writings contraries would continue to play a central role, but we no longer hear of forward-trending "progression." And whereas Urizen would remain a central figure in his mythic thinking, Orc would dwindle from view, and a whole new cast of symbolic characters would need to be invented.

6. ATOMS AND VISIONARY INSIGHT

UNDERLYING Blake's critique of the psychological, political, and religious assumptions of his time was a conviction that modern ways of thought blind us to the fullness of experience. As a stopgap measure in their retreat from belief, eighteenth-century agnostics were fond of recommending deism (from the Latin *deus*), also known as natural religion, which claimed that anything worth knowing about the deity could be deduced rationally from the orderly processes of nature. Just as a clock must be the work of a skilled clockmaker, so the solar system must be the product of a clockmaker-god. Such a god, of course, need have no interest whatever in human beings, and Blake thought that an impersonal, detached deity like that was no god at all. But neither was the orthodox Jehovah. The god Blake did acknowledge was the very human Jesus whose benevolent presence pervades *Songs of Innocence.*

Blake's attack on natural religion, and the symbolism with which he counters it, are embodied in an unpublished lyric in his notebook, which has no title and no accompanying picture.

> Mock on Mock on Voltaire Rousseau
> Mock on Mock on! 'tis all in vain!
> You throw the sand against the wind
> And the wind blows it back again

And every sand becomes a gem
Reflected in the beams divine
Blown back they blind the mocking eye
But still in Israel's paths they shine

The atoms of Democritus
And Newton's particles of light
Are sands upon the Red Sea shore
Where Israel's tents do shine so bright[1]

Always sparing with punctuation, Blake used none at all here except for a pair of exclamation points. He evidently wanted each line to carry its own separate weight, not to slot neatly into place in tidy syntax.

Voltaire and Rousseau were leading figures in the Enlightenment, so called because it aspired to shed light on the dark places of superstition and tyranny. After the French Revolution the remains of these two great philosophes were reinterred next to each other in the Pantheon, but in life they had thought of themselves as opposites. The worldly, sophisticated Voltaire was a cynical wit, a rich landowner, and an admirer of philosopher-kings. Rousseau was a loner and hermit, a spokesman for "natural" simplicity, and the theorist of a radically new political system that would embody the "general will" of all citizens. From Blake's point of view, however, the affinities were deeper than the differences. He saw both Voltaire and Rousseau as believers in natural religion, and his own conviction was that the natural world as understood by modern thinkers was a barrier against truth, not a window into it.

What Blake did approve of in the Enlightenment was its campaign against institutional religion. Voltaire had a favorite slogan, *Écrasez l'infâme:* "Crush the infamous thing," meaning the Catholic Church, which controlled French education, imposed orthodox theological doctrine, and rigorously censored publications. He rejected most of orthodox doctrine as moralizing thought control, and so did Blake, who agreed that it was wrong to take the Bible as literally and factually true. "Voltaire was commissioned by God," he said, "to expose that."[2]

In Blake's view, the thinkers of the Enlightenment performed a necessary act of destruction with their critique of orthodoxy, but they didn't know how to reconstruct. In an inspired metaphor, he exploits the fact that although grains of sand can look like inert particles, if thrown up into sunlight they sparkle like jewels. The philosophes made that happen when they stirred up the sands of superstition, but because they foolishly faced into the wind, the sharp crystals stung their eyes into spiritual blindness.

There is another way to think about sand, though. Theorists of science in Blake's day thought that nature is best understood through mathematical laws, which supposedly described the interaction of atoms, far too tiny to be seen. Atoms were not conceived of as force fields, as they would be today; they were more like identical marbles in a bag. The ancient philosopher Democritus had imagined them as unbreakably solid building blocks, and in empiricist philosophy they were held to constitute everything that exists, including ourselves. As for the so-called secondary qualities that we perceive as color and taste and odor, they have no real existence at all. They are merely illusions that our brains construct from the sense data that stream in on us. As summarized by a modern historian of science, "The world that people had thought themselves living in [before empiricism] — a world rich with color and sound, redolent with fragrance, filled with gladness, love and beauty, speaking everywhere of purposive harmony and creative ideals — was now crowded into minute corners of the brains of scattered organic beings. The really important world outside was a world hard, cold, colorless, silent, and dead; a world of quantity, a world of mathematically computable motions in mechanical regularity."[3]

Blake understood these implications and utterly despised them. "Deduct from a rose its redness," he wrote, "from a lily its whiteness, from a diamond its hardness, from a sponge its softness, from an oak its height, from a daisy its lowness, and rectify everything in nature as the philosophers do, and then we shall return to chaos."[4]

Blake and Newton

Isaac Newton was a major culture hero in the eighteenth century, much as Albert Einstein would be in the twentieth. And like Einstein, Newton advanced theories that only specialists could grasp. His masterpiece was *Philosophiae Naturalis Principia Mathematica — Mathematical Principles of Natural Philosophy*. For nonexperts the math was impossibly difficult, but Newton's other classic, *Opticks,* was a book that ordinary readers could understand. Using prisms and lenses, he conducted a series of experiments on the properties of light, showing that a prism breaks seemingly white light into all the colors of the spectrum. Alexander Pope wrote a memorable epitaph:

> Nature and Nature's laws lay hid in night;
> God said, "Let Newton be!" and all was light.

With similar awe, Blake's contemporary Wordsworth described a statue at Trinity College, Cambridge, where Newton had once lived and taught:

> Newton with his prism and silent face,
> The marble index of a mind for ever
> Voyaging through strange seas of thought, alone.[5]

Blake would certainly not have disagreed that raindrops and prisms reveal the colors of the rainbow. What he objected to was Newton's claim that like everything else, light was composed of minute particles, which he called corpuscles. At the creation of the universe, Newton wrote, God "formed matter in solid, massy, hard, impenetrable, movable particles," which resemble each other just as much "as the sands on the shore."[6] Whenever we open our eyes, the stream of particles strikes our retinas and triggers signals in the brain. Blake invokes Newton's "sands on the shore" for a very different purpose: for him they suggest the Sinai Desert—"sands upon the Red Sea shore"—through which the Israelites journeyed from Egyptian captivity to the Promised Land. Newton described the ways in which light always behaves; Blake invokes a great symbolic story, the Exodus from bondage to freedom. The light that illuminates that journey is a spiritual force, not a hailstorm of material particles.

Infinity and Eternity

There is also a grain of sand in another of Blake's notebook poems:

> To see a world in a grain of sand
> And a heaven in a wild flower,
> Hold infinity in the palm of your hand
> And eternity in an hour.

One of Blake's favorite writers was the seventeenth-century German mystic Jacob Boehme, who wrote, "When I take up a stone or clod of earth and look upon it, then I see that which is above and that which is below; yea, I see the whole world therein." That kind of mysticism is very different from the kind that dismisses the visible world as mere illusion. Far from wanting to escape to a "higher" realm, Blake, like Boehme, sought richer apprehension of this one. "I can look at a knot in a piece of wood," he once said, "till I am frightened at it." Perhaps surprisingly, he was friendly with the far better known painter John Constable. Once, leafing through Constable's sketchbook, Blake commented on a drawing of trees, "Why, this is not drawing, but inspiration." "I never knew it before," Constable replied, no doubt with a smile. "I meant it for drawing." It is the same real world that we inhabit all the time but seen with new freshness, or with what Robert Frost calls "strangeness."[7]

Infinity, the empiricists thought, was a meaningless concept, since we are unable to comprehend a universe that goes on forever without end. Likewise eternity was meaningless, since all we can ever actually know is the ticktock of each successive second. Blake would agree that those were hopelessly abstract ways of trying to imagine infinity and eternity, but for him both were immediate and concrete. Infinity is present here and now in the real world we inhabit, not far away in unimaginable endlessness. Eternity, likewise, is present in each moment of lived experience; it is the river of time in which we are continuously immersed. He coined a memorable term for it—"the Eternal Now"—and he would have appreciated Ludwig Wittgenstein's statement, "If we take eternity to mean not infinite temporal duration but timelessness, then eternal life belongs to those who live in the present." "Eternity is in love with the productions of time," Blake wrote in *The Mar-*

riage of Heaven and Hell; elsewhere he called time "the mercy of Eternity."[8] Perhaps that means that for mortal men and women, the vastness of Eternity would be overwhelming if we were fully conscious of it. Mercifully, we are aware only of the onward flow of time in which we are immersed.

Although Blake criticized Newton's assumptions as reductive, he nevertheless had a generous admiration for Newton's genius. The great physicist is the subject of an extraordinary picture (color plate 18), though without knowing that its title is *Newton* one would be hard put to guess what it shows. Here Newton is very much alone, as in Wordsworth's lines, but not gazing into the heavens as the statue does. On a lichen-encrusted rock at the bottom of the sea, he sits in a constricted posture, compressed almost into a ball, the very opposite of the wide-flung limbs in pictures such as *Albion Rose.* Tracing a geometric diagram with a pair of compasses, he stares with intense concentration at a little scroll.

Whereas the Newton of history was a gaunt, ascetic professor, this Newton is a muscular athlete. Hunched over though he is, his powerful body, with clearly articulated muscles, contrasts vividly with the simplified diagram that he believes to be a true picture of reality. Much as Michelangelo would, Blake has thus translated intellectual power into a physical equivalent.[9] Newton is shown on the sea floor because Blake adopted from Neoplatonic philosophy the symbolism of water as suffocating materiality. But by implication nothing is stopping him from getting up off his rock and rising to the surface, into the world of sunlight and fresh air. Nor does he show any interest in the intricate and beautiful life-forms that cover his rock. Newton is a mighty genius, but also the prisoner of a reductive intellectual program. Blake's intention in this picture is not to deny his greatness but to suggest the imaginative bondage that his intellectual system imposed.

It is interesting that when Blake did try to study geometry, he couldn't see the point of formal proofs as opposed to immediate intuition. Thomas Taylor, whose translations of Plato Blake used, undertook to tutor him. According to someone who knew Taylor, they got as far as the fifth proposition in Euclid, "which proves that any two angles at the base of an isosceles triangle must be equal. Taylor was going through the demonstration, but was interrupted by Blake exclaiming, 'Ah,

29. *Newton,* by Eduardo Paolozzi

never mind that—what's the use of going to prove it? Why, I see with my eyes that it is so, and do not require any proof to make it clearer.'"[10]

A note about the process by which Blake produced this print can add to our appreciation, and it accounts for the striking contrast between the enamel-like human form and the blurry vegetation. A painter friend of his explained how it was done:

When he wanted to make his prints in oil, he took a common thick millboard, and drew in some strong ink or colour his design upon it strong and thick. He then painted upon that in such oil colours and in such a state of fusion that they would blur well. He painted roughly and quickly, so that no colour would have time to dry. He then took a print of that on paper, and this impression he coloured up in watercolours, repainting his outline on the millboard when he wanted to take another print. This plan he had recourse to because he could vary slightly each impression; and each having a sort of accidental look, he could branch out so as to make each one different. The accidental look they had was very enticing.[11]

Blake has thus given visual embodiment to the contrast between the clarity of the human form and the confused, stifling materiality of the world as Newton and the empiricists conceived of it.

In modern times Blake's *Newton* inspired a remarkable sculpture by Eduardo Paolozzi (figure 29), erected in 1995 outside the British Library in London. Constructed of weighty metal plates that are visibly bolted together, and peering through tight-fitting eyeglasses that resemble goggles, this Newton provides a thought-provoking reimagining of Blake's picture. A commentator calls him "a three-dimensional machine man," reinforcing Blake's critique of Newtonian science by emphasizing its artificiality.[12]

7. "THE GATE IS OPEN"

A Vision of Light

B Y 1800 commercial jobs were distressingly few, and more than ever, the Blakes were pinched by poverty. Then an unexpected offer appeared. A well-to-do poet and patron of artists, William Hayley, invited them to settle on the south coast near his country home in Sussex, in a thatched cottage with a view of wheat fields and the sea. His kindly plan was to promote Blake's work among his friends and neighbors. The brick and flint cottage, little changed over the years and still thatched, survives to this day (figure 30).

The move to the village of Felpham was a major undertaking. What with the disassembled printing press and the complete stock of engraved copper plates, sixteen heavy boxes were needed. Blake's sister, Catherine—his mother, sister, and wife all had the same name—helped with the move.

In a recently discovered letter to George Cumberland, a fellow radical, Blake included some verses that indicate his emotional state at the time. Discouraged by condescension and neglect, he claimed to be sick of the great city where he had spent his first forty-three years, and to be thrilled by the beauty and peace of the countryside.

Dear generous Cumberland, nobly solicitous for a friend's welfare: behold me

30. Blake's cottage at Felpham

Whom your friendship has magnified, rending the manacles of London's
   dungeon dark;
I have rent the black net and escaped. See my cottage at Felpham in joy
Beams over the sea, a bright light over France, but the web and the veil I
   have left
Behind me at London resists every beam of light, hanging from heaven to
   earth
Dropping with human gore. Lo! I have left it! I have torn it from my limbs,
I shake my wings ready to take my flight! Pale, ghastly pale, stands the city
   in fear.[1]

Just before setting out, Blake had written to Hayley at his home in Eartham, a few miles from Felpham: "Eartham will be my first temple and altar. My wife is like a flame of many colours of precious jewels whenever she hears it named. . . . My fingers emit sparks of fire with expectation of my future labours." This was more than metaphor, since Blake was interested in the "animal magnetism" theorized by the physicist Franz Anton Mesmer, who gave his name to mesmerism. The notion was that sick people could be cured by magnetizing an invisible bodily fluid that was related somehow to electricity. Hayley owned an "electrical machine" from which he received healing "shower baths," and a few years later Blake reported to him that Catherine's rheumatism was benefiting from "electrical magic."[2]

At first, all was exhilarating. Shortly after arrival Blake wrote to Thomas Butts, a civil servant who was his loyal patron and affectionate friend, "A roller and two harrows lie before my window. I met a plow on my first going out at my gate the first morning after my arrival, and the plowboy said to the plowman, 'Father, the gate is open.' I have begun to work and find that I can work with greater pleasure than ever." Butts replied sympathetically, "You have the plow and the harrow in full view, and the gate, you have been prophetically told, is open. Can you then hesitate joyfully to enter into it?"[3]

A week later Blake described an extraordinary experience, this time in ecstatic verse:

> To my friend Butts I write
> My first vision of light.
> On the yellow sands sitting,
> The sun was emitting
> His glorious beams
> From heaven's high streams;
> Over sea over land
> My eyes did expand
> Into regions of air
> Away from all care,
> Into regions of fire
> Remote from desire,
> The light of the morning

Heaven's mountains adorning.
In particles bright
The jewels of light
Distinct shone and clear —
Amazed and in fear
I each particle gazed
Astonished amazed,
For each was a man
Human formed; swift I ran
For they beckoned to me
Remote by the sea. . . .
My eyes more and more
Like a sea without shore
Continue expanding,
The heavens commanding,
Till the jewels of light
Heavenly men beaming bright
Appeared as one man
Who complacent began
My limbs to enfold
In his beams of bright gold. . . .
And the voice faded mild,
I remained as a child,
All I ever had known
Before me bright shone.

A psychologist might call this a state of altered consciousness, and in religious terms it is a mystical experience — not the kind that seeks to escape from sensory experience but the kind that transforms it. "The extrovertive mystic," a philosopher writes, "using his physical senses, perceives the multiplicity of external material objects — the sea, the sky, the houses, the trees — mystically transfigured so that the One, or the Unity, shines through them."[4] The whole of nature is humanized for Blake in this way, as in *A Sunshine Holiday*. And although he describes his senses as heightened, they are calm and "remote from desire." He is a child again, readmitted to the world of Innocence.

It is notable that the sun always had a special emotional charge for Blake. He imagined a questioner demanding, "What, when the sun rises do you not see a round disk of fire somewhat like a guinea?" "O no no," he would reply, "I see an innumerable company of the heavenly host, crying Holy Holy Holy is the Lord God Almighty." Blake not only perceives the sun as a heavenly host, he hears the host singing. The sun also appears, with spectacular beauty, in a watercolor entitled *Hyperion*, inspired by a rather casual allusion in a poem by Thomas Gray. Hyperion was a Greek name for the sun god, and Gray imagined his "glittering shafts" dispelling a series of afflictions—Labor, Disease, Sorrow, and so on.[5] In Blake's magnificent image (color plate 19), Hyperion is an archer in a celestial chariot, and his sunbeams are the arrows routing the spectres below.

"I Am under the Direction of Messengers from Heaven"

It wasn't long before the euphoria began to wane. Hayley was well meaning and generous, but also officious and given to controlling his protégés. He saw the world, Gilchrist said, through "a fog of amiability," and at times could be absurd: "A persevering and fearless rider, he was in the eccentric habit of using an umbrella on horseback to shade his eyes; the abrupt unfurling of which was commonly followed, naturally enough, by the rider's being forthwith pitched on his head."[6] One is reminded of the White Knight in *Through the Looking Glass.*

Hayley expected his generosity to be repaid with a steady diet of compliments, and Blake's notebook contains a number of acerbic epigrams:

> To H——
> Thy friendship oft has made my heart to ache,
> Do be my enemy for friendship's sake.

> On H—— the Pickthank
> I write the rascal thanks till he and I
> With thanks and compliments are quite drawn dry.

One might suppose that Blake made up the word "pickthank," but Shakespeare uses it, and there is a character called Pickthank in *Pilgrim's Progress.*[7]

1. *Pity*

2. *A Sunshine Holiday*

3. *Songs of Innocence*, title page, copy Z, plate 3

I have no name
I am but two days old. —
What shall I call thee?
I happy am
Joy is my name. —
Sweet joy befall thee!

Pretty joy!
Sweet joy but two days old.
Sweet joy I call thee:
Thou dost smile.
I sing the while
Sweet joy befall thee.

4. *Infant Joy, Songs of Innocence*, copy Z, plate 25

The Blossom.

Merry Merry Sparrow
Under leaves so green
A happy Blossom
Sees you swift as arrow
Seek your cradle narrow
Near my Bosom.

Pretty Pretty Robin
Under leaves so green
A happy Blossom
Hears you sobbing sobbing
Pretty Pretty Robin
Near my Bosom

5. *The Blossom, Songs of Innocence,* copy Z, plate 11

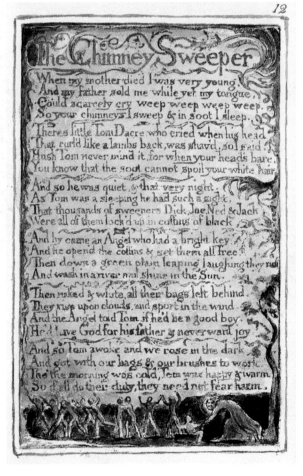

6. *The Chimney Sweeper, Songs of Innocence,* copy Z, plate 12

7. *Songs of Innocence and of Experience,*

title page, copy C, plate 2

8. *The Sick Rose, Songs of Experience, copy Z, plate 39*

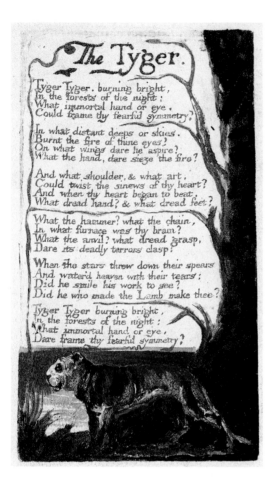

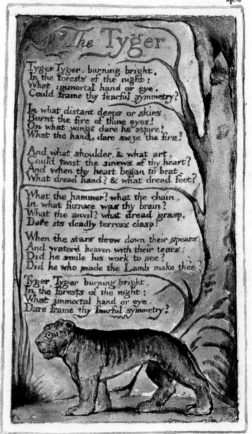

9. *The Tyger, Songs of Experience,* copy F, plate 42

10. *The Tyger, Songs of Experience,* copy Z, plate 42

11. *Albion Rose*

12. *The Marriage of Heaven and Hell,*

title page, copy D, plate 1

I have always found that Angels have the vanity to speak of themselves as the only wise; this they
do with a confident insolence sprouting from systematic reasoning:

Thus Swedenborg boasts that what he writes is
new; tho' it is only the Contents or Index of already
publish'd books

A man carried a monkey about for a shew, & because he was a little wiser than the monkey, grew
vain, and concievd himself as much wiser than seven men. It is so with Swedenborg; he shews the
folly of churches & exposes hypocrites, till he imagines that all are religious. & himself the single
one

13. *The Marriage of Heaven and Hell,* copy D, plate 21

PRELUDIUM

The shadowy daughter of Urthona stood before red Orc
When fourteen suns had faintly journey'd o'er his dark abode:
His food she brought in iron baskets, his drink in cups of iron;
Crown'd with a helmet & dark hair the nameless female stood;
A quiver with its burning stores, a bow like that of night,
When pestilence is shot from heaven; no other arms she need:
Invulnerable tho' naked, save where clouds roll round her loins,
Their awful folds in the dark air: silent she stood as night;
For never from her iron tongue could voice or sound arise;
But dumb till that dread day when Orc assay'd his fierce embrace.

Dark virgin; said the hairy youth, thy father stern abhorr'd;
Rivets my tenfold chains while still on high my spirit soars;
Sometimes an eagle screaming in the sky, sometimes a lion,
Stalking upon the mountains, & sometimes a whale I lash
The raging fathomless abyss, anon a serpent folding
Around the pillars of Urthona, and round thy dark limbs,
On the Canadian wilds I fold, feeble my spirit folds.
For chaind beneath I rend these caverns; when thou bringest food
I howl my joy; and my red eyes seek to behold thy face
In vain! these clouds roll to & fro, & hide thee from my sight.

14. *America: A Prophecy, Preludium,* copy M, plate 3

15. *Europe: A Prophecy,* title page, copy E, plate 2

16. *America: A Prophecy,* copy M, plate 9

Enitharmon slept,
Eighteen hundred years: Man was a Dream!
The night of Nature and their harps unstrung:
She slept in middle of her nightly song,
Eighteen hundred years, a female dream!

Shadows of men in fleeting bands upon the winds:
Divide the heavens of Europe:
Till Albions Angel smitten with his own plagues fled with his bands
The cloud bears hard on Albions shore:
Fill'd with immortal demons of futurity:
In council gather the smitten Angels of Albion
The cloud bears hard upon the council house; down rushing
On the heads of Albions Angels.

One hour they lay buried beneath the ruins of that hall:
But as the stars rise from the salt lake they arise in pain,
In troubled mists o'erclouded by the terrors of struggling times.

17. *Europe: A Prophecy,* copy A, plate 10

18. *Newton*

O'er her warm cheek, and rising bosom, move
The bloom of young desire, and purple light
of Love.

II. 1.

Man's feeble race what ills await!
Labour, and Penury, the racks of Pain,
Disease, and Sorrow's weeping train,
And Death, sad refuge from the storms of Fate!
The fond complaint, my song, disprove,
And justify the laws of Jove.
Say, has he given in vain the heav'nly Muse?
Night, and all her sickly dews,
Her spectres wan, and birds of boding cry,
He gives to range the dreary sky:
Till down the eastern cliffs afar
Hyperion's march they spy, and glitt'ring
shafts of war.

II. 2.

19. *Hyperion*

20. *Milton*, copy D, plate 16

21. *The Book of Urizen*, copy A, plate 14

22. *The Book of Urizen*, copy F, plate 17

23. *The Song of Los,* copy E, plate 4

24. *Milton,* copy D, plate 47

25. *Jerusalem*, copy E, plate 6

And this the form of mighty Hand. sitting on Albions cliffs
Before the face of Albion. a mighty threatning Form.
His bosom wide & shoulders huge overspreading wondrous
Bear Three strong sinewy Necks & Three awful & terrible Heads
Three Brains in contradictory council brooding incessantly.
Neither daring to put in act its councils, fearing each other.
Therefore rejecting Ideas as nothing & holding all Wisdom
To consist. in the agreements & disagreents of Ideas.
Plotting to devour Albions Body of Humanity & Love.

Such Form the aggregate of the Twelve Sons of Albion took; & such
Their appearance when combind: but often by birth-pangs & loud groans
They divide to Twelve: the key-bones & the chest dividing in pain
Disclose a hideous orifice; thence issuing the Giant-brood
Arise as the smoke of the furnace. shaking the rocks from sea to sea.
And there they combine into Three Forms, named Bacon & Newton & Locke,
In the Oak Groves of Albion which overspread all the Earth.

Imputing Sin & Righteousness to Individuals: Rahab
Sat deep within him hid: his Feminine Power unreveald
Brooding Abstract Philosophy. to destroy Imagination, the Divine-
Humanity A Three-fold Wonder: feminine: most beautiful: Three-fold
Each within other. On her white marble & even Neck, her Heart
Inorb'd and bonified: with locks of shadowing modesty, shining
Over her beautiful Female features, soft flourishing in beauty
Beams mild, all love and all perfection, that when the lips
Recieve a kiss from Gods or Men. a threefold kiss returns
From the pressd loveliness: so her whole immortal form three-fold
Three-fold embrace returns: consuming lives of Gods & Men
In fires of beauty melting them as gold & silver in the furnace
Her Brain enlabyrinths the whole heaven of her bosom & loins
To put in act what her Heart wills; O who can withstand her power
Her name is Vala in Eternity: in Time her name is Rahab

The Starry Heavens all were fled from the mighty limbs of Albion   His

26. *Jerusalem*, copy E, plate 70

The Argument

I loved Theotormon
And I was not ashamed
I trembled in my virgin fears
And I hid in Leutha's vale!

I plucked Leutha's flower,
And I rose up from the vale;
But the terrible thunders tore
My virgin mantle in twain.

27. *Visions of the Daughters of Albion,* copy G, plate 3

✧　✧　✧

Then Theotormon broke his silence. and he answered.

Tell me what is the night or day to one oerflowd with woe?
Tell me what is a thought? & of what substance is it made?
Tell me what is a joy? & in what gardens do joys grow?
And in what rivers swim the sorrows, and upon what mountains

28. *Visions of the Daughters of Albion,* copy G, plate 6

29. *The Nightmare,* by Henry Fuseli

30. *Visions of the Daughters of Albion,* frontispiece, copy G, plate 2

31. *Satan Watching the Caresses of Adam and Eve*

32. *The Book of Urizen*, copy C, plate 18

When on the highest lift of his light pinions he arrives
At that bright Gate. another Lark meets him & back to back
They touch their pinions tip tip; and each descend
To their respective Earths & there all night consult with Angels
Of Providence & with the Eyes of God all night in slumbers
Inspired: & at the dawn of day send out another Lark
Into another Heaven to carry news upon his wings
Thus are the Messengers dispatchd till they reach the Earth again
In the East Gate of Golgonooza, & the Twenty-eighth bright
Lark. met the Female Ololon descending into my Garden
Thus it appears to Mortal eyes & those of the Ulro Heavens
But not thus to Immortals, the Lark is a mighty Angel.

For Ololon step'd into the Polypus within the Mundane Shell
They could not step into Vegetable Worlds without becoming
The enemies of Humanity except in a Female Form
And as One Female, Ololon and all its mighty Hosts
Appear'd: a Virgin of twelve years nor time nor space was
To the perception of the Virgin Ololon but as the
Flash of lightning but more quick the Virgin in my Garden
Before my Cottage stood for the Satanic Space is delusion

For when Los joind with me he took me in his firy whirlwind
My Vegetated portion was hurried from Lambeths shades
He set me down in Felphams Vale & prepard a beautiful
Cottage for me that in three years I might write all these
    Visions
To display Natures cruel holiness: the deceits of Natural
    Religion
Walking in my Cottage Garden, sudden I beheld
The Virgin Ololon & addressd her as a Daughter of Beulah

Virgin of Providence fear not to enter into my Cottage
What is thy message to thy friend: what am I now to do
Is it again to plunge into deeper affliction? behold me
Ready to obey, but pity thou my Shadow of Delight
Enter my Cottage, comfort her, for she is sick with fatigue

Blakes Cottage
at Felpham.

33. *Milton*, copy C, plate 39

✧ ✧ ✧

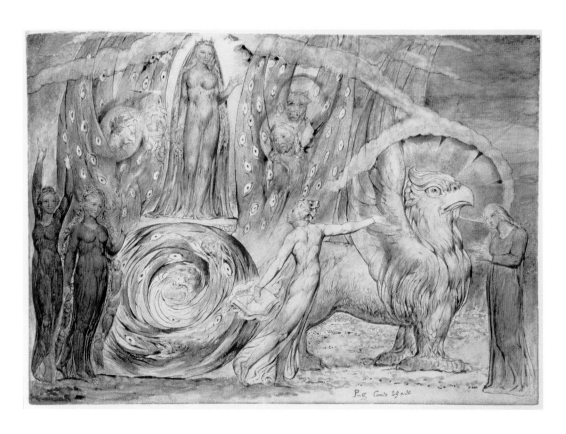

34. Beatrice Addressing Dante from the Car

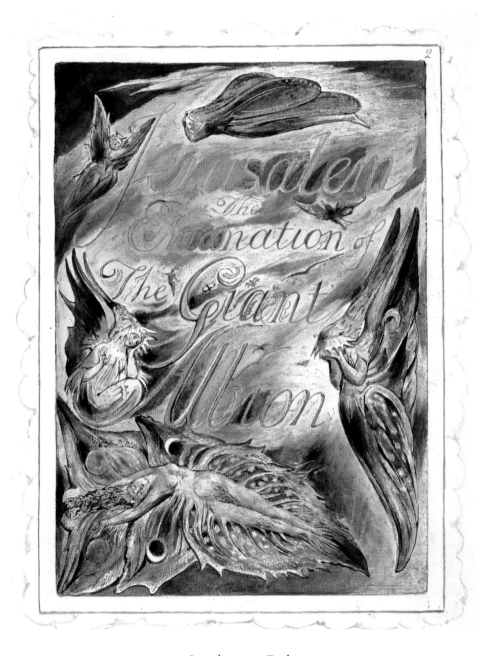

35. *Jerusalem*, copy E, plate 2

36. *The Ancient of Days, Europe,* frontispiece, copy E, plate 1

37. The Book of Urizen, copy F, plate 5

38. Elohim Creating Adam

39. *Jerusalem*, copy E, plate 76

All Human Forms identified even Tree Metal Earth & Stone. all
Human Forms identified living going forth & returning wearied
Into the Planetary lives of Years Months Days & Hours reposing
And then Awaking into his Bosom in the Life of Immortality.
And I heard the Name of their Emanations they are named Jerusalem

The End of The Song
of Jerusalem

40. *Jerusalem*, copy E, plate 99

Blake's distress had deeper causes, too. In *Milton* he refers bitterly to those who "dare to mock with the aspersion of madness." He knew all too well that he was often called mad, and it is hard to doubt that deep psychic disturbances do indeed lie at the heart of his work. Blake scholars used to reject the suggestion defensively, but to do that is to misrepresent the nature of his achievement. In a valuable study entitled *Madness and Blake's Myth,* Paul Youngquist comments that nobody denies that Van Gogh was intermittently insane, or that the startling colors and astounding energy in his paintings owe much to his psychic distress.[8]

Even before going to Felpham, Blake was afflicted with what was then called melancholy, and would now be called clinical depression. It is possible that there were manic-depressive symptoms too, in which case the "vision of light" at Felpham could be seen as an episode of extreme elation. Two months before the move he wrote to Cumberland, "I begin to emerge from a deep pit of melancholy, melancholy without any real reason for it, a disease which God keep you from and all good men."[9]

A constant source of unease was Blake's fear that his neglect of remunerative work was a shameful indulgence to be overcome. In the letter to Cumberland he went on to say, "I myself remember when I thought my pursuits of art a kind of criminal dissipation and neglect of the main chance, which I hid my face for not being able to abandon as a passion which is forbidden by law and religion, but now it appears to be law and Gospel too." In other words, Blake had decided that to create art in his own unique mode was actually a religious duty. There was a long-standing Protestant tradition of dedication to one's vocation or calling, and Blake was rediscovering his.

As time went on, drudging at uncongenial tasks was profoundly discouraging, and it was especially galling that Hayley, who regarded himself as a major poet, showed not the slightest interest in Blake's illuminated books. *Milton,* begun in 1804 after Blake's return to London, contains a heavily allegorized drama in which Hayley tries in vain to usurp Blake's prophetic role — a spiritual quarrel of which Hayley himself probably had no inkling. One line in the poem is especially telling: "Corporeal friends are spiritual enemies."[10]

Suddenly, in August 1803, there was a shocking crisis. Soldiers were quartered nearby, to be on hand at the coast in the event of a French invasion, and one of them blundered drunkenly into Blake's garden. He refused to leave, there was a quarrel, and Blake hustled him away. The soldier then declared that Blake had uttered damning statements against the king. What Blake had feared for many years now came to pass: he was to be put on trial for sedition. Hayley lost no time engaging a first-rate lawyer, and at the trial, early the next year, witnesses testified that they had been nearby and had heard no seditious language. Blake was acquitted, and in a letter to Butts he acknowledged, "Perhaps the simplicity of myself is the origin of all offenses committed against me." He enclosed a wrenchingly painful poem:

> O why was I born with a different face,
> Why was I not born like the rest of my race?
> When I look each one starts! when I speak I offend
> Then I'm silent and passive and lose every friend.
>
> Then my verse I dishonour; my pictures despise,
> My person degrade and my temper chastise,
> And the pen is my terror, the pencil my shame
> All my talents I bury, and dead is my fame.

("Pencil," in those days, meant "paintbrush.") Blake was taking to heart the fate of the servant who buried his talent instead of investing it: "For unto every one that hath shall be given, and he shall have abundance: but from him that hath not shall be taken away even that which he hath. And cast ye the unprofitable servant into outer darkness: there shall be weeping and gnashing of teeth."[11]

Whether or not there was an element of bipolar disorder, Blake also experienced phenomena that would now be called schizoid. He heard voices, saw visions, believed that forces beyond himself directed him to write, and at times nursed paranoid suspicions against his friends. Not even Hayley was exempt:

> When H——y finds out what you cannot do
> That is the very thing he'll set you to.
> If you break not your neck 'tis not his fault
> But pecks of poison are not pecks of salt,
> And when he could not act upon my wife
> Hired a villain to bereave my life.

Although Hayley was suspected of preferring men to women, it is possible that he did make advances to Catherine. It is inconceivable, however, that he paid the drunken soldier to accuse Blake. Curiously, that last line—"Hired a villain to bereave my life"—was lifted verbatim from a Gothic ballad that Blake had written in his teens.[12]

Blake felt a special kinship with the poet William Cowper, who had died just before Blake's move to Felpham and whose biography Hayley was engaged in writing. Cowper was institutionalized for insanity in his early thirties, and afterward experienced a conversion to Methodism. He then wrote hymns, including *Light Shining Out of Darkness* with its well-known lines, "God moves in a mysterious way / His wonders to perform." But for Cowper that was no comforting faith, for he learned in a dream that he was condemned to eternal damnation. His harrowing poem *The Castaway* takes as its metaphor an able-bodied sailor who, in a fierce gale, falls from a ship that has no way to turn back and rescue him. In the line from *The Castaway* that Mr. Ramsay booms out in Virginia Woolf's *To the Lighthouse*, "We perished, each alone."

Still more harrowing is Cowper's *Lines Written during a Period of Insanity,* describing a biblical sinner whom the earth swallowed up:

> Him the vindictive rod of angry justice
> Sent quick and howling to the center headlong;
> I, fed with judgment, in a fleshly tomb, am
> Buried above ground.

Blake didn't believe in damnation, but he did empathize with Cowper's distress. Hayley saw the similarity. To Cowper's cousin Lady Hesketh he wrote that he was befriending Blake "from a motive that I know our dear angel Cowper would approve, because this poor man, with an admirable quickness of apprehension and with uncommon powers of mind, *has often appeared to me on the verge of insanity.*" The emphasis is Hayley's. He added that Blake was fortunate to have "an invaluable helpmate, perhaps the only woman on earth who could have perfectly suited him as a wife."[13] Unfortunately, when Blake completed a portrait of Cowper for the projected biography, Lady Hesketh was appalled by it. She thought it revealed all too clearly that her cousin had been insane.

Years later Blake acquired Johann Spurzheim's *Observations on the Deranged Manifestations of the Mind, or Insanity,* perhaps in order to investigate the possibility that he might indeed be mad. Spurzheim remarks that "religion is a fertile cause of insanity" and that Methodism supplies "numerous cases." To this Blake retorted in the margin, "Cowper came to me and said, 'O that I were insane, always. I will never rest. Can you not make me truly insane? I will never rest till I am so. O that in the bosom of God I was hid! You retain health and yet are as mad as any of us all—over us all—mad as a refuge from unbelief—from Bacon, Newton, and Locke.'" This is strikingly similar to the claim of the counterculture psychiatrist R. D. Laing that schizophrenia can be a refuge from the collective madness of society, "a successful attempt not to adapt to pseudo-social realities."[14] As Blake describes it, Cowper's mistake was to accept a cruel theology of damnation. If he could have opened his imagination to true religion, he would then have been received into God's bosom. Even so, his contemporaries would have continued to regard him as insane.

The turmoil of the Felpham period convinced Blake that to obey Hayley and confine himself to "the mere drudgery of business" would be to fail in his solemn calling. To Butts he wrote, "I am under the direction of messengers from Heaven daily and nightly. . . . But if we fear to do the dictates of our angels and tremble at the tasks set before us, if we refuse to do spiritual acts because of natural fears or natural desires! Who can describe the dismal torments of such a state!"[15]

It was with this conviction that Blake returned to London in September 1803, where he resumed work on a vast symbolic poem he had begun six years previously, at first entitled *Vala* and afterward *The Four Zoas: The Torments of Love and Jealousy in the Death and Judgment of Albion the Ancient Man.* It grew to 140 pages in manuscript, some carefully copied out and the rest densely scribbled over, and was never published. But elements from it would be incorporated in the two long "prophecies," *Milton* and *Jerusalem,* which were his first works in relief etching since 1795.

An Artistic Conversion

If the years at Felpham were the seedbed of the great myth that informs those poems, the decisive impulse to dedicate himself to it came to Blake in 1804, in still another conversion experience. This one was artistic as well as spiritual. He wrote joyfully to Hayley:

> I have entirely reduced that spectrous Fiend to his station, whose annoyance has been the ruin of my labours for the last passed twenty years of my life. . . . I was a slave bound in a mill among beasts and devils; these beasts and these devils are now, together with myself, become children of light and liberty, and my feet and my wife's feet are free from fetters. O lovely Felpham, parent of immortal friendship, to thee I am eternally indebted for my three years' rest from perturbation and the strength I now enjoy! Suddenly, on the day after visiting the Truchsessian Gallery of pictures, I was again enlightened with the light I enjoyed in my youth, and which has for exactly twenty years been closed from me as by a door and by window-shutters.

What happened was that after a lifetime of knowing the old masters only in engraved copies, Blake came face to face with actual paintings. These were a nine-hundred-piece collection which an Austrian, Count Truchsess, hoped to sell to the British nation. Among them were, according to the catalog, a *Last Judgment* by Michelangelo, a triptych of the Virgin attributed to his school, a *Woman Taken in Adultery* by Giulio Romano, and several paintings by Claude Lorrain and Nicolas Poussin, whom Blake is known to have admired. There were also a large number of Dutch and Flemish paintings, including seven by Antony van Dyck, eight by Rembrandt van Rijn, and five by Rubens.[16]

It was soon apparent to experts that most of these paintings were fakes and practically worthless, but a skillful copy can give a good sense of the original. Blake suddenly grasped that he had allowed himself to stray from his artistic vision. He was usually careful about dates, and when he mentions "exactly" twenty years of error, he must have been remembering his father's death in 1784, when a small inheritance allowed him to open a print shop and optimistically launch an artistic career. Since then he had tried conscientiously to imitate the most admired Venetian and Dutch painters, Titian and Rembrandt above all, but at the Truchsessian Gallery he suddenly realized how destructively his imagination had been invaded by theirs. Venetian painting, as already noted, featured colors that merged into each other, altogether unlike Blake's own characteristic distinct outlines and solid colors.

And Dutch painting was minutely realistic in a way that seemed to him the very opposite of visionary insight. He would have agreed with Michelangelo's statement: "In Flanders they paint with a view to external exactness. They paint stuffs and masonry, the green grass of the fields, the shadow of trees, and rivers and bridges, which they call landscapes, with many figures on this side and many figures on that. And all this, though it pleases some people, is done without reason or art." Michelangelo also commented that a great painting might depict a single human figure, and Blake thought so too.[17]

This Truchsessian Gallery revelation was so crucial a turning point that Blake's two long prophetic poems, though not completed for many years after that, both bear the date "1804" on their title pages.

8. UNDERSTANDING BLAKE'S MYTH

"I Must Create a System"

FREUD once observed, "No one who, like me, conjures up the most evil of those half-tamed demons that inhabit the human breast, and seeks to wrestle with them, can expect to come through the struggle unscathed." Each version of Blake's myth ends in an apocalypse that makes all things new, but in his actual experience it was the struggle with those demons that tormented him. Still, the endless quest for self-knowledge was valuable in itself. Freud also said, "Turn your eyes inward, look into your own depths, learn first to know yourself! Then you will understand why you were bound to fall ill; and perhaps you will avoid falling ill in future." In Blake's more optimistic words,

> O search and see: turn your eyes inward: open O thou world
> Of love and harmony in man: expand thy ever lovely gates.[1]

Another psychiatrist, Anthony Storr, notes that creative people are often distinguished by "an exceptional degree of division between opposites" and that they possess "an exceptional awareness of this division." Artistic creation can be an attempt to resolve that inner division, and it was surely this motivation that kept Blake laboring at his vast, complicated myth even though he did so in complete obscurity. Only four copies of *Milton* were ever printed in his lifetime, and five of *Jerusalem*. William Hayley, long before Blake knew him, had called for a new kind of epic that would embody "extremes of harmony and discord," for which a "new mythology" would need to be created in order to express the "copious spring of visionary force."[2] Right under his nose Blake was doing exactly that, and Hayley, who may never even have looked at his poems, was too conventional to realize it.

As he continued to work on *The Four Zoas* and then to quarry the manuscript for *Milton* and *Jerusalem*, Blake's unique myth grew richer, subtler, and stranger. "I must create a system," he wrote in *Jerusalem*, "or be enslaved by another man's." "System" does not mean intellectualized abstraction, for "I will not reason and compare: my business is to create." Instead, it means a dynamic myth of the self and of the entire universe, drawing on existing philosophies and mythologies but uniquely Blake's own. He speaks also of "striving with systems to deliver individuals from those systems." The expression "striving with" can be understood in two senses: working within his own personal system, but also using it to wrestle with the systems of others.[3]

The early Lambeth Books—*The Marriage of Heaven and Hell, Visions of the Daughters of Albion, America, Europe*—had been inspired by hope for revolutionary change. Now, a decade later, the emphasis is on an interior breakthrough and mutual forgiveness.

> Trembling I sit day and night, my friends are astonished at me,
> Yet they forgive my wanderings, I rest not from my great task!
> To open the eternal worlds, to open the immortal eyes
> Of man inwards into the worlds of thought: into Eternity,
> Ever expanding in the bosom of God, the human imagination.
> O Saviour pour upon me thy spirit of meekness and love:
> Annihilate the selfhood in me, be thou all my life![4]

This Saviour is the Jesus of the *Songs of Innocence,* fully human, but also a divine presence that is greater than any individual person.

Blake's myth went through many permutations, and each of the three long poems explores it from a different perspective. *The Four Zoas* develops a symbolism of the self as constituted by four psychic components, the Zoas, who collapse into fragmentation and then struggle to regain wholeness. *Milton* is about the Puritan poet's quest to renounce his errors, reunite with his feminine element, and overcome selfhood. And *Jerusalem* is about the rehabilitation of the universal man, Albion, who is at once the English people and all of humanity.

A foundational idea is expressed in verses that Blake sent from Felpham to his friend Thomas Butts:

> Now I a fourfold vision see
> And a fourfold vision is given to me.
> 'Tis fourfold in my supreme delight
> And threefold in soft Beulah's night
> And twofold always. May God us keep
> From single vision and Newton's sleep.

Single vision is the positivist worldview of empiricism, sometimes called Ulro by Blake, which accepts nothing as real unless it can be mathematically expressed and measured. Twofold vision belongs to Generation, the cycle of birth and death, haunted always by mortality. In some ways Beulah (a biblical name meaning "the married land") resembles the Christian idea of heaven:

> There is a place where contrarieties are equally true;
> This place is called Beulah. It is a pleasant lovely shadow
> Where no dispute can come. . . .
> Beulah is evermore created around Eternity, appearing
> To the inhabitants of Eden around them on all sides.
> But Beulah to its inhabitants appears within each district
> As the beloved infant in his mother's bosom round encircled
> With arms of love and pity and sweet compassion. But to
> The sons of Eden the moony habitations of Beulah
> Are from Great Eternity a mild and pleasant rest.[5]

This is very like Blake's Innocence, and it differs from the traditional heaven in important ways: it is fully alive to sexual pleasure, and it is a temporary place of rest, not a final destination.

As was evident in *A Sunshine Holiday,* from Beulah one can go either down or up. Below is Generation, the realm of birth and death, in which sexual relations can turn possessive and even sadistic—the world of Experience. Above is Eden: not the peace that passes understanding or the saints' everlasting rest, as preachers commonly described it, but an active strife of contraries that reflects the dynamism of human nature. Eden experiences a kind of warfare, but spiritual warfare that is creative and constructive.

It was a profound insight that no heaven worth imagining could exist without energetic activity. Like many of his contemporaries, including Hegel of whom he may never have heard, Blake believed that conflict and opposition are fundamental to life. And it follows that although his ideal Eden aspires to unity, such a state can never be static. Its inhabitants, a brotherhood of Eternals, are entirely capable of confusion and error, and one or more of them may fall back into the lower levels of existence. Just such a fall, described as nightmarish slumber, happens to "Albion the Ancient Man" at the beginning of *The Four Zoas*.

Trying to Understand the Long Poems

Many parts of the long poems are difficult, at times impenetrably so. Even specialists can be frustrated by Blake's obscurity; the time is long past when critics followed Northrop Frye in dismissing as imaginatively impaired anyone who found him obscure. One commentary on *The Four Zoas* compares trying to understand it to picking up a bowling ball that has no finger holes.[6]

The fourth and final book of *Jerusalem* is headed by this quatrain:

> I give you the end of a golden string,
>   Only wind it into a ball:
> It will lead you in at Heaven's gate,
>   Built in Jerusalem's wall.

That invitation is far from easy to act on. A leading specialist observes that although *Jerusalem* can be thrilling to read, "If anyone has been able to follow that string I don't know it." Another says, "As a prophet Blake seems to presuppose a reader equipped like himself. It seems unlikely that any such reader has yet appeared."[7]

Coleridge was familiar with Blake's Neoplatonic sources, but even the *Songs of Innocence and of Experience* provoked this comment from him: "You perhaps smile at *my* calling another poet a mystic; but verily I am in the very mire of commonplace common sense compared with Mr. Blake, apo- or rather ana-calyptic poet and painter." "Apocalyptic" means "taking off a veil," as in the apocalypse in the Book of Revelation. "Anacalyptic," then, would mean "putting on a veil," which is indeed what Blake does, inventing new symbols and deploying them in bewildering ways. Coleridge also referred acutely to Blake's "despotism in symbols."[8]

Blake's long prophecies used to be called epics, but that makes no sense. An epic is a narrative based on strict chronology. Even when the narration begins in the middle, as in the *Iliad* or *Paradise Lost,* the essential sequence is never in question. More recently it has been fashionable to call Blake's method cinematic, but in films the continuity of scenes is normally established by careful editing. Blake has no interest in conventional continuity, and in his poems multiple versions of the "same" events occur over and over again. Since he changed the order of plates in the various copies, they don't even recur in the same sequence.

A better analogy than film is music. One commentator calls the poems symphonic, with "broken continuities, stop-and-start development, repetitions, key changes, and tempo contrasts." Another says that they resemble oratorios with solos and choruses; a third speaks persuasively of "performing Blake."[9]

For Blake the most important model is the final and most baffling book in the Bible, the Book of Revelation. Remarkably, what the eighth-century theologian Alcuin of York says of that book can be applied word for word to Blake's *Jerusalem:*

> This is the sequence of the narration. Sometimes it starts with the arrival of the Lord and carries through to the end of time. Sometimes it starts with the arrival of the Lord, and before it finishes, it returns to the beginning, and by repeating in different figures both what it has left out and what it has said, it hastens to the second coming of the Lord. . . . Sometimes, in order to narrate, it temporarily abandons its themes and introduces something totally unconnected. . . . Sometimes, in this kind of style, a figure is changed in such a way that it is confused, as it were, with other things so that it signifies something quite other than what it began to represent.[10]

It helps to read Blake's poems aloud. In an address "To the Public" with which *Jerusalem* begins, he calls himself "a true orator" for whom even blank verse is too confining; and in *The Four Zoas* he declares, "The living voice is ever living in its inmost joy." He was greatly interested in a theory lately advanced by Bishop Robert Lowth that Hebrew poetry was based on rhythm and parallelism, and his increasingly long poetic lines refuse metrical regularity in any familiar sense. They are sometimes called "fourteeners," an old-fashioned term for the style of verse favored by some earlier writers, with seven stresses to a line instead of the five of pentameter, as in Arthur Golding's 1567 translation of Ovid:

> Now have I brought a work to end which neither Jove's fierce wrath,
> Nor sword, nor fire, nor fretting age with all the force it hath. . . .

But Blake's stresses, though always rhythmic, are unpredictable:

> The sóng of the áged móther which shóok the héavens with wráth
> Héaring the márch of lóng resóunding stróng heróic vérse
> Márshalled in órder for the dáy of intelléctual báttle.[11]

Most readers will probably hear seven stresses in the middle line, but six in the first line and five in the last.

David Fuller has performed a valuable experiment by recasting the printed layout of Blake's lines as if they were modernist poetry, which approximates what happens if one reads them aloud with proper expression. Here is a passage from *The Four Zoas* that may well seem congested and awkward as Blake wrote it:

> His nostrils breathe a fiery flame, his locks are like the forests
> Of wild beasts, there the lion glares, the tyger and wolf howl there,
> And there the eagle hides her young in cliffs and precipices.
> His bosom is like starry heaven expanded, all the stars
> Sing round. There waves the harvest and the vintage rejoices, the springs
> Flow into rivers of delight; there the spontaneous flowers
> Drink, laugh and sing, the grasshopper, the emmet and the fly;
> The golden moth builds there a house and spreads her silken bed.

How different the same words seem in the patterns that the speaking voice would give them!

> His nostrils breathe a fiery flame.
> His locks are like the forests of wild beasts,

there the lion glares,
  the tyger and wolf howl there,
  and there the eagle hides her young in cliffs and precipices.
His bosom is like starry heaven expanded; all the stars sing round.
  There waves the harvest and the vintage rejoices,
    the springs flow into rivers of delight;
  there the spontaneous flowers drink, laugh and sing,
    the grasshopper the emmet and the fly;
  the golden moth builds there a house and spreads her silken bed.[12]

Satanic Mills and Arrows of Desire

Though Blake no longer expected imminent political and social revolution, there was never anything otherworldly about his message, which always focused on imaginative renovation of this world. Expressions of profound moral outrage appear throughout *Milton* and *Jerusalem*, together with occasional lyric passages of great beauty. One of these lyrics, commonly known as *Jerusalem* though Blake didn't call it that, may be his best-loved poem, and it has inspired people who hold a wide range of social and political opinions. Confusingly, it doesn't in fact come from the poem entitled *Jerusalem* but instead is from *Milton.*

And did those feet in ancient time
Walk upon England's mountains green:
And was the holy Lamb of God
On England's pleasant pastures seen!

And did the countenance divine
Shine forth upon our clouded hills?
And was Jerusalem builded here,
Among these dark Satanic mills?

Bring me my bow of burning gold:
Bring me my arrows of desire:
Bring me my spear: O clouds unfold!
Bring me my chariot of fire!

> I will not cease from mental fight,
> Nor shall my sword sleep in my hand
> Till we have built Jerusalem
> In England's green and pleasant land.

Immediately following this poem in *Milton*, Blake quotes Moses: "Would to God that all the Lord's people were prophets."[13]

"And did those feet" recalls a legend that Joseph of Arimathea brought the Holy Grail—the chalice used at the Last Supper—to Glastonbury in England, and that Jesus then came to bless the church that housed it. Feet are emphasized to confirm his physical presence on the land, with an allusion as well to Isaiah: "How beautiful upon the mountains are the feet of him that bringeth good tidings, that publisheth peace; that bringeth good tidings of good."[14]

That was an apocryphal legend, but the chariot of fire is in the Bible—not that Blake thought of the Bible as literally true. When Elijah bequeathed his mantle of prophecy to Elisha, "Behold, there appeared a chariot of fire and horses of fire, and parted them both asunder; and Elijah went up by a whirlwind into heaven." As Blake adapts the image, it represents the visionary breakthrough he has personally experienced and hopes to share. He says elsewhere, referring to his now-lost painting of the Last Judgment, "If the spectator could enter into these images in his imagination, approaching them on the fiery chariot of his contemplative thought; if he could enter into Noah's rainbow or into his bosom, or could make a friend and companion of one of these images of wonder which always entreats him to leave mortal things as he must know, then would he arise from his grave, then would he meet the Lord in the air, and then he would be happy." "Enter in" implies active participation, not passive viewing; we are being invited to escape from the living death of mortal existence.[15]

"Arrows of desire" suggests the erotic energy of Blake's Orc, and "mental fight" recalls the seventeenth-century revolutionaries who sought to re-create the kingdom of God on earth. Cromwell's soldiers went into battle singing:

> The Lord begins to honour us,
> The saints are marching on;

> The sword is sharp, the arrows swift
> To destroy Babylon.

But for Blake the combat is spiritual, not military. As he says in his final prophetic work, the one that is actually named *Jerusalem,*

> Our wars are wars of life and wounds of love,
> With intellectual spears, and long winged arrows of thought.[16]

The meaning of the "dark Satanic mills" has been much debated, since the industrial system was only in its infancy, and since mills in Blake's poems can refer to repetitive processes of any kind. But it is not wrong to think of factories. A powerful passage in *Jerusalem* explicitly contrasts modern industrialism with traditional labor:

> Then left the Sons of Urizen the plow and harrow, the loom,
> The hammer and the chisel, and the rule and compasses. From London
>   fleeing
> They forged the sword on Cheviot, the chariot of war and the battle-ax,
> The trumpet fitted to mortal battle, and the flute of summer in
>   Annandale,
> And all the arts of life they changed into the arts of death in Albion.
> The hourglass contemned, because its simple workmanship
> Was like the workmanship of the plowman; and the water wheel
> That raises water into cisterns, broken and burned with fire,
> Because its workmanship was like the workmanship of the shepherd;
> And in their stead, intricate wheels invented, wheel without wheel,
> To perplex youth in their outgoings, and bind to labours in Albion
> Of day and night the myriads of eternity, that they may grind
> And polish brass and iron hour after hour laborious task!

"Wheel without wheel" refers to the cogwheels that drive machinery, and brass and iron went into armaments for Britain's foreign wars. Some years earlier a French visitor described an English cannon foundry: "Amongst these warlike machines, these terrible death-dealing instruments, huge cranes, every kind of windlass, lever and tackle for moving heavy loads, were fixed in suitable places. Their creaking, the piercing noise of the pulleys, the continuous sound of hammering, the ceaseless energy of the men keeping all this machinery in motion, presented a sight as interesting as it was new." Blake thought such developments were satanic, not "interesting."[17]

The *Jerusalem* lyric unites two ideals that are normally thought of as opposites. One is an Arcadian myth of a golden age in the past, and the other is activist anticipation of utopia in the future. "Blake's poem," A. D. Nuttall observes, "combines the two with dream-like intensity, the green England trodden by the feet of Christ, and the holy city we shall build together when tyranny and oppression are obliterated from this happy land."[18] The move from "I" to "we" in the final stanza is a call to collective commitment: "I will not cease . . . Till *we* have built."

For this reason *Jerusalem* has always appealed strongly to reformers. After Sir Charles Hubert Hastings Parry set it to the now familiar melody in 1916, it acquired the name *Jerusalem* and became the anthem of the women's suffrage movement and later of the Women's Institute; still later it was sung at the conclusion of a 1981 film that took its title from the poem, *Chariots of Fire*. To be sure, not everyone in Britain saw that as appropriate use of Blake's lyric. It struck some as an expression of British triumphalism at a time when Margaret Thatcher was waging war in the Falklands. And Blake might not have cared much for the use a recent Conservative prime minister made of the poem. When Prince William married Kate Middleton in 2011, David Cameron exclaimed, "There is something special about singing *Jerusalem* in Westminster Abbey with the orchestra behind you. You think the roof is going to lift off and there is no better place and no better country to be in. Just wonderful."[19]

More congenial to Blake would be Jez Butterworth's 2009 play *Jerusalem,* an ironic yet exhilarating view of what actually did become of England's green and pleasant land. The raffish antihero draws a blank after rattling off correct answers to Trivial Pursuit questions:

> Who wrote the words to the popular hymn Jerusalem?
> Pause.
> Ah, fuck. I know this. Fuck. It's . . . .[20]

Surprisingly, in two of the four surviving copies of *Milton*, Blake deleted this poem. Nobody knows why.

London and Blake's Myth

Robert Southey, poet laureate from 1813 to 1843, was shown the hundred plates of *Jerusalem* and thought the poem "perfectly mad." In support of that judgment he remarked, "Oxford Street is in Jerusalem." Blake does say that. Not just Oxford Street, in fact, but the whole of London can be seen as Jerusalem in its spiritual form.

> The Lamb of God creates himself a bride and wife
> That we his children evermore may live in Jerusalem
> Which now descendeth out of heaven, a city yet a woman,
> Mother of myriads, redeemed and born in her spiritual palaces,
> By a new spiritual birth regenerated from death.[21]

But if London ought to be an ideal Jerusalem in spirit, in reality it is all too tragically a Babylon. An extended lyric in *Jerusalem* vividly evokes that contrast, and is pervaded by local references to the city in which Blake spent nearly all of his life:

> The fields from Islington to Marybone,
> To Primrose Hill and Saint Johns Wood,
> Were builded over with pillars of gold,
> And there Jerusalem's pillars stood.
>
> Her little ones ran on the fields,
> The Lamb of God among them seen,
> And fair Jerusalem his bride
> Among the little meadows green.
>
> Pancras and Kentish Town repose
> Among her golden pillars high;
> Among her golden arches which
> Shine upon the starry sky.
>
> The Jews Harp House and the Green Man,
> The ponds where boys to bathe delight,
> The fields of cows by Willan's farm,
> Shine in Jerusalem's pleasant sight.

She walks upon our meadows green,
The Lamb of God walks by her side;
And every English child is seen
Children of Jesus and his bride.

Forgiving trespasses and sins
Lest Babylon with cruel Og,
With moral and self-righteous law,
Should crucify in Satan's synagogue!

What are those golden builders doing
Near mournful ever-weeping Paddington,
Standing above that mighty ruin
Where Satan the first victory won,

Where Albion slept beneath the fatal tree,
And the Druids' golden knife
Rioted in human gore,
In offerings of human life?

They groaned aloud on London Stone,
They groaned aloud on Tyburn's brook;
Albion gave his deadly groan,
And all the Atlantic mountains shook.

"Cruel Og" is an Old Testament giant in league with Babylon, the antitype of Jerusalem. But the other names are all real places, familiar to Blake from his boyhood when there was still open countryside within easy walking distance. "The beauty of those scenes in his youth," Gilchrist writes, "was a lifelong reminiscence with Blake, and stored his mind with lifelong pastoral images." The Green Man pie house and the Jew's Harp teahouse lay on the way from Paddington to Islington, separate villages then although soon to be swallowed up in Regent's Park, and as late as Dickens's time there were still ponds at Willan's farm (see frontispiece map). The "golden builders" were occupied with the city's ongoing expansion, and there may be an allusion to the honey-colored limestone in the terraces that were going up at

Regents Park. Paddington, a village of poverty-stricken Irish laborers, is described as "ever-weeping" because builders had dug up bones of Puritan leaders who had been beheaded and buried there.[22]

London Stone was the central milestone from which distances were measured. Blake associates it with official tyranny because it was close to Newgate Prison as well as to Saint Paul's Cathedral. As for the "fatal tree," that was the gallows at Tyburn at the corner of Hyde Park, not far from the Blakes' residence after returning from Felpham, where the hanging of criminals had still been shocking public spectacles when they were young. The title of an important modern work on crime and punishment in the eighteenth century is borrowed from Blake: *Albion's Fatal Tree*.[23]

A passage in *Milton* assembles details from an earlier neighborhood, the one in Lambeth where the Blakes had lived in the 1790s. What look like classical names are actual London ones, invoked for ironic effect:

> Beginning at Jerusalem's inner court, Lambeth ruined and given
> To the detestable gods of Priam, to Apollo; and at the Asylum
> Given to Hercules, who labour in Tirzah's looms for bread,
> Who set pleasure against duty: who create Olympic crowns
> To make learning a burden, and the work of the Holy Spirit strife.
> To Thor and cruel Odin who first reared the polar caves,
> Lambeth mourns, calling Jerusalem; she weeps and looks abroad
> For the Lord's coming, that Jerusalem may overspread all nations.[24]

The Blakes' Lambeth address, to which they had moved in 1790 when there was hope of increasing income, was No. 13 Hercules Buildings, the most spacious quarters they ever had (figure 31). It was a brick row house with two rooms on each of three floors, and a kitchen in a damp basement. The massive rolling press stood in the front room on the ground floor, and the studio was in back, with plenty of light for painting and engraving. It overlooked a garden that harbored a privy and also a vine and a fig tree. When the house was eventually razed in 1918 the tree and vine were still flourishing.[25]

If the house was pleasant, much of the neighborhood was not. Not far away was the "asylum" mentioned in the poem, a workhouse for orphaned girls that was intended to train "a supply of diligent and sober domestics for the use of that pub-

31. No. 23 Hercules Buildings

lic which, by its contributions, has so nobly acquired a right to their services." Blake always made clear what he thought of ostensibly charitable institutions like that:

> Children are sold to trades
> Of dire necessity, still laboring day and night, till all
> Their life extinct, they took the spectre form in dark despair.

Tirzah, whom we will meet again, is Blake's name for an ominous nature goddess who binds down mortals to the restricted life of the five senses. Odin and his son Thor are Norse gods of war, and "the detestable gods of Priam" preside over the Trojan War. To be sure, the Apollo of classical mythology is not particularly warlike, but Blake names him because a derelict pleasure garden around the corner from his house was called Apollo Gardens. "Jerusalem's inner court" refers to the courtyards of Lambeth Palace, headquarters of the established church that seemed indifferent to human misery.[26]

London should aspire to be Jerusalem, but is all too clearly Babylon, the scene of suffering and exploitation on a massive scale.

> There Babylon is builded in the waste, founded in human desolation. . . .
> But Albion is cast forth to the potter, his children to the builders
> To build Babylon because they have forsaken Jerusalem.
> The walls of Babylon are souls of men; her gates the groans
> Of nations; her towers are the miseries of once happy families.
> Her streets are paved with destruction, her houses built with death,
> Her palaces with Hell and the grave; her synagogues with torments
> Of ever-hardening despair squared and polished with cruel skill.

The groans recall the anguished cries in the lyric *London,* and the potter comes from a text in Zechariah that Christians saw as an anticipation of Judas: "I took the thirty pieces of silver, and cast them to the potter in the house of the Lord." As for Satan's synagogue, that is Blake's name for the false religion that honors the cruel powers of this world. "Man must and will have some religion; if he has not the religion of Jesus, he will have the religion of Satan, and will erect the Synagogue of Satan." It is called a synagogue because it embodies the vengeful law of the Old Testament instead of the New Testament spirit of forgiveness. "Urizen called together the Synagogue of Satan in dire Sanhedrim / To judge the Lamb of God to death as a murderer and robber."[27]

Few people who sing "Till we have built Jerusalem / In England's green and pleasant land" are aware of how deep is the pessimism from which it springs. And few people, also, realize that this hopeful lyric is embedded in a massive prophetic poem that explores the fragmentation of self and world with harrowing intensity.

9. THE ZOAS AND OURSELVES

The Four Living Creatures

WHEN Blake first invented the bearded, patriarchal Urizen and his antagonist, the flamey-haired Orc, he may have thought of them simply as representing the perennial impulses of authoritarian control and youthful rebellion. Soon afterward, however, he evidently decided that he needed a whole cast of characters to dramatize the dynamics of psychic experience. These he called Zoas, adapting a term from the Book of Revelation.[1] *Zoon* in Greek means a living creature, and Saint John on Patmos sees four of them bearing a vision of God in the air. Blake was studying Greek with William Hayley at Felpham in the early 1800s, and there he anglicized the plural *zoa* as "Zoas." The never-printed poem *The Four Zoas* was the proving ground in which he gradually got to know them. As he developed his personal myth, it grew challengingly complicated and increasingly strange.

No doubt to prevent readers from drawing on prior associations, Blake made up new (and exotic-sounding) names for his Zoas. In general terms, Urizen, who continues to play a major role in the myth, represents reason and moral law. Orc dwindles in significance in these later poems and is replaced by his counterpart in Eternity, Luvah, the emotions. And there are two further Zoas who had not appeared previously. Urthona, mentioned in passing in *America* but not yet a Zoa there, is creative imagination. Tharmas, the fourth, is passive and shadowy most of the time. At one point he is called the "parent power," and he seems to represent an instinctual wholeness that keeps the entire structure intact.[2] These four beings, or forces, are alive in each person. They are the foundational elements of the self.

The reason Blake invented the Zoas seems clear, and is evidence of his profound originality. Existing psychologies were rigidly hierarchical, distributing aspects of the psyche into discrete elements, and placing one of them firmly in control at the top. In the classical model that Christian thinkers took over, reason presides and the passions are kept in subjection below, with the will as an executive agent to make sure they stay there. Or as Plato describes it in the *Phaedrus,* the charioteer of the soul, representing reason, drives an ill-matched pair of horses, one of which is positive moral emotions and the other irrational appetites.

In these traditional models, the ideal is authoritarian stability. Much the same can be said of Freud's model, though he adds the concept of the superego as the internalized moral code, and in his system Plato's unruly horse becomes the anarchic energies of the repressed id. "Our mind," Freud writes, "is no peacefully self-contained unity. It is rather to be compared to a modern state in which a mob, eager for enjoyment and destruction, has to be held down forcibly by a prudent superior class." One can imagine what Blake would have said about that analogy—class warfare in which privileged superiors discipline the mob. More largely, he would never have accepted Freud's claim that repression, even if painful, is necessary. For Freud, to resist instinctual gratification is a sign of psychic health; for Blake it is a definition of sickness.[3]

More congenial to Blake's conception than Freud's is Jung's, which is not surprising, since Jung was interested in many of the same sources that Blake drew on. The Jungian category of thinking could be said to correspond to Urizen, intuition to Urthona, emotion to Luvah, and sense perception to Tharmas. The four interact dynamically, much as the Greek and Hindu gods do, with no controlling element on top.

In Blake's view, the Zoas are not abstractions. We have noted his tendency to humanize everything, and that is what he does with psychic experience. Each Zoa is an active character who thinks and desires and suffers; each forms alliances, competes, and fights with the others. Borrowing from various mythic and kabbalistic sources, Blake postulates a universal humanity whom he calls Albion. When Albion falls asleep in Eternity, or rather falls into nightmare, his constituent Zoas break apart and struggle for supremacy. Only when they learn to interact cooperatively can the wholeness of the self be restored.

No one knows how Blake pronounced the names of the Zoas. Two of them, Tharmas and Urthona, seem obvious enough. (The latter recalls "earth owner," and may have been suggested by a character in one of the faux-Gaelic poems by Ossian fabricated in the 1760s by James Macpherson.) Luvah perhaps sounded like "lover," which would be appropriate to his role. The real puzzle is Urizen. It is generally agreed that the name derives from a Greek word meaning "horizon," but it may also imply the English "your reason." So is it "Your-EYE-zon" or "Your REA-son"? Possibly neither, since in many places the rhythm of the verse seems to call for the accent to fall on the first syllable, "YOUR-izen." Blake may not have cared much about the pronunciation.

Ezekiel's Vision

The source for John's vision in the Book of Revelation is a similar vision experienced by Ezekiel during the Babylonian captivity. Blake illustrated that text in a remarkable painting that brings out how complex the relationship of his Zoas is, and also how dynamic. The text in Ezekiel is filled with weird images, and needs to be quoted at length:

> Now it came to pass in the thirtieth year, in the fourth month, in the fifth day of the month, as I was among the captives by the river of Chebar, that the heavens were opened and I saw visions of God. . . . I looked, and behold, a whirlwind came out of the north, a great cloud, and a fire infolding itself, and a brightness was about it, and out of the midst thereof as the colour of amber, out of the midst of the fire. Also out of the midst thereof came the likeness of four living creatures. And this was their appearance: they had the likeness of a man, and every one had four faces, and every one had four wings. . . . As for the likeness of their faces, they four had the face of a man, and the face of a lion, on the right side; and they four had the face of an ox on the left side; they four also had the face of an eagle. Thus were their faces,

and their wings were stretched upward; two wings of every one were joined one to another, and two covered their bodies. . . . Their appearance and their work was as it were a wheel in the middle of a wheel. When they went, they went upon their four sides: and they turned not when they went. As for their rings, they were so high that they were dreadful; and their rings were full of eyes round about them four.[4]

This extraordinary vision, mysterious but also inspiring, is invoked in a well-known spiritual: "Ezekiel saw the wheel / Way up in the middle of the air." Christian interpreters drew on it to symbolize the four Evangelists: a winged man or angel is Matthew, a winged lion Mark (as in the Piazza San Marco in Venice), a winged ox Luke, and an eagle John. The "rings," incidentally, which are hard to make any sense of, are the *rims* of the wheels in most modern translations.

Blake didn't hesitate to give visual embodiment to Ezekiel's hard-to-visualize imagery. It has so many disparate parts, indeed, that he was the first major artist since Albrecht Dürer to depict the actual vision rather than just the prophet writing about it. A painting by Raphael, *The Vision of Ezekiel,* does represent the four creatures, together with a winged angel and God enthroned above, but Raphael ignores the wheels and rings and eyes.[5]

Blake's picture (figure 32), painted in 1805, is not entirely faithful to the original either. There is no lion or ox or eagle, and only human faces are shown. Each of these must be fourfold, though the fourth face of the central figure can't be seen, the two at the side margin show only two faces each, and a fourth figure is presumably hidden altogether at the back. These, then, are Blake's Zoas, and all four are human. Recumbent at the bottom is the tiny figure of Ezekiel himself, an "astonished dreamer," as Bentley calls him.[6]

The central figure in the picture, gazing directly at us, has the two sets of wings that Ezekiel describes, and seated between the raised pair of wings is God on his throne. God's right hand is lifted in blessing, but his expression seems somber and uneasy. Blake could never have endorsed the traditional interpretation of Ezekiel's vision as the Hebrew Merkabah, chariot of an omnipotent God. In *Paradise Lost* Ezekiel's chariot is the vehicle in which Christ crushes the rebel angels; in our day (with the spelling Merkavah) it is the most powerful tank in the Israeli army.

32. Ezekiel's Vision

The idea of wheels coordinating their motion "within" each other held great appeal for Blake. He thought of this cooperative energy as altogether different from the grinding, externalized gears of industrial machinery:

> . . . Wheel without wheel, with cogs tyrannic
> Moving by compulsion each other: not as those in Eden, which
> Wheel within wheel in freedom revolve in harmony and peace.[7]

So for Blake the spiritual heart of Ezekiel's vision is not a presiding deity on an uncanny chariot, but the dynamic forces within the self. As for the eyes within the whirling wheels, he imagined them as successive intuitions of the divine, which he called the Seven Eyes of God; they will be considered later.

In Eternity the Zoas interact harmoniously:

> Four mighty ones are in every man; a perfect unity
> Cannot exist but from the universal brotherhood of Eden,
> The Universal Man. To whom be glory evermore amen.

In the margin next to these lines in *The Four Zoas,* Blake cites two texts from the Gospel of John, both of which refer to Jesus: "That they all may be one; as thou, Father, art in me, and I in thee, that they also may be one in us. . . . And the Word was made flesh, and dwelt among us."[8] The divine principle that integrates the self is no patriarch on high, but God in human form.

Emanations

As he developed his symbolism of the Zoas, it evidently struck Blake that he needed to account for the female element in the psyche, and he provided each Zoa with a feminine "emanation." The term came from Neoplatonism, where it referred to forces that emanate from the divine being in order to create the world. The original title of *The Four Zoas,* begun three years before the move to Felpham, was *Vala,* and Blake now made Vala the feminine counterpart of Luvah. Ahania is Urizen's emanation, Enitharmon is Urthona's, and Enion is Tharmas's. Vala and Enitharmon often act aggressively and even cruelly; Ahania and Enion are gentler but also less distinct.

Tracing the interactions of not just four characters but eight produces complications that can be desperately hard to keep in focus. At times, Blake himself may have had trouble doing so, especially since he believed he was transmitting a message that had been "given" to him, rather than making it up to suit himself. He knew also that our deepest psychic experiences remain mysterious as well as many-sided. In *Milton* he acknowledges, "Man cannot know / What passes in his members till periods of space and time / Reveal the secrets of Eternity."[9]

For many readers, what emerges most powerfully in *The Four Zoas* is not the detailed narrative, if indeed it can be called a narrative, but rather the poetic power with which Blake evokes the threat of psychic breakdown. The stress and anguish of that breakdown are made woundingly apparent when each male Zoa suffers the loss of his feminine element. Here, for example, is a magnificent passage in which first Urizen and then Tharmas cries out in anguish when his emanation—Ahania and Enion, respectively—has been torn away:

> Ahania fell far into non-entity,
> She continued falling. Loud the crash continued loud and hoarse;
> From the crash roared a flame of blue sulphureous fire, from the flame
> A dolorous groan that struck with dumbness all confusion,
> Swallowing up the horrible din in agony on agony,
> Through the confusion like a crack across from immense to immense,
> Loud strong a universal groan of death, louder
> Than all the wracking elements, deafened and rended worse
> Than Urizen and all his hosts in curst despair down rushing.
> But from the dolorous groan one like a shadow of smoke appeared,
> And human bones rattling together in the smoke and stamping
> The nether abyss and gnashing in fierce despair, panting in sobs
> Thick short incessant bursting sobbing, deep despairing stamping
>   struggling
> Struggling to utter the voice of man struggling to take the features of man,
>   struggling
> To take the limbs of man. At length emerging from the smoke
> Of Urizen, dashed in pieces from his precipitant fall,
> Tharmas reared up his hands and stood on the affrighted ocean;
> The dead reared up his voice and stood on the resounding shore,

Crying "Fury in my limbs, destruction in my bones and marrow!
My skull riven into filaments, my eyes into sea jellies
Floating upon the tide wander bubbling and bubbling,
Uttering my lamentations and begetting little monsters
Who sit mocking upon the little pebbles of the tide
In all my rivers and on dried shells that the fish
Have quite forsaken. O fool fool to lose my sweetest bliss!
Where art thou Enion? ah too near too cunning, too far off
And yet too near."

Andrew Lincoln says, "The rhythms and distorted syntax of the passage vividly enact the desperate struggle for life and expression. The verse itself bursts its bounds and re-forms."[10]

That is how Urizen and Tharmas experience the breakup of the self, but it is no single event, and there can be no correct version of the story, as Milton insisted there was when he told the story of the Fall in *Paradise Lost*. It is an ongoing torment that takes place in the nightmare of Albion. In dreams, as Freud says, thoughts and images "are turned about, broken into fragments and jammed together, almost like pack-ice." Each Zoa and each emanation experiences a different version of the psychic catastrophe, and in *The Four Zoas* there are no fewer than fourteen competing accounts.[11]

To arrest this chaotic suffering, and to begin the labor of reconstruction, will be the task of the Zoa of imagination. In Eternity his name is Urthona, but Blake apparently decided that after the collective breakup of the primal Albion, he is so changed that he needs a new name in his "fallen" state. That name is Los, and in *Milton* and *Jerusalem* he is the hero of Blake's myth. Los is also the source of creative inspiration: "He is the spirit of prophecy, the ever apparent Elias"—another name for Elijah, who was taken up into heaven in a whirlwind.[12] Blake would work out this relationship in *Milton: A Poem in Two Books,* which was first conceived at Felpham and then worked on for years afterward. It is called *Milton* because Blake imagined uniting as well with his great English predecessor, summoning the spirit of John Milton from Eternity to reinforce the prophetic mission inspired by Los.

10. THE PROPHETIC CALL

Bringing Milton Back

WHEN he created the Lambeth Books, particularly *The Marriage of Heaven and Hell, Visions of the Daughters of Albion,* and *America: A Prophecy,* Blake was a man with a social message. At Felpham he became convinced that he was more than that: he felt called to be a prophet in the line that stretched from Isaiah and Ezekiel through John of Patmos. "Mark well my words!" he exclaims in *Milton,* "they are of your eternal salvation." And in *Jerusalem* he testifies, as his predecessors had, that the prophet's obligation is heavy:

> Trembling I sit day and night, my friends are astonished at me,
> Yet they forgive my wanderings, I rest not from my great task!
> To open the eternal worlds, to open the immortal eyes
> Of man inwards into the worlds of thought: into Eternity,
> Ever expanding in the bosom of God, the human imagination.
> O Saviour pour upon me thy spirit of meekness and love:
> Annihilate the selfhood in me, be thou all my life!
> Guide thou my hand which trembles exceedingly upon the rock of ages.[1]

As Blake understood the role of prophecy, it was to give expression to an individual's perception of truth. No biblical prophet was infallible, far from it. Nor did prophecy cease after the Bible was compiled. Blake regarded Milton as the most recent of the prophets, and as he worked to elaborate his own personal myth, he became obsessed with his great predecessor.

As a feat of imagination, *Paradise Lost* was exceptionally appealing to Blake. "To paint things as they are," Samuel Johnson said, "requires a minute attention, and employs the memory rather than the fancy." That was just the kind of art that Blake despised. But Johnson went on to say, "Milton's delight was to sport in the wide regions of possibility; reality was a scene too narrow for his mind. He sent his faculties out upon discovery, into worlds where only imagination can travel, and delighted to form new modes of existence, and furnish sentiment and action to superior beings, to trace the counsels of hell, or accompany the choirs of heaven." Blake would agree with all of that, except to insist that the world of imagination is the true reality, not an escape from it.[2]

In *The Marriage of Heaven and Hell* Blake had criticized Milton's theology but honored him as "a true poet." At Felpham he began to think about Milton more deeply. William Hayley owned many books by and about Milton, and had written a biography in which he speculated about what would happen if Milton could return to earth to correct mistaken interpretations of his life and writings. That suggestion may well have given Blake the idea of bringing Milton back in a poem of his own. But in Blake's opinion it was Milton himself, and not just his interpreters, who needed correction.[3]

Milton begins with a long "Bard's song" that presents a heavily disguised version of Blake's spiritual struggle with Hayley. That struggle played itself out within Blake's consciousness, and in all probability Hayley never suspected it. He was never the real target anyway, since Blake gratefully acknowledged how kindly his intentions were. Insofar as Hayley does play a role in *Milton,* it is by embodying the conventional worldly expectations that Blake had long struggled against and that he had hoped to be liberated from in Felpham. Disillusionment came when he realized that if he followed Hayley's advice, he would be in artistic bondage just as much as before.

As the poem's title indicates, its true target is Milton, whom Hayley was seeking to coopt as self-appointed custodian of his reputation. Blake's attitude toward Milton was deeply complicated. As creator of a mighty mythic narrative, he was an inspiration; as defender of a repressive belief system, he was an obstacle.

> Say first! what moved Milton, who walked about in Eternity
> One hundred years, pondering the intricate mazes of Providence.
> Unhappy though in heaven, he obeyed, he murmured not, he was silent
> Viewing his sixfold emanation scattered through the deep
> In torment! To go into the deep, her to redeem and himself perish:
> What cause at length moved Milton to this unexampled deed?
> A Bard's prophetic song!

The Bard is an idealized version of Blake; the "sixfold emanation" is Milton's three wives and three daughters, the collective female counterpart over whom he supposedly tyrannized during his lifetime. Since his death, his spirit has been confined unhappily to the bleak heaven he depicted in *Paradise Lost,* presided over by a tyrant God who declares imperiously in that poem, "What I will is fate."[4]

Blake's aggressive critique of Milton furnishes one of Harold Bloom's examples of the "anxiety of influence," in which a "strong poet" achieves his own vision by wrestling with an intimidating predecessor. Blake himself would have said that he was uniting with Milton, not displacing or rejecting him, and that he was rescuing what was inspired in Milton's vision by purging it of error.[5]

The majestic title page for *Milton* (figure 33) shows a naked, muscular figure with his back to us, advancing resolutely into flames of renewal. With his right hand he breaks open his name, MIL–TON, pushing forward into our world and into Blake's poem. At the bottom of the plate his own mandate in *Paradise Lost* is quoted: "To justify the ways of God to men."[6] Milton believed that he could justify God by showing that humankind is responsible for its own suffering. Blake will seek to "justify" a conception of the divine very different from that of the seventeenth-century Calvinist.

The Milton who wrote *Paradise Lost* was personally authoritarian, and it is time to free him from his self-righteous ego, or in Blake's terms from the "false body" of selfhood.

33. *Milton*, copy C, title page

❖ ❖ ❖

> This is a false body: an incrustation over my immortal
> Spirit; a selfhood, which must be put off and annihilated alway
> To cleanse the face of my spirit by self-examination,
> To bathe in the waters of life: to wash off the not human.
> I come in self-annihilation and the grandeur of inspiration
> To cast off rational demonstration by faith in the Saviour,
> To cast off the rotten rags of memory by inspiration.[7]

Milton's immortal spirit lives on, but the ragged garment of his selfhood—the historical Milton, with all his limitations and biases—must be "annihilated." In the picture that illustrates these lines (color plate 20) he is again naked, as he was on the title page, but now he is facing us. His face is Christlike, and the sun rises behind him while a radiant halo surrounds his head.

Since it is Blake in Felpham who has summoned Milton back to earth, a crucial event in the poem is their direct encounter. It is described, however, in imagery of surpassing weirdness:

> Then first I saw him in the zenith as a falling star
> Descending perpendicular, swift as the swallow or swift,
> And on my left foot falling on the tarsus, entered there;
> But from my left foot a black cloud redounding spread over Europe.

Milton the man no longer exists; it is his spirit that hurtles down from the heavens, taking the form of a shooting star and not a person. The star strikes Blake's foot, perhaps since he thought of feet as our point of contact with the physical world. It is Jesus' feet that are invoked in the lyric in *Milton* known as *Jerusalem:* "And did those feet in ancient time / Walk upon England's mountains green!"[8]

Though not always consistently, Blake generally saw negative implications in the left or "sinister" side. With surprising specificity, he identifies the point of contact here as the tarsus. That is the upper part of the foot that joins the ankle, but Blake must have chosen it because it is also a biblical name: Saul of Tarsus was struck down on the road to Damascus and became Saint Paul. The black cloud may be the false elements of Milton's former beliefs, now dispersing. Or, since the cloud seems to spread from Blake himself, perhaps he too is complicit in errors that must be exposed and rejected.[9]

The moment of Milton's descent is illustrated with not one image but two, each occupying a full page. The first (figure 34) is positioned as a divider between the two books of *Milton*. Blake, identified as "William" in the caption, staggers backward at the very instant when the shooting star, trailing light, is about to strike his foot. In one copy of the poem he is naked; in the other three, as here, he wears diaphanous briefs through which his body can be seen. A number of commentators are convinced that his penis is erect, but if so it is very tactfully represented.[10]

The other image (figure 35) is altogether surprising. It comes a few plates later, not facing this one as might be expected, but obviously a mirror image of it. Its caption, "Robert," would have baffled any contemporary viewer, since that name appears nowhere in the poem. This is Blake's much-loved younger brother, who had died in his teens and whom Blake continued to regard as a kind of alter ego in Eternity. The star may represent Robert's astral body as imagined in Neoplatonic philosophy, a spiritual projection that can revisit earth from the afterlife.[11]

A few months before he moved to Felpham, Blake sent a moving letter of consolation to Hayley, whose teenage son had just died after a long and painful illness.

> I am very sorry for your immense loss, which is a repetition of what all feel in this valley of misery and happiness mixed. . . . I know that our deceased friends are more really with us than when they were apparent to our mortal part. Thirteen years ago I lost a brother, and with his spirit I converse daily and hourly in the spirit, and see him in my remembrance in the regions of my imagination. I hear his advice and even now write from his dictate—forgive me for expressing to you my enthusiasm which I wish all to partake of since it is to me a source of immortal joy even in this world. By it I am the companion of angels. May you continue to be so more and more, and to be more and more persuaded that every mortal loss is an immortal gain. The ruins of time builds mansions in Eternity.[12]

All Christians are supposed to believe that their loved ones enjoy eternal life. What is exceptional in Blake is his conviction that Robert has not ascended to some remote heaven, but continues to communicate with him "daily and hourly." So the letter to Hayley moves from reminiscence—"thirteen years ago"—to "even now" as the words flow from the pen.

It is hard to know how literally to take Blake's claim that he communicates directly with Robert. Remarks that are scattered throughout his works suggest that the contact must be with Robert's essential spirit, which lives on in Eternity but is no longer identical with the young sibling who died in 1787. Blake always criticized orthodox preaching that encouraged people to endure suffering in this life with the promise that their individual selfhood would survive unchanged in Heaven. Similarly, as the paired "William" and "Robert" pictures suggest, Blake's union with Milton is spiritual and symbolic. After it occurs, we do not see Milton walking the earth with Blake as a novelistic character might. And in any case, the heart of the poem is not so much Blake's union with Milton as Blake's union with Los.

Los Falling, Los Creating

Los first made his appearance in two of the short Lambeth Books, *The Book of Urizen* and *The Book of Los*. In *Milton* he emerges not as a rebel but as a formidable rival creator to Urizen. Urizen attempts to create after the fashion of the biblical Jehovah: "God said, Let there be light: and there was light." In contrast, Los creates with intense physical labor, a blacksmith hammering recalcitrant iron on his anvil. This creator is an artist and a craftsman, and in the late *Jerusalem* Blake imagines himself as an avatar of Los, a blacksmith who uses the Thames as the trough in which to cool the molten metal:

> Round from heaven to earth down falling with heavy blow
> Dead on the anvil, where the red hot wedge groans in pain,
> He quenches it in the black trough of his forge; London's River
> Feeds the dread forge, trembling and shuddering along the valleys.[13]

The "he" in this passage is Rintrah, one of the sons of Los, who was associated in *The Marriage of Heaven and Hell* with prophetic wrath.

In conceiving this blacksmith creator, Blake may well have been thinking of Hephaestus, known to the Romans as Vulcan, the artificer of Olympus who creates the great shield of Achilles. But most important, surely, was Blake's own experience as an artist and craftsman. A writer like Shelley could think of creativity as wholly

34. *Milton*, copy C, plate 31

35. *Milton*, copy C, plate 36

mental: "The mind in creation is as a fading coal which some invisible influence, like an inconstant wind, awakens to transitory brightness." But Blake's poems were not fully realized until sharp tools had gouged them into copper plates or until acid had raised the metal outline into relief—"melting apparent surfaces away, and displaying the infinite which was hid," as he says in *The Marriage of Heaven and Hell*.[14]

Still, even if Blake was a worker in metal, a tidy engraver's studio is very different from a hot and smoke-filled smithy, such as he and his contemporaries would have seen constantly—even in the city, horses needed to be shod. It must have been the blacksmith's associations with flames and muscular energy that appealed to Blake. Perhaps he was thinking of a well-known series of paintings, all entitled *A Blacksmith's Shop*, by Joseph Wright of Derby. In the most striking of these, a glowing forge stands out from a shadowy background, and at the center a white-hot metal bar lies beneath the blacksmith's hammer. Blake may also have remembered Ben Jonson's use of blacksmith imagery in his tribute to Shakespeare, which likewise captures the heat and effort of the forge, as well as the effect of creation on the artist himself:

> And that he
> Who casts to write a living line, must sweat . . .
> Upon the muses' anvil: turn the same,
> (And himself with it) that he thinks to frame.

At the end of *A Portrait of the Artist as a Young Man*, Stephen Dedalus invokes the same analogy, with a moral emphasis that is very Blakean: "I go to encounter for the millionth time the reality of experience and to forge in the smithy of my soul the uncreated conscience of my race."[15]

As with Blake's other invented characters, no one knows how he pronounced "Los." The name is suggestive of "loss," and may have been pronounced that way, though it seems easier somehow to make it rhyme with "close."

Just as the other Zoas do, Los experiences a fall when Albion slips into nightmare; that was when all four Zoas, together with their emanations, broke apart into competing entities. In Eternity, where he represented the unfallen imagination, he was known as Urthona, and the very presence of the new name is a symptom of the disaster.

What, exactly, Los is falling *from* is not made clear, since Blake never tries to describe the mysterious life of Eternity or what the Eternals themselves might be like. Their mode of existence is drastically different from our own, so we can only guess at it; at the end of *Jerusalem* Blake describes the unfallen Zoas as "the four living creatures, chariots of humanity divine, incomprehensible."[16] For that matter, Albion himself is none too easy to understand. Although all four Zoas were once fully integrated within him, they are now bitterly divided, and their quarrelsome interaction is what fills the poems.

One of the final Lambeth Books, *The Book of Los,* published in 1795, describes Los's fall in verse that is tumbling and unstable:

> Falling, falling! Los fell and fell,
> Sunk precipitant heavy down down
> Times on times, night on night, day on day;
> Truth has bounds, error none. Falling, falling,
> Years on years, and ages on ages
> Still he fell through the void, still a void
> Found for falling, day and night without end,
> For though day or night was not, their spaces
> Were measured by his incessant whirls
> In the horrid vacuity bottomless.[17]

The vertiginous fall threatens to go on forever, since error has no bounds. Los tumbles through the void for "ages on ages," before time as we know it even exists — "day or night was not." But as he spins it is he himself who begins to define day and night, "measured by his incessant whirls."

In Blake's myth, Los is consistently associated with the measurement of time. While he was falling he measured time involuntarily, but was somehow able to arrest his fall; thereafter he measures time more constructively with rhythmic blows of his blacksmith's hammer. Blake is not a narrative poet in any conventional sense, and we are not told how the change from fall to reconstruction takes place. Perhaps it can't be narrated; it is a psychic turn that is felt but not fully understood.

Los had already appeared as a blacksmith measuring time in *The Book of Urizen,* published one year before *The Book of Los:*

> The eternal prophet heaved the dark bellows
> And turned restless the tongs, and the hammer
> Incessant beat; forging chains new and new,
> Numb'ring with links hours, days and years.

The Eternals, whatever they are, inhabit a perpetual Now, but in our fallen world we desperately need the structuring that is given by time. Thus, in *Milton:*

> Time is the mercy of Eternity; without time's swiftness,
> Which is the swiftest of all things, all were eternal torment.[18]

Terrified by formlessness, Urizen tries to create a world of petrified stability. Los rightly breaks it asunder, but that act precipitates his own fall. As described in *The Book of Los,*

> The prophetic wrath, struggling for vent
> Hurls apart, stamping furious to dust
> And crumbling with bursting sobs; heaves
> The black marble on high into fragments.
> Hurled apart on all sides, as a falling
> Rock, the innumerable fragments away
> Fell asunder; and horrible vacuum
> Beneath him and on all sides round.

Having smashed Urizen's rigid and sterile universe, Los wields his mighty hammer to rebuild Urizen himself. In allegorical terms, one might say that imagination comes to the rescue of self-crippled reason.

> Los beat on the anvil, till glorious
> An immense orb of fire he framed. . . .
> Nine ages completed their circles
> When Los heated the glowing mass, casting
> It down into the deeps, the deeps fled
> Away in redounding smoke; the sun
> Stood self-balanced, and Los smiled with joy.
> He the vast spine of Urizen seized
> And bound down to the glowing illusion.[19]

"Smiled with joy" recalls "and did he smile his work to see" in *The Tyger*, published just one year previously. In a sense Los, like Urizen, plays the part of a Neoplatonic or Gnostic demiurge who creates the material world. In this unusually short work—*The Book of Los* has just five plates—the following words all appear: "hands," "feet," "immortal," "furnaces," "anvil," "hammer," "framed," "deeps," and "seizing." That is the very same vocabulary as in *The Tyger*.[20]

As usual with Blake, there are multiple versions of every "event," and in an account in *The Book of Urizen* there is no smiling Los:

> A vast spine writhed in torment
> Upon the winds; shooting pained
> Ribs, like a bending cavern
> And bones of solidness, froze
> Over all his nerves of joy.

Exhausted by the effort and horrified at the hideous creature he has fabricated,

> In terrors Los shrunk from his task:
> His great hammer fell from his hand.

The image that illustrates these lines (color plate 21) shows Los experiencing the "dismal woe" that is described just above the image, with a huge fluted column projecting weirdly from his body. It seems grotesquely phallic, and architectural as well; Erdman thinks it's a leaning tower like that of Pisa, about to topple over. We don't see the "vast spine" and ribs mentioned in the poem, but Urizen is indeed shockingly skeletal, with neck vertebrae disturbingly visible. Still, the work of reconstruction is under way, and as David Bindman says, he is now "sentient enough to agonize in the flames of the forge."[21] His ankles are shackled to the ground.

There are many ways to imagine creativity, and the blacksmith's labor is not the only one. Further on in *The Book of Urizen*, Los somehow extrudes a globe of organic "life blood" from his head:

> The globe of life blood trembled
> Branching out into roots,
> Fibrous, writhing upon the winds;

> Fibres of blood, milk and tears,
> In pangs, eternity on eternity.

Anatomists at the time understood the organs to be composed of fibers, and they identified three different types of fluid-bearing vessels. These were blood, lacteals, and tears—the very ones that emerge from Los's bloody globe. In the picture that corresponds to these lines (color plate 22) he presses his hands forcibly against his head while his hair drips down upon the globe like bloody rain.[22]

In still another poem on this theme, *The Song of Los,* published in the same year as *The Book of Los,* a weary Los is depicted at rest with a blood-red sun before him (color plate 23). Here he seems melancholy and even tender, though oddly chubby. The just-created sun gives off crimson beams, while a greater source of light and energy spills from beyond it. Los is *a* creator, but he is not *the* creator. Creation is an ongoing expression of energy, not the primal event described in Genesis.

In the densely colored images in the books of this period there is no etching at all, just paint laid directly on the plate and touched up as needed after printing. Robert Essick describes what can be seen in the particular copy that is reproduced here:

> The design is built up by multiple layers of color printing, painting, and perhaps blotting. The major elements of the design were printed in thick, opaque colors that formed large dendritic patterns. These can be seen in areas untouched by subsequent layers, such as the background and just below the figure's left knee. The man and hammer were then painted with thick colors, but the suns received further printings or blottings. Below the hammer are a number of short hairs stuck to the paper—very likely the remains of a stubble brush used to daub on colors. . . . Subsequent layers of color shimmer above the paper to form a "glowing illusion" like the sun described in the Book of Los.[23]

In reproduction, unfortunately, these subtle effects disappear.

Los as Watchman, Los in the Sun

When he was first imagining the role of Los, Blake concentrated on mythic origins. In *Milton* and in its sequel, *Jerusalem,* Los enters our world, and in the frontispiece to *Jerusalem* (figure 36) we see him doing so. He is dressed as a night watchman; the sun is now a "globe of fire," not blood, and serves as his lantern. Strange dark rays shine from inside the archway, and a wind blows Los's hair and clothing to one side. His hat is a broad-brimmed one such as Blake himself was accustomed to wear, and his garment—blue in the sole colored copy of *Jerusalem*—is perhaps a printer's smock. One item is hardly British, however: the sandal, which for Blake symbolizes prophetic vocation. And again we hear of the left foot, which in *Milton* was the place where Milton's spirit entered Blake as a falling star. Here he speaks in his own voice:

> All this vegetable world appeared on my left foot
> As a bright sandal formed immortal of precious stones and gold;
> I stooped down and bound it on to walk forward through Eternity.

"Sounds solid," Stephen Dedalus reflects as he walks with eyes closed on a Dublin beach, "made by the mallet of Los Demiurgos. Am I walking into eternity along Sandymount Strand?"[24]

Los's left hand is raised in a gesture that is hard to read. Is he registering apprehension? Just keeping his balance? He is gazing to the right; what does he see that we can't? Above the archway some lines of verse were originally engraved, deleted from the printed version but recoverable from a proof sheet, and one of them describes this moment: "He entered the door of death for Albion's sake inspired."[25]

Two biblical texts help to clarify the significance of the watchman. One is in Isaiah: "Watchman, what of the night? The watchman said, The morning cometh, and also the night: if ye will inquire, inquire ye: return, come." And since by entering death's door Los is enacting a Christlike role, the Gospel of John is relevant too: "I am the door: by me if any man enter in, he shall be saved."[26]

Just as Milton unites with Blake in Felpham, so does Los, as described at length in a verse letter to Butts. (It is worth remarking that if Blake had not had Butts for

36. *Jerusalem*, copy E, frontispiece

a sympathetic correspondent, some of his most memorable statements and poems would not exist.) Setting out from Felpham to meet his sister, who was coming from London for a visit, Blake finds the way threateningly blocked by family demons:

> With my father hovering upon the wind
> And my brother Robert just behind
> And my brother John the evil one
> In a black cloud making his moan,
> Though dead they appear upon my path
> Notwithstanding my terrible wrath.
> They beg they entreat they drop their tears
> Filled full of hopes filled full of fears,
> With a thousand angels upon the wind
> Pouring disconsolate from behind
> To drive them off, and before my way
> A frowning thistle implores my stay.
> What to others a trifle appears
> Fills me full of smiles or tears,
> For double the vision my eyes do see
> And a double vision is always with me.
> With my inward eye 'tis an old man grey,
> With my outward a thistle across my way.
> "If thou goest back," the thistle said
> "Thou art to endless woe betrayed,
> For here does Theotormon lower
> And here is Enitharmon's bower
> And Los the terrible thus hath sworn
> Because thou backward dost return
> Poverty envy old age and fear
> Shall bring thy wife upon a bier."[27]

("Theotormon" here is one of the sons of Los.)

This is a vision, not a hallucination. But if to other people a thistle is just a thistle, to Blake it looms as a figure of stern reproof, accusing him of failing to support his depressed and sickly wife. Catherine was ill a good deal of the time at Felpham, and Blake evidently felt that she was reproaching him for failing to bring in more income—but the way to do that would be to abandon his original work and to drudge full-time at tiresome commissions secured by Hayley. By invoking Los, the thistle uses Blake's own mythic character against him, provoking a crisis of self-doubt. He passes the test and kicks the thistle aside. Suddenly an epiphany bursts upon him:

> Then Los appeared in all his power;
> In the sun he appeared descending before
> My face in fierce flames; in my double sight
> 'Twas outward a sun, inward Los in his might. . . .
> With the bows of my mind and the arrows of thought,
> My bowstring fierce with ardour breathes,
> My arrows glow in their golden sheaves.
> My brothers and father march before,
> The heavens drop with human gore.
> Now I a fourfold vision see
> And a fourfold vision is given to me.
> 'Tis fourfold in my supreme delight
> And threefold in soft Beulah's night
> And twofold always. May God us keep
> From single vision and Newton's sleep.

Strikingly, the family members are all male. There is no mention of Blake's mother, or for that matter of the sister who is about to arrive. And why do the heavens drip with "human gore"? Has Blake wounded the familial blocking figures with his arrows of thought?

At any rate, the mandate must not be refused, and the bow and arrows are the ones that Blake will invoke again in the lyric that introduces *Milton:* "Bring me my bow of burning gold, / Bring me my arrows of desire." When this episode is recapitulated in *Milton,* the relatives and the blood are no longer mentioned.

> While Los heard indistinct in fear, what time I bound my sandals
> On, to walk forward through Eternity, Los descended to me,
> And Los behind me stood, a terrible flaming sun, just close
> Behind my back. I turned round in terror, and behold,
> Los stood in that fierce glowing fire; and he also stooped down

And bound my sandals on in Udan-Adan. Trembling I stood
Exceedingly with fear and terror, standing in the vale
Of Lambeth: but he kissed me and wished me health,
And I became one man with him arising in my strength.
'Twas too late now to recede; Los had entered into my soul:
His terrors now possessed me whole! I arose in fury and strength.[28]

This moment is illustrated by a full-page design (color plate 24) in which an impressively muscular Blake—as usual, blond—pauses from strapping on his sandal and turns "in terror" as Los steps forward out of the sun. (Commentators suggest that his name implies the sun—*sol,* its Latin name, spelled backward.) Why is Blake's head positioned at the level of Los's crotch? Mitchell long ago suspected "homoerotic implications," while a more recent commentator objects that the conjunction of head and loins may be merely a botched attempt to suggest three-dimensional depth. Christopher Hobson, in his judicious *Blake and Homosexuality,* argues that Blake was tolerant of all sexual practices but not personally homosexual, and points out that in this picture "Blake's posture of twisting to face someone behind him is an unlikely configuration for an actual sexual act or kiss."[29] But even if, as does seem likely, no literal sexual encounter is implied, the location of the head is surely not accidental. As in *The Marriage of Heaven and Hell* and in *America,* energy is libidinal, and Los is transmitting that potency to Blake.

Painful though the struggle was, Blake has accepted his prophetic calling—but that is only the beginning. Acting as an avatar of the inspiring Los, he must now strive to bring about a breakthrough into Eternity. Each of the three major prophecies—*The Four Zoas, Milton,* and *Jerusalem*—ends with an apocalypse, which is described in imagery from the Book of Revelation that was once familiar to everybody, as in "Mine eyes have seen the glory of the coming of the Lord; / He is trampling out the vintage where the grapes of wrath are stored." According to Revelation, that apocalypse lies in the future, when the entire universe will end. In Blake's myth it is an interior Last Judgment that takes place "whenever any individual rejects error and embraces truth."[30] It is thus constructive, not destructive, apprehending Eternity within the world of time.

11. BREAKTHROUGH TO APOCALYPSE

Mastering the Spectre

LONG as *Jerusalem* is—and it is very long—it is not really a poem in which events "happen." Even Northrop Frye, its most passionate admirer, conceded that it is a "dehydrated epic." It is far from obvious that it should be called an epic at all. Frye also says, "Each part of *Jerusalem* presents a phase of imaginative vision simultaneously with the body of error which it clarifies." Not everyone will agree that what goes on is clarifying, but the myriad forms of error are displayed in bewildering detail. For example, Blake expects us to make sense of a succession of twenty-seven "churches" in human history, the first nine of which are "hermaphroditic," the second nine "female males," and the final nine "male females." There are passages of great eloquence throughout the poem but also long pedestrian stretches, such as a ninety-line passage listing correspondences between British names and biblical ones (a brief excerpt will suffice):

> And the names of the thirty-two counties of Ireland are these:
> Under Judah and Issachar and Zebulun are Lowth Longford
> Eastmeath Westmeath Dublin Kildare Kings County
> Queens County Wicklow Catherloh Wexford Kilkenny. . . .[1]

One threat, in particular, permeates *Jerusalem*. Far more than in *Milton*, and more even than in *The Four Zoas*, Blake is preoccupied by what he calls the Female

Will. The culmination of the poem will be Albion's reunion with his emanation Jerusalem, though she is more like a daughter than an equal partner. But it is a confederacy of nature goddesses that dominates the poem. Vala seduces Albion away from Jerusalem, and she is abetted thereafter by characters called Tirzah and Rahab. Blake's symbolism of the female is of great importance to him, but most readers today are likely to find it repellent; it will be taken up separately later on.

There is also a male incarnation of error, and here Blake addresses his experience as an artist in a powerfully imaginative way. A picture near the beginning of *Jerusalem* shows Los resting after hard labor at his blazing forge (color plate 25). Hovering above him is a new addition to the cast of characters, the Spectre. As the text on this plate indicates, it has separated out from Los himself, "divided from his back," and is threatening him with doubts about his vocation.

> In pain the Spectre divided, in pain of hunger and thirst,
> To devour Los's human perfection; but when he saw that Los
> Was living, panting like a frighted wolf and howling
> He stood over the Immortal, in the solitude and darkness:
> Upon the darkening Thames, across the whole island westward,
> A horrible Shadow of Death, among the furnaces, beneath
> The pillar of folding smoke; and he sought by other means
> To lure Los: by tears, by arguments of science, and by terrors:
> Terrors in every nerve, by spasms and extended pains.

Yet Los is unafraid. In the picture he gazes up at the howling Spectre, whose hands are pressed against its ears to shut out anything he might say, and "answered unterrified to the opaque blackening fiend."[2]

The symbolism of the Spectre is a striking example of the zeitgeist at work. Many writers at the time were fascinated by the idea of a shadowy double or doppelgänger (the word was coined by Jean Paul Richter in 1796); the best known is the monster that acts out Dr. Frankenstein's unconscious aggression, successively strangling his brother, his best friend, and his fiancée. At times Blake imagines a spectre as emerging when a Zoa and his emanation split apart. At other times it represents an interior division that is somehow present from the very start: "Man is born a spectre or Satan and is altogether an evil, and requires a new selfhood continually and must continually be changed into his direct contrary."[3] By now, when Blake speaks of Satan he no longer means the figure of fiery energy in *The Marriage of Heaven and Hell;* rather, he has in mind a "state" of negativity and resistance that individuals may fall into but may also escape from. When the mild-mannered William Hayley seeks to dominate Blake, he is described as being temporarily in the state of Satan.

As Blake's sympathy with the "mad" poet Cowper confirms, he did have fears of despair. In its separated state the Spectre cries out in anguish,

> O that I could cease to be! Despair! I am despair,
> Created to be the great example of horror and agony; also my
> Prayer is vain. I called for compassion: compassion mocked;
> Mercy and pity threw the grave stone over me, and with lead
> And iron bound it over me for ever.[4]

Threatening though the Spectre is, there is no possibility of rejecting it outright, for it is an essential element in the self. When Albion fell into nightmare and his constituent Zoas broke away, the Zoa formerly known as Urthona split into three elements: Los, Enitharmon, and the Spectre. All must be reintegrated. Enitharmon plays what Blake regards as a "feminine" role in artistic creation, adding coloring to Los's firm outlines. As for the Spectre, it represents the practical execution of Blake's visionary conceptions, which are not embodied until words and images have been etched into metal plates.

In its separated state, the Spectre seeks to intimidate Los, or even to destroy him.

> While Los spoke, the terrible Spectre fell shuddering before him,
> Watching his time with glowing eyes to leap upon his prey.

But Los proves more powerful, and he forces the Spectre to cooperate in the work of imaginative creation. "Take thou this hammer," he commands, "and in patience heave the thundering bellows, / Take thou these tongs: strike thou alternate with me, labour obedient." The hammer is obviously phallic in the picture, and there can be no doubt that sexual energy is implied. Just how the bat-winged "fiend" is

supposed to wield the hammer is far from clear, however; we are probably not expected to visualize it.

> Therefore Los stands in London building Golgonooza,
> Compelling his Spectre to labours mighty. Trembling in fear,
> The Spectre weeps, but Los unmoved by tears or threats remains.
> "I must create a system, or be enslaved by another man's;
> I will not reason and compare: my business is to create."
> So Los, in fury and strength, in indignation and burning wrath.
> Shudd'ring the Spectre howls, his howlings terrify the night.
> He stamps around the anvil, beating blows of stern despair.[5]

Golgonooza is Blake's city of artistic creation, of which more presently.

Once tamed and assimilated, the Spectre pretty much drops out of sight. What
evidently matters to Blake is the *idea* of its role in creation, rather than its continued
activity as a character in the poem. Or to put it differently, in its separated state the
Spectre is all too vividly real, as we will see later in a powerful notebook poem that
begins, "My Spectre around me night and day / Like a wild beast guards my way."[6]
Reintegrated into the creative self, it ceases to have a distinct existence of its own.

This disappearance of the Spectre is characteristic of Blake's prophecies. In a
very broad sense, each of them has a plot, but not in an ordinary cause-and-effect
way. They are more like kaleidoscopic dreams than coherent narratives. Each is a
dizzying medley of refractions, repetitions, and metamorphoses. Though Albion
disappears from view most of the time, in effect he is constantly present throughout, since everything that happens is the shifting imagery of his ongoing nightmare.
In the original draft of *The Four Zoas*, entitled *Vala*, the subtitle was *The Death and
Judgment of the Ancient Man, a Dream of Nine Nights*. But we never get to know Albion;
it is his discordant components that are all too visibly alive.

Apocalypse

In *Milton* and *Jerusalem,* the culminating apocalypse—the breakthrough into Eternity when Albion awakens—is only briefly described, but in *The Four Zoas* it is

described at great length. The chronology of these three works is not entirely clear, but their sequence is. Blake began *The Four Zoas* in 1797 and revised that never-engraved manuscript at various times. Some of its material was recycled in the fifty-plate *Milton* in 1804, which was first printed in 1811. By then Blake had gotten started on *Jerusalem,* possibly as early as 1808, and he continued to enlarge that poem over many years. In its final form it filled a hundred plates, divided rather arbitrarily into four books of equal size, and was printed at last in 1820. And although each of the final two prophecies ends with an apocalypse, it is almost endlessly deferred and surprisingly anticlimactic when it finally arrives.

In *The Four Zoas,* it is Los who precipitates the apocalypse by ripping Urizen's rigid heavens apart:

> His right hand branching out in fibrous strength
> Seized the sun, his left hand like dark roots covered the moon,
> And tore them down, cracking the heavens across from immense to
>   immense.
> Then fell the fires of Eternity with loud and shrill
> Sound of loud trumpet thundering along from heaven to heaven,
> A mighty sound articulate: "Awake ye dead and come
> To judgment from the four winds, awake and come away!"[7]

This breakthrough is a colossal expansion of the liberation of humanity that had been anticipated in *America: A Prophecy.* Now, however, the cruelty is far more shocking than in that optimistic early work.

> The tree of Mystery went up in folding flames;
> Blood issued out in mighty volumes pouring in whirlpools fierce
> From out the flood gates of the sky. The gates are burst, down pour
> The torrents black upon the earth, the blood pours down incessant;
> Kings in their palaces lie drowned, shepherds their flocks their tents
> Roll down the mountains in black torrents, cities villages
> High spires and castles drowned in the black deluge; shoal on shoal
> Float the dead carcasses of men and beasts driven to and fro on waves
> Of foaming blood beneath the black incessant sky till all
> Mystery's tyrants are cut off and not one left on earth. . . .

From the clotted gore and from the hollow den
Start forth the trembling millions into flames of mental fire,
Bathing their limbs in the bright visions of Eternity.

The grapes of wrath from Revelation are explicitly invoked:

But in the wine presses the human grapes sing not nor dance,
They howl and writhe in shoals of torment, in fierce flames consuming.[8]

Insofar as a historical apocalypse has taken place, this may refer to the bloodshed of the French Revolution and the counterrevolutionary wars that followed. Insofar as the apocalypse is internal, it is the psychic pain that accompanies any deep, far-reaching change, which entails a drastic reordering of the self.

It is apparent that by the time Blake engraved *Milton* and *Jerusalem,* he no longer thought that an apocalyptic liberation of humanity could be fully attained. In *Milton* it never occurs at all, but is only described as about to happen. At the end of *Milton* two sons of Los very briefly anticipate the event:

Rintrah and Palamabron view the human harvest beneath.
Their winepresses and barns stand open; the ovens are prepared,
The wagons ready. Terrific lions and tygers sport and play,
All animals upon the earth are prepared in all their strength
To go forth to the great harvest and vintage of the nations.

In *Jerusalem* the apocalypse does happen, but it is more like a release from frustration than a fulfilling breakthrough. As Essick comments, "*Jerusalem* is highly repetitious in its imagery and actions. We are tossed about with maximum sound and fury but appear to get nowhere until suddenly, on the last few plates, the poem ends with an apocalyptic big-bang."[9]

Traditional Blake scholarship used to celebrate the apocalypse as fully achieved, rather than acknowledging that it is a fantasized alternative to life as people actually experience it. The comments of a psychoanalyst who is familiar with Blake's writings are worth pondering. Ronald Britton observes that a dread of psychic fragmentation and of the void is characteristic of borderline personalities, and he suggests that Blake's apocalyptic breakthrough can be seen as compensatory fantasy: "He unashamedly propounds as the route to salvation what in psychoanalysis has been called infantile megalomania. In this state, he claims, we are what we imagine we are, and our imagination is our share of the divine."[10]

Generations of critics have indeed echoed Frye's extravagant claim that "imagination creates reality, and as desire is a part of imagination, the world we desire is more real than the world we passively accept." In what possible sense more real? Britton's persuasive conclusion is that what is most powerful in Blake's poems is the representation of Experience, "a sadder and grimmer place than in *The Songs of Innocence,* and less blissful than Beulah, but with the great advantage of being as real as it sounds."[11] And this may well be the reason why the apocalypse, when it finally comes, seems almost cursory in *Milton* and *Jerusalem.* For Blake it is a deeply longed-for goal, but his real subject is the arduous struggle to get there.

The Stubborn Structure

The struggle to achieve the breakthrough is where Golgonooza, Los's city of art, comes in. It may not be the oddest name Blake invented, but it is certainly odd. Various imaginative associations have been proposed. The most obvious is that Christ was crucified at Golgotha, "the place of the skull," so the name may imply self-sacrifice. In any event Golgonooza is imperfect, an all too temporary city of imagination that Los erects against the forces of destruction.

> Here on the banks of the Thames Los builded Golgonooza,
> Outside of the gates of the human heart, beneath Beulah
> In the midst of the rocks of the altars of Albion. In fears
> He builded it, in rage and in fury. It is the spiritual fourfold
> London: continually building and continually decaying desolate!

An illustration in *Jerusalem* shows a pair of winged angels with their heads in their hands, facing each other across a circle that contains this inscription: "Continually Building. Continually Decaying because of Love and Jealousy."[12] The same could be said of Blake's myth—it was forever being rebuilt.

In Eternity, buildings and works of art are unnecessary. The Eternals—

shadowy and impossible to visualize, as always—communicate in an imaginative mode that we can only guess at.

> They conversed together in visionary forms dramatic, which bright
> Redounded from their tongues in thunderous majesty.

For us, however, communication is hard work. Referring to Bowlahoola and Allamanda (generally thought to mean the stomach and nervous system), Blake declares,

> I call them by their English names: English, the rough basement.
> Los built the stubborn structure of the language, acting against
> Albion's melancholy, who must else have been a dumb despair.[13]

English is Blake's rough basement, as Italian would be Dante's, because thoughts have to be communicated through words. But words are generic and degenerate into clichés, so Blake strives continually, like Los at the forge, to force the stubborn structure of language into new shapes. That includes making up "English names" that nobody ever heard before.

The final plate of *Jerusalem* presents a richly thought-provoking image, but before we look at it we need to consider an earlier image in the poem, a gigantic version of the prehistoric stone structures known as trilithons (color plate 26). Familiar from the surviving example at Stonehenge, the ancient stone circles were believed in Blake's time to have been built by Druids. At first sight this image is attractive. "The firm drawing," an art historian says, "in the thick yet graceful lines, is lightly printed and freely and delicately coloured, so the stones are felt as colossal, of enormous mass, but also have a lovely airy cool space around them."[14] The colors are indeed delicate: green fields and hills, the sky in two shades of blue, and a mild yellow sun glowing at the exact center of the plate.

Still, this is not a positive image. The tiny human figures are dwarfed by the enormous rectangular blocks that tower above them, the very opposite of living form. In his address "To the Jews" in *Jerusalem* Blake declares, "Your ancestors derived their origin from Abraham, Heber, Shem, and Noah, who were Druids, as the Druid temples (which are the patriarchal pillars and oak groves) over the whole earth witness to this day." Worshipping a threatening goddess of nature in dark oaken groves, the Druids sought to propitiate her with human sacrifice, and they sponsored a vicious culture of war:

> The wicker man of Scandinavia, in which cruelly consumed
> The captives reared to heaven howl in flames among the stars;
> Loud the cries of war on the Rhine and Danube with Albion's sons.
> Away from Beulah's hills and vales break forth the souls of the dead
> With cymbal, trumpet, clarion, and the scythed chariots of Britain.

Blake didn't make up the wicker man. No less an authority than Julius Caesar reported that the Gauls appeased their gods by filling huge wickerwork effigies with living men and then setting them on fire.[15] Current events mingle here with ancient legend: "Albion's sons" were fighting on the Rhine and Danube.

Stonehenge, though mistakenly attributed to Druids, was rightly surmised to have had something to do with tracking the sun and measuring time. To Blake this means that it was disastrously implicated in natural religion.

> They build a stupendous building on the plain of Salisbury, with chains
> Of rocks round London Stone: of reasonings, of unhewn demonstrations
> In labyrinthine arches (mighty Urizen the architect) through which
> The heavens might revolve and Eternity be bound in their chain.
> Labour unparalleled! a wondrous rocky world of cruel destiny,
> Rocks piled on rocks reaching the stars, stretching from pole to pole.
> The building is natural religion and its altars natural morality,
> A building of eternal death, whose proportions are eternal despair.[16]

With this as context, we may turn to the final plate of *Jerusalem* (figure 37). At the center stands Los at his ease, in the pose of the classical Apollo Belvedere, with genitals clearly visible, leaning on his tongs and hammer. He looks weary, and well he should. Building the city of art has been hard labor, gripping red-hot metal with the tongs, while the great hammer—much larger than any actual blacksmith's hammer—pounded it into shape.

To the right, Los's dark emanation Enitharmon is associated with a crescent moon from which bloody fibers drip down. In her left hand she holds a distaff (or

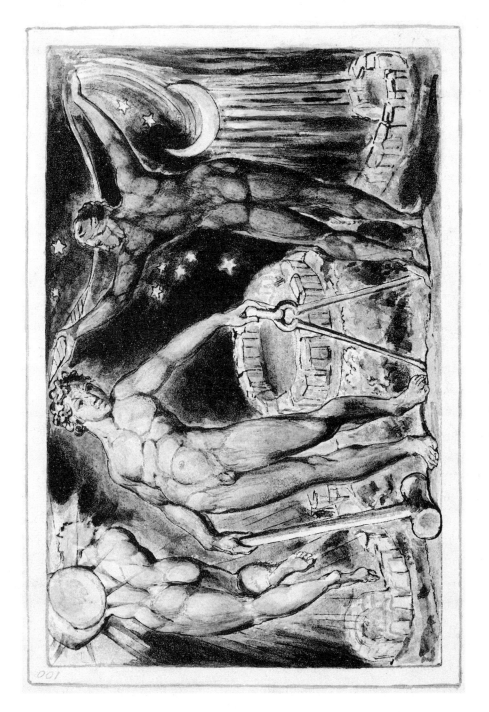

37. *Jerusalem*, copy E, plate 100

possibly a shuttle) with which to weave mortal bodies. That is the work of Generation, at once necessary and entrapping. At the left, an assistant springs into the air, bearing a sun on his shoulder like a bricklayer's hod. Commentators generally agree that this must be the Spectre, but actually they are just guessing. If they are right, then he is now trusted to carry the sun that was once the lantern with which Los, dressed as a watchman, "entered the door of death." That was shown in the frontispiece to *Jerusalem,* bookending the poem with this final plate. In the body of the poem the Spectre was threatening and batlike; now—if this identification is correct—he is fully human. The divided selves of Los are reunited at last, and fully cooperative.[17] But how this has come to pass is never shown or explained. Blake is piercingly eloquent about conflict and suffering but unwilling or unable to give a convincing account of the breakthrough into wholeness.

But what is the winding structure in the background? This might seem to be yet another strange Blakean invention, but in fact he took it, as we have already noted, directly from a book called *Abury: A Temple of the British Druids,* by the antiquarian William Stukeley (figure 38). The modern name of the town is Avebury, and the prehistoric remains there were in ruins when Stukeley saw them, having been pillaged over the centuries for local buildings. His illustration is therefore an imaginative reconstruction, based on a mistaken belief that the central circle had originally been flanked by two wings in the form of a serpent, supposedly reflecting the influence of Egyptian religion. Stukeley also imagined Christian parallels: "The circle meant the supreme fountain of all being, the Father; the serpent, the divine emanation from him which was called the Son; the wings, the other divine emanation from them which was called the Spirit." Blake had his own ideas about what serpent temples were for, and as early as *Europe* he made Avebury a symbol of repression, expanding to fill the whole of Britain as it "stretches out its shady length along the island white." (Whiteness is implied in the name "Albion.")[18]

What we find in this culminating plate of *Jerusalem,* then, is symbolism that is equivocal, and almost certainly meant to be. From one point of view Los has recreated and detoxified the old images. In Mitchell's interpretation, "The serpent temple is Golgonooza, the city of art-in-progress, the 'new Golgotha' which is both the new place of sacrifice (self-annihilation) that replaces the old doctrine of atone-

A Scenographic view of the Druid temple of ABVRY in north Wiltshire, as in its original.

TAB.VIII.
P.14

ABVRY

W.Stukeley Delin.

Præhonorabili Dño Dño. Philippo Dño. Hardwick, summo magnæ Brittanniæ Cancellario tabulam, L.M.D. W.Stukeley.

38. Avebury, as reconstructed by William Stukeley

ment, and the new 'place of the skull,' the new consciousness of eternity in time rather than beyond it."[19] But from another point of view, the temple's symmetry is more suggestive of Urizen than of Los, whose expression in this picture seems gloomy rather than triumphant. The symbols are perplexingly mixed, too. The tongs and hammer were for shaping metal in a forge, but the serpent temple must have been hewn out of massive stones. When and how did Los do that—or did he do it? Perhaps the temple doesn't represent Golgonooza at all, but instead invokes the natural world that resists transformation right up to the very end.

Is the message that the poem *Jerusalem* has likewise done all it can, and that what happens next is up to us? "It is the poem itself," Peter Otto says, "the very vehicle which has taken us to this point, which now must be cast off."[20] *Jerusalem* would turn out to be the last prophetic book Blake ever wrote.

12. "THE TORMENTS OF LOVE AND JEALOUSY"

William and Catherine

CATHERINE BLAKE was an active partner in producing the illuminated books, assisting with the printing process and sometimes applying watercolors to the final product. In *The Four Zoas,* Enitharmon, Los's emanation, enacts a similar role: "First he drew a line upon the walls of shining heaven / And Enitharmon tinctured it with beams of blushing love." Catherine's loyalty to William was unquestioned. When Hayley got to know the couple at Felpham he described her in his verbose style as "perhaps the very best wife that ever mortal possessed, at least one that most admirably illustrates that expressive appellation 'a helpmate.'" Hayley added, "They have been married more than seventeen years and are as fond of each other as if their honeymoon were still shining. . . . The good woman is so truly the half of her good man that they seem animated by one soul."[1]

Thomas Butts told a story about calling on the Blakes in the 1790s, soon after their move to Lambeth, and finding them naked in their garden reading *Paradise Lost.* "Come in!" Blake cried, "it's only Adam and Eve, you know." Bentley dismisses this anecdote as apocryphal, but Aileen Ward isn't so sure. She points out that a rebuttal by Butts's grandson came long afterward and might reflect Victorian uneasiness about nudity rather than actual knowledge. Certainly Blake celebrated nakedness in his pictures and poems — "Intense! naked! a human fire fierce glowing" — and if Butts reacted in shock, Blake's remark might have been intended to tease him.[2]

Nevertheless, there were serious tensions in the marriage, which surface repeatedly in poems in Blake's notebook and throughout his great myth. Early on, Gilchrist heard, there had been a remarkable confrontation:

> One day a dispute arose between Robert and Mrs. Blake. She, in the heat of discussion, used words to him his brother (though a husband too) thought unwarrantable. A silent witness thus far, he could now bear it no longer, but with characteristic impetuosity when stirred, rose and said to her: "Kneel down and beg Robert's pardon directly, or you never see my face again!" A heavy threat, uttered in tones which, from Blake, unmistakably showed it was meant. She, poor thing! thought it very hard, as she would afterwards tell, to beg her brother in law's pardon when she was not in fault! But being a duteous, devoted wife, though by nature nowise tame or dull of spirit, she did kneel down and meekly murmur, "Robert, I beg your pardon, I am in the wrong." "Young woman, you lie!" abruptly retorted he: "I am in the wrong!"[3]

There is no way to know what the dispute was about, or what words were so offensive.

Some poems in Blake's notebook express an ideal of mutual pleasure:

> What is it men in women do require?
> The lineaments of gratified desire.
> What is it women do in men require?
> The lineaments of gratified desire.

If Alexander Pope had written the first two lines — not that he would have — the final two lines would have undercut them with some witty reversal, showing that women and men want different things. The surprise in Blake's anti-epigram is the frank acknowledgment that they both want the same thing: to see in each other unmistakable signs of gratification. But on the same notebook page there is a cynical alternative:

> In a wife I would desire
> What in whores is always found,
> The lineaments of gratified desire.

Whores appear gratified because they're paid to do so.[4]

Most of the notebook poems on love and sex are about conflictedness, not gratification. The ancients associated myrtle with Venus, but Blake's *To My Myrtle* presents a grim picture:

> To a lovely myrtle bound,
> Blossoms show'ring all around,
> O how sick and weary I
> Underneath my myrtle lie.
> Why should I be bound to thee,
> O my lovely myrtle tree?

And still more succinctly:

> Grown old in love from seven till seven times seven,
> I oft have wished for Hell for ease from Heaven.

As for Catherine, someone who knew the couple in old age remembered her saying, "I have very little of Mr. Blake's company, he is always in Paradise."[5] That is usually taken as evidence of profound admiration, and Bentley inscribed it just below the title of his biography, *The Stranger from Paradise.* But surely it is ironic!

Free Love or Frustration and Defilement?

Most of the poets known as Romantics were discreet about sex. Wordsworth barely acknowledges it; Coleridge and Keats are eloquent about unhappiness in love but don't refer to sex directly; and Shelley's allusions are idealized and hazy. Byron had a well-deserved reputation as an irresistible seducer, but even so, his poems are relatively inexplicit about sex. Only Blake addresses the subject repeatedly and in depth. Of course the others couldn't have done so even if they had wanted to, aiming as they did at commercial publication and a wide audience.

Thanks to a few declarations in the earliest works, particularly *The Marriage of Heaven and Hell,* Blake is widely thought to celebrate free love enthusiastically and to regard repression as easily overcome. According to the Voice of the Devil, "Those who restrain desire do so because theirs is weak enough to be restrained." Conversely, the way to perceive existence as infinite is "by an improvement of sensual enjoyment." But before long Blake would take a far gloomier view of erotic relations, and in his myth sexuality would become an ominous trap.

Visions of the Daughters of Albion, one of the early Lambeth Books, has a more connected narrative than most of Blake's poems. In it a young woman named Oothoon awakens to her sexuality but is almost immediately raped by a brutal male. Regarding her as defiled, her intended partner then repudiates her angrily. She proclaims an ideal of free love and tries to win him back, but without success.

By the end of this remarkable work, the obstacles to gratification seem both inevitable and insoluble. *Visions of the Daughters of Albion* has affinities with the pioneering feminist analysis of Mary Wollstonecraft in *A Vindication of the Rights of Woman,* published just one year before Blake's poem. Since she and Blake were both connected with the same liberal publisher (he as an illustrator), it is quite possible that they knew each other. In a repeated refrain in *Visions* that is also the final line of the poem, the Daughters of Albion, speaking for all English women, share in Oothoon's frustration and pain: "The Daughters of Albion hear her woes, and echo back her sighs."[6]

The third plate of the poem, entitled "The Argument," is exceptionally beautiful (color plate 27) and has evident affinities with a little notebook lyric entitled *Eternity:*

> He who binds to himself a joy
> Does the wingèd life destroy
> But he who kisses the joy as it flies
> Lives in Eternity's sun rise.[7]

A magnificent sunrise is indeed blazing behind Oothoon in the picture, and she does kiss the joy as it flies.

The verses that appear on this plate, however, as contrasted with the notebook poem, seem disconcertingly out of harmony with the picture:

> I loved Theotormon
> And I was not ashamed;
> I trembled in my virgin fears
> And I hid in Leutha's vale!
>
> I plucked Leutha's flower
> And I rose up from the vale;
> But the terrible thunders tore
> My virgin mantle in twain.

Theotormon, not previously named, is the wooer who rejects Oothoon. The vale, commentators agree, is the female genitals.[8] But why does a deflowering or rape follow immediately after Oothoon plucks the flower? Even if sexuality is experienced initially as innocent pleasure, that is only for the briefest time.

The lines that begin the next plate help to elucidate what is going on, but also complicate it further.

> Enslaved, the Daughters of Albion weep: a trembling lamentation
> Upon their mountains; in their valleys, sighs toward America.
> For the soft soul of America, Oothoon wandered in woe
> Along the vales of Leutha seeking flowers to comfort her;
> And thus she spoke to the bright Marygold of Leutha's vale:
> "Art thou a flower! art thou a nymph! I see thee now a flower,
> Now a nymph! I dare not pluck thee from thy dewy bed!"
> The golden nymph replied, "Pluck thou my flower, Oothoon the mild,
> Another flower shall spring, because the soul of sweet delight
> Can never pass away." She ceased and closed her golden shrine.
> Then Oothoon plucked the flower saying, "I pluck thee from thy bed,
> Sweet flower, and put thee here to glow between my breasts,
> And thus I turn my face to where my whole soul seeks."

The picture in "The Argument" shows Oothoon placing the flower-nymph between her breasts, kissing it instead of seeking to bind it down. The Marygold—probably spelled that way to suggest a woman's name—is described as glowing, because according to Erasmus Darwin, marigolds actually emit flashes of light.[9]

Now the rape is more clearly recounted. The rapist is Bromion, from a Greek word meaning "roarer" or "thunderer," and he describes himself as a slave owner. Immediately after "rending" Oothoon, he addresses her lover Theotormon, whom he advises insultingly to marry her before she bears Bromion's child:

> Bromion rent her with his thunders. On his stormy bed
> Lay the faint maid, and soon her woes appalled his thunders hoarse.
> Bromion spoke: "Behold this harlot here on Bromion's bed,
> And let the jealous dolphins sport around the lovely maid;
> Thy soft American plains are mine, and mine thy north and south.
> Stamped with my signet are the swarthy children of the sun.
> They are obedient, they resist not, they obey the scourge;
> Their daughters worship terrors and obey the violent.
> Now thou mayest marry Bromion's harlot, and protect the child
> Of Bromion's rage, that Oothoon shall put forth in nine moons' time."

The action is set in America because Blake is suggesting an analogy between the African slaves there and women in England, whom Wollstonecraft explicitly compared to slaves. She added, however, "When I call women slaves, I mean in a political and civil sense." Blake would agree with that, but in *Visions of the Daughters of Albion* he is also critiquing psychic and sexual repression.[10]

Oothoon's name was adapted from Oithóna, the heroine of one of James Macpherson's Ossianic prose poems, who likewise suffers rape, is avenged by her lover, and then commits suicide anyway because she is convinced that she has been irrevocably defiled. Unlike Oithóna, Oothoon denies that she is defiled, much less that she is a harlot as Bromion contemptuously calls her, but Theotormon rejects her all the same. His name suggests "God-tormented."

Appealing directly to Theotormon's repressive God, Oothoon cries out to Urizen (who is mentioned here for the first time in Blake's poems):

> O Urizen! Creator of men! Mistaken demon of heaven:
> Thy joys are tears! thy labour vain, to form men to thine image.
> How can one joy absorb another? are not different joys
> Holy, eternal, infinite! and each joy is a love!

To Theotormon, Oothoon protests eloquently,

How can I be defiled when I reflect thy image pure?
Sweetest the fruit that the worm feeds on, and the soul preyed on by woe,
The new washed lamb tinged with the village smoke and the bright swan
By the red earth of our immortal river.

Defiantly she proclaims erotic freedom: "I cry, Love! Love! Love! happy happy love! free as the mountain wind!"[11] "Sweetest the fruit that the worm feeds on" sounds like an explicit contradiction of the symbolism in *The Sick Rose*.

But what exactly is meant by "free" love, and why does Oothoon describe Theotormon's image as "pure"? Striving to win him back, she makes a remarkable proposal:

Silken nets and traps of adamant will Oothoon spread,
And catch for thee girls of mild silver or of furious gold;
I'll lie beside thee on a bank and view their wanton play
In lovely copulation bliss on bliss with Theotormon.
Red as the rosy morning, lustful as the first-born beam,
Oothoon shall view his dear delight, nor e'er with jealous cloud
Come in the heaven of generous love; nor selfish blightings bring.

Critics disagree about the implications of this statement. Perhaps Oothoon is simply happy in the expectation that Theotormon is going to be happy, although that would seem reminiscent of the self-abnegating clod in *The Clod and the Pebble*. Or perhaps she expects to derive gratification of her own from voyeuristically observing the "lovely copulation." Even in Beulah, as we learn in *Jerusalem,*

Every female delights to give her maiden to her husband;
The female searches sea and land for gratification to the
Male genius.

Oothoon's proposal to trap golden and silver girls, as Helen Bruder observes, is a harem fantasy. The reason Blake wants women to be liberated is so that they can give pleasure to men.[12]

Another speech of Oothoon's, together with its illustration (color plate 28), seems disturbingly masochistic:

> Oothoon weeps not: she cannot weep! her tears are locked up;
> But she can howl incessant, writhing her soft snowy limbs
> And calling Theotormon's eagles to prey upon her flesh.
> "I call with holy voice! kings of the sounding air,
> Rend away this defiled bosom that I may reflect
> The image of Theotormon on my pure transparent breast."
> The eagles at her call descend and rend their bleeding prey;
> Theotormon severely smiles; her soul reflects the smile,
> As the clear spring mudded with feet of beasts grows pure and smiles.
> The Daughters of Albion hear her woes and echo back her sighs.[13]

Contradicting what she said before, Oothoon now describes her bosom as "defiled" and invites Theotormon's eagles to "rend" it, much as Bromion rent her at the beginning. In the picture, she displays herself provocatively like a seductive Leda.

Blake must have been thinking of a celebrated painting by his close friend Henry Fuseli, *The Nightmare* (color plate 29), which depicts a woman in a very similar pose. Educated as a minister in his native Zurich, where he was known as Johann Heinrich Füssli, Fuseli had been working for years as a painter in England. Blake found in him a kindred spirit, inspired by the German *Sturm und Drang* movement to create imagery of intense emotion. *The Nightmare* was exhibited in 1782 at the annual Royal Academy show, reproduced in a print that sold thousands of copies, and constantly imitated and parodied.[14]

In this nighttime scene a gnomelike incubus crouches heavily on a woman's body, while behind them a pop-eyed horse thrusts its head through heavy curtains. In Samuel Johnson's 1755 *Dictionary* "nightmare" is defined thus: "*Night* and *mara*, a spirit that in the heathen mythology was related to torment or suffocate sleepers. A morbid oppression in the night, resembling the pressure of weight upon the breast." Actually it is only a verbal coincidence that female horses are called mares, but popular lore did associate nightmares with evil horses.

No one was quite sure what Fuseli's picture meant, but its sexual intensity is obvious, and Erasmus Darwin described the sleeper as orgasmic:

> Back o'er her pillow sinks her blushing head,
> Her snow-white limbs hang helpless from the bed,

> While with quick sighs, and suffocative breath,
> Her interrupted heart-pulse swims in death.

In a collection of aphorisms Fuseli specified that an ideal woman should be "poised between pure helpless virginity and sainted ecstasy."[15] Perhaps he was thinking of Bernini's *Saint Teresa in Ecstasy,* which he would have seen when he studied in Rome.

In most copies of *Visions of the Daughters of Albion,* the poem does not begin with "The Argument" at all, or even with the title page that shows Oothoon running freely over the sea, but opens instead with a startling frontispiece (color plate 30) that must bewilder anyone who comes to it before reading the poem. It doesn't illustrate any actual incident, but rather suggests the symbolic meaning of the poem as a whole. The rocky outcrop in midocean recalls the lost Atlantis, whose submergence into watery chaos Blake often invokes as a symptom of the fall. The identity of the three figures becomes clear as one reads on: Bromion the "roarer" is indeed roaring at the left, Theotormon hides his face at the right, and in the middle a disconsolate Oothoon is bound back to back with Bromion, who is himself shackled with a heavy ankle fetter. Her loathsome connection with the rapist remains a permanent burden. In all three, contortion is painfully extreme.

Since these are not novelistic characters but symbolic ones, it makes sense to think of them as conflicting aspects of human consciousness. No external force has bound them together; they are self-shackled and entangled, as in the "mind-forged manacles" in *London.* It is possible to see the whole image as a human head, with the lurid sun as a single staring eye. That is suggested explicitly in the poem:

> Instead of morn arises a bright shadow, like an eye
> In the eastern cloud; instead of night a sickly charnel house.

The overarching cavern would then be the top of the skull, as in another poem from the same period:

> Once open to the heavens and elevated on the human neck,
> Now overgrown with hair and covered with a stony roof.[16]

Bromion might represent the element of the self that desires sex possessively and brutally, while Theotormon would be the fearful, moralizing element that represses it. Oothoon is hopelessly trapped in the sadomasochistic dynamic. She defiantly proclaims free love, but in vain, and the Daughters of Albion echo back her sighs.

The Chain of Jealousy

The subtitle of *The Four Zoas* is *The Torments of Love and Jealousy in the Death and Judgment of Albion the Ancient Man.* Jealousy played a significant role in the Blakes' relationship. It is not known whether Catherine showed interest in other men, but she was definitely aware of her husband's interest in other women. Gilchrist heard from people who knew them that "there had been stormy times in years long past, when both were young; discord by no means trifling while it lasted. But with the cause (jealousy on her side, not wholly unprovoked), the strife had ceased also." Whether there were actual affairs is not known, but what is known is that William suggested that like an Old Testament patriarch he should have more than one wife. Writing in German for discretion, Crabb Robinson reported him saying "that from the Bible he has learned that eine Gemeinschaft der Frauen statt finden sollte" — wives should be in common.[17]

Enitharmon may be expressing Blake's own view when she exclaims,

> The joy of woman is the death of her most best beloved
> Who dies for love of her
> In torments of fierce jealousy and pangs of adoration.[18]

Here jealousy is blamed on the female, but at other times Blake recognizes that it can breed obsessively within the jealous male.

One of Blake's illustrations for *Paradise Lost, Satan Watching Adam and Eve* (color plate 31), addresses the psychology of jealousy with exceptional insight. Puritan though he was in theology, Milton was never morally puritanical, and in *Paradise Lost* he makes it clear that before the Fall sex was both sensual and innocent:

> Iris all hues, roses, and jessamine
> Reared high their flourished heads between, and wrought
> Mosaic; underfoot the violet,
> Crocus, and hyacinth with rich inlay

> Broidered the ground, more coloured then with stone
> Of costliest emblem. . . .
>   Here in close recess
> With flowers, garlands, and sweet-smelling herbs
> Espousèd Eve decked first her nuptial bed,
> And heavenly choirs the hymenean sung.[19]

Blake's picture captures the delicate floral beauty. Milton doesn't mention lilies, but Blake shows them — Adam is even plucking one — since they were associated iconographically with purity. The nuptial bed is a massive couch of pale pink roses, and more roses hang from the palm branches that frame the two figures. Eve plucks a rose, and Adam wears a rose garland.

In *Paradise Lost* Satan gazes "with jealous leer malign," bitterly acknowledging his own isolation:

> Sight hateful, sight tormenting! Thus these two
> Imparadised in one another's arms,
> The happier Eden, shall enjoy their fill
> Of bliss on bliss, while I to hell am thrust
> Where neither joy nor love, but fierce desire,
> Among our other torments not the least,
> Still unfulfilled with pain of longing pines.

In Blake's picture, however, Satan's expression doesn't look malign at all. On the contrary, he seems sad and perplexed. And he is not really looking at the lovers. His gloomy gaze is fixed instead on the golden-scaled serpent that coils around him while he strokes its flame-red head. Rossetti was struck by this image: "Satan holds the serpent — an amazingly subtle, prismatic-hued serpent — which seems in horrid counsel with him, draining his vitals. Satan has a languid, almost 'sentimental' air, yet very terrible."[20] Another way of putting it might be that the scene is narcissistic and autoerotic.

Nor is Satan the only one who gazes at the serpent. So does Eve, for she is looking, not lovingly at Adam as one would expect, but past him. Meanwhile Adam's hand cradles her head in a mirror image of Satan's hand cradling the serpent's head. Adam's face and Satan's likewise mirror each other.[21]

In terms of Blake's system, Milton's Garden of Eden is actually a vision of Beulah, the state of existence below the true Eden. Beulah is the "married land" where contraries are equally true, but from which the sexes may plunge down into Generation. The Satan in Blake's picture is Adam's doppelgänger, embodying an instinctive jealousy that is inherent in love. At this moment in *Paradise Lost* Adam and Eve have no one to be jealous of, since they are the only two human beings in existence. But Satan already embodies what awaits. Both Adam and Eve have vacant expressions, as if in a trance.

Jealousy, in this conception, is all about obsession with self. One of La Rochefoucauld's terse maxims is: "In jealousy there is more self-love than love." As Blake imagines it, jealousy is like a chain that grows from within, as depicted in a remarkable picture in *The Book of Urizen* (color plate 32). Orc in this poem is the son of Los and his emanation Enitharmon; he is still sexual as he was in *America,* but he is no longer liberated. As soon as he is born, his father is overwhelmed by suffocating jealousy:

> No more Los beheld Eternity.
> In his hands he seized the infant;
> He bathed him in springs of sorrow,
> He gave him to Enitharmon.
> They named the child Orc, he grew
> Fed with milk of Enitharmon.
> Los awoke her; O sorrow and pain!
> A tight'ning girdle grew
> Around his bosom. In sobbings
> He burst the girdle in twain,
> But still another girdle
> Oppressed his bosom. In sobbings
> Again he burst it. Again
> Another girdle succeeds.
> The girdle was formed by day:
> By night was burst in twain,
> These falling down on the rock
> Into an iron chain

> In each other link by link locked.
> They took Orc to the top of a mountain.
> O how Enitharmon wept!
> They chained his young limbs to the rock
> With the chain of jealousy
> Beneath Urizen's deathful shadow.[22]

In the picture all three figures are naked. The boy looks up at his mother (is his mouth reaching for her breast?), but she averts her face. Los gazes at them gloomily, yet his shoulder twists away; he is not part of the embrace. From his breast a heavy, bloody chain of jealousy descends to his left foot, which it conceals. His left arm seems to be missing, too, replaced by the idle hammer that hangs down like a prosthetic limb.

The same symbolic event is narrated in *The Four Zoas,* where Los binds Orc when he arrives at puberty and at the same time is cripplingly self-bound.

> But when fourteen summers and winters had revolved over
> Their solemn habitation Los beheld the ruddy boy
> Embracing his bright mother and beheld malignant fires
> In his young eyes, discerning plain that Orc plotted his death.
> Grief rose upon his ruddy brows; a tightening girdle grew
> Around his bosom like a bloody cord. In secret sobs
> He burst it, but next morn another girdle succeeds. . . .
> Enitharmon beheld the bloody chain of nights and days
> Depending from the bosom of Los and how with griding pain
> He went each morning to his labours with the spectre dark,
> Called it the chain of jealousy.

"Griding" is a Miltonic word meaning "piercing": "So sore / The griding sword with discontinuous wound / Passed through him."[23]

Freud's Oedipus complex comes to mind. Unlike Blake, however, Freud locates oedipal jealousy in a small boy who has no possibility of taking his mother away from his father but who punishes himself nevertheless for wanting to violate the incest taboo. In Blake's version jealousy begins in the father, not the son, when he becomes aware that the boy not only has reached puberty but is showing sexual awareness of his mother. And if she doesn't actively encourage it, she permits the suggestive embrace, even as her tormented husband looks helplessly on.

The Forbidden Shrine

Blake often articulated the insight that to prohibit something is to make it more desirable, anticipating Nietzsche's aphorism, "Christianity gave Eros poison to drink; he did not die of it, but degenerated into Vice." Is unrestrained sexuality forbidden because it's bad, or bad only because it's forbidden? In a prologue that appears in two of the surviving copies of *Europe,* a mocking fairy says that "five windows light the caverned man," meaning the five senses. With the sense of touch he may "pass out what time he please," connecting freely with the world and its gratifications—"but he will not; / For stolen joys are sweet, and bread eaten in secret pleasant." The allusion is to the Book of Proverbs: "Stolen joys are sweet, and bread eaten in secret pleasant."[24]

One of the most disturbing poems Blake ever wrote directly follows *The Garden of Love* in his notebook, and may well have been originally conceived as a Song of Experience.

> I saw a chapel all of gold
> That none did dare to enter in,
> And many weeping stood without
> Weeping mourning worshipping.
>
> I saw a serpent rise between
> The white pillars of the door,
> And he forced and forced and forced,
> Down the golden hinges tore,
>
> And along the pavement sweet
> Set with pearls and rubies bright
> All his slimy length he drew
> Till upon the altar white

> Vomiting his poison out
> On the bread and on the wine.
> So I turned into a sty
> And laid me down among the swine.

The chapel doors suggest a symbol that occurs frequently in the prophecies: the vagina as the holy of holies in the temple of Jerusalem, which it was forbidden to view. In Blake's interpretation, what is hidden is not holiness but "secret lust, when hid in chambers dark the nightly harlot / Plays in disguise in whispered hymn and mumbling prayer."[25] Back in the early days of *The Marriage of Heaven and Hell,* his message might have been that abolishing secrecy could liberate sex for frank and open enjoyment. In the later poems, however, that no longer seems so easy. On the contrary, it is precisely hiddenness and mystery that make sex alluring—but also entrapping and obsessional.

The *Four Zoas* manuscript contains a number of erotic drawings; others were erased after Blake's death, presumably by someone who found them too shocking (a few of the erased drawings can be dimly made out with the aid of infrared photography). One remarkable pencil sketch (figure 39) could stand as an illustration for *I saw a chapel all of gold.* In it the goddess of nature, regularly identified as such in Blake's pictures by her spiky crown, does indeed have a Gothic chapel between her legs. Blake probably knew about an especially transgressive form of Gnosticism, the Ophitic ("serpent-worshipping") cult, which expressly invoked a symbolism of phallic assault. As a scandalized Saint Epiphanius described their ritual, loaves of bread were placed on an altar, a serpent was put on them, and each of the faithful ate of the loaves after kissing the serpent on the mouth. To the Ophites the serpent symbolized the forbidden knowledge of the Garden of Eden, and more specifically sexual initiation.[26] To Blake it connotes degradation. Ejaculation is horribly evoked as the slimy serpent brutally forces the doors, finally "vomiting his poison out / On the bread and on the wine"—the stress on "vomiting" is especially shocking. The bread and wine of shared communion have been defiled by brutal lust, and that lust, in turn, was provoked by the alluring but hidden shrine. So the self-loathing speaker lies down in a pigsty, like the Prodigal Son in Christ's parable.

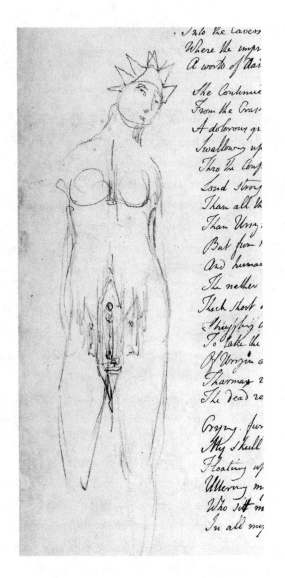

39. *Vala* manuscript, page 86

That sexual desire entices us to gaze at specific body parts must seem to most people a simple fact, and indeed an agreeable one. Blake, however, seems to have found it disturbing. Even in peaceful Beulah, we find the ominous shrine, "beautiful" but therefore entrapping.

> Humanity knows not of sex: wherefore are sexes in Beulah?
> In Beulah the female lets down her beautiful tabernacle,
> Which the male enters magnificent between her cherubim,
> And becomes one with her, mingling condensing in self-love
> The rocky law of condemnation and double generation and death.[27]

By contrast with male and female sex, Blake imagines his Eternals as enjoying a mysterious union like that of Milton's angels, total rather than genital.

> Embraces are cominglings: from the head even to the feet,
> And not a pompous high priest entering by a secret place.

No one has ever been able to explain what Blake's ideal "cominglings" are supposed to be like.[28] At any rate, this is clearly not the body we are currently equipped with.

Blake is not really a prophet of unconflicted sexuality, and his vision is closer to the tragic one that Freud expresses: "Something in the nature of the sexual instinct itself is unfavourable to the achievement of absolute gratification."[29]

13. THE FEMALE WILL

"Mother of My Mortal Part"

ALTHOUGH Blake criticized patriarchy, in important ways he was by no means opposed to it. As a man, he hated authoritarian control and was suspicious of fathers even when they were well-intentioned. But he took for granted male superiority over female. In *Milton,* to be sure, Milton's spirit is reconciled with the sixfold emanation—his three wives and three daughters—over whom he supposedly tyrannized in life. But that reunion is asserted theoretically, not demonstrated.

As Blake's obsessive image of the secret shrine suggests, he tended to think of female sexuality as an insidious threat. That erotic relations involve power is a familiar fact. As the old metaphor of being in someone's "thrall" suggests, it can feel like a kind of slavery. Blake definitely saw it that way. And his indictment of the female, in his later poems, enlarges in scope until it is blamed for almost everything—even war. The most fundamental charge is that it is the female who binds us down to mortal existence, for it is women who give birth.

Conventional religion taught that the only good thing about sex is that it leads to reproduction. According to Blake that was exactly what is bad. It was common to imagine nature as maternal: "O Nature, O my mother," Rousseau exclaims, "I am under your protection alone." Even the skeptic Hume refers to "nature herself."[1]

Blake was sympathetic to actual mothers, as the *Songs of Innocence* makes clear, but he had no use whatever for the sentimental ideal of Mother Nature.

As in the picture *A Sunshine Holiday,* the state that Blake calls Generation—the human life cycle from birth to death—is highly equivocal in significance. Our goal, he repeatedly asserts, should be an interior apocalypse that breaks through to Eternity, and we should aspire to the genderless "cominglings" of the Eternals—whatever those may be. His suspicion of Generation is already evident in a miniature book of emblems entitled *For Children: The Gates of Paradise.* The date of that work is 1793, the same year as *Visions of the Daughters of Albion* and *Songs of Experience.* In traditional emblems, brief texts accompanied allegorical pictures to convey conventional didactic lessons. Blake means to instruct in a very different way, encouraging suspicion of life experience as it is normally understood.[2]

The first tiny image in *For Children* is captioned "What is Man!" It shows a caterpillar feeding on a leaf, with a baby-faced larva or chrysalis on another leaf below (figure 40). Here begins the cycle from birth to death; we have seen that Blake sometimes calls man "a worm of sixty winters."[3] It is true that a butterfly, traditionally symbolic of immortality, will one day emerge from its chrysalis and soar into the air. But meanwhile, childbirth has brought yet another vulnerable mortal into the world.

The second emblem (figure 41) illustrates ironically where babies come from, in the sort of preposterous fiction that children used to be told. A mother is pulling an infant out of the earth, with an already-harvested babe cradled in her dress. When Blake retouched these emblems years later, with the new title *For the Sexes: The Gates of Paradise,* he added some explanatory verses entitled "The Keys of the Gates." On this picture he comments:

> My eternal man set in repose,
> The female from his darkness rose,
> And she found me beneath a tree
> A mandrake and in her veil hid me.[4]

It is in Albion's slumbrous "repose" that the sexes separate from each other—"the female from his darkness rose." As for the mandrake, since its bifurcated root re-

40. *For Children: The Gates of Paradise,* copy D, plate 1

sembles human legs, it was regularly associated with procreation, as in the story of Jacob and Leah in Genesis, or Donne's line, "Get with child a mandrake root."[5]

What did Blake think children could possibly grasp in this strange little book? Perhaps it wasn't really meant for children at all, but intended rather to challenge the conventional attitudes of adults by subverting the complacent message of ordinary emblems. The revised title, *For the Sexes,* makes the message clearer: to accept the cycle from birth to death as inevitable means enslavement to the natural world.

The final emblem is captioned, "I have said to the worm: Thou art my mother and my sister" (figure 42). Mortal bodies subside into the ground from which an earthworm emerges, wrapping itself around a seated figure who is cowled like a traditional image of death. According to "The Keys of the Gates," she represents the female in all of her manifestations:

41. *For Children: The Gates of Paradise,* copy D, plate 3

42. *For Children: The Gates of Paradise,* copy D, plate 18

The door of death I open found
And the worm weaving in the ground.
Thou'rt my mother from the womb,
Wife, sister, daughter to the tomb,
Leaving to dreams the sexual strife
And weeping over the web of life.[6]

In Blake's late prophecies the maternal creator of the mortal body is given the name Tirzah, the capital in the Old Testament of the ten lost tribes, and therefore opposed to Jerusalem. At some stage he added a final poem to *Songs of Experience* entitled *To Tirzah:*

Whate'er is born of mortal birth
Must be consumèd with the earth
To rise from Generation free;
Then what have I to do with thee?

The sexes sprung from shame and pride,
Blowed in the morn, in evening died.
But mercy changed death into sleep;
The sexes rose to work and weep.

Thou mother of my mortal part
With cruelty didst mould my heart,
And with false self-deceiving tears
Didst bind my nostrils eyes and ears;

Didst close my tongue in senseless clay
And me to mortal life betray.
The death of Jesus set me free;
Then what have I to do with thee?

"Blowed" means "bloomed," as in Wordsworth's "the meanest flower that blows." The fourth line of *To Tirzah* repeats what Jesus says to his mother just before he turns water into wine: "Woman, what have I to do with thee?"[7] As Blake adapts the question, it is addressed not to Mary but to Tirzah, "mother of my mortal part."

"The sexes sprung from shame and pride" refers to the orthodox story of the Fall. In Genesis, Adam and Eve experience shame at their nakedness after committing the original sin, and they are condemned by God to work with the sweat of their brows. But in Blake's Eden there are no distinct sexes, and the existence of sex in the world of Generation is a consequence of the primal disintegration rather than of sin. As for work, it is valuable in itself, not a punishment that should have been avoided.

"The death of Jesus," as Blake understands it, is entirely different from the orthodox doctrine of atonement, in which the Son of God sacrificed himself as our surrogate in order to appease an angry Father. In Blake's myth, Jesus' death symbolizes the self-sacrifice in which everyone should participate.

> Jesus said, "Wouldest thou love one who never died
> For thee, or ever die for one who had not died for thee?
> And if God dieth not for man and giveth not himself
> Eternally for man, man could not exist, for man is love
> As God is love. Every kindness to another is a little death
> In the divine image, nor can man exist but by brotherhood."[8]

Brotherhood, not motherhood. Blake's attack on Tirzah as mortal mother is nothing less than an attack on nature itself—or rather, nature herself, since in his opinion nature in its fallen form is the responsibility of the female. First she entices the male into reproduction by luring him into her secret tabernacle, and then she perpetuates the cycle of fallen existence by giving birth. In *Jerusalem* Los exclaims,

> I hear the screech of childbirth loud pealing, and the groans
> Of death in Albion's clouds dreadful uttered over all the earth.
> What may man be? who can tell! but what may woman be?
> To have power over man from cradle to corruptible grave.

Helen Bruder, pondering Blake's views on gender, concludes that he was "by turns a searching critic of patriarchy but *also* a hectoring misogynist." She lists a whole anthology of archetypes that turn up repeatedly in his poems: virgin, maid, mother, harlot, nymph, queen.[9]

Alicia Ostriker distinguishes still further between four different Blakes. One is the prophet of free love and unchained desire, but only in the earliest works. The second sees the female as an "emanation" that should never have acquired separate existence at all. The third believes that female sexuality is a seductive trap, and the fourth holds that actual women—Catherine Blake not least—should be subordinate to men and devote their being to them. In some early notes Blake wrote, "Let the men do their duty and the women will be such wonders; the female life lives from the light of the male. See a man's female dependents, you know the man." It was in this sense that he called Catherine his "shadow of delight."[10] She was never a mother, and Blake may have thought that that was just as well.

Emanations and the Female Will

Although the emanations play a crucial role in Blake's later poems, he never makes clear why they must always be female. Commentators used to argue that they are female only in a metaphorical sense, representing the agency through which each Zoa interacts with the world. Frye, fond of the word "total," defines the emanation as "the total form of all the things a man loves and creates." But why "a man"? Tristanne Connolly crisply observes, "From a female point of view, the female is not other."[11]

An analogy with Jung's concept of the anima is sometimes proposed, but it fails at just this point, since Blake does not represent women as having a complementary animus. And whereas Jung is concerned to give both anima and animus full value, Blake is preoccupied with an alleged domination of the female principle over the male. His concept of the emanation makes man the creator of woman, just as in Genesis Eve is constructed from Adam's rib. His bitter complaint that women have power over men from cradle to grave is an irrational contradiction of the facts of life, a refusal to accept the natural power of the female.

Perhaps the most favorable image of an emanation in Blake's poems is the descent in *Milton* of Ololon, Milton's emanation. Blake would have known Johnson's trenchant verdict: "It has been observed that they who most loudly clamour for liberty do not most liberally grant it. What we know of Milton's character in domestic relations is that he was severe and arbitrary. His family consisted of women; and there appears in his books something like a Turkish contempt of females, as subordinate and inferior beings. That his own daughters might not break the ranks, he suffered them to be depressed by a mean and penurious education. He thought woman made only for obedience, and man only for rebellion."[12]

As Blake imagines it, Ololon descends from the sky to his Felpham cottage, and by implication she will unite there with Catherine as Milton does with Blake. Her name may have been suggested by a Greek word meaning a cry of joy. This moment is illustrated in a charming picture (color plate 33) in which Blake looks up from the cottage garden while a winged Ololon glides down as if on a tightrope. Since he believed that eternity is fully present in each moment of time, the events in the poem are understood to be simultaneous rather than successive. Susan Fox explains, "Milton's descent came before Ololon's, but hers is completed first. Milton descended to find her, and she is waiting for him when he arrives—although it was his descent that precipitated hers." Thus the crucial event "takes place in a single instant which takes Blake fifty pages to describe."[13]

Throughout Blake's myth, however, what we usually see is not reconciliation but rupture and strife between Zoas and emanations. After he developed the symbol of the spectre in *The Four Zoas,* he imagined each emanation splitting apart from her Zoa in the same catastrophe that detaches the spectre from the integrated self. A harrowing notebook poem describes the plight of the now-divided consciousness. It is not always clear who is speaking, but the general meaning is clear.

> My spectre around me night and day
> Like a wild beast guards my way;
> My emanation far within
> Weeps incessantly for my sin.
>
> A fathomless and boundless deep,
> There we wander there we weep;
> On the hungry craving wind
> My spectre follows thee behind.
>
> He scents thy footsteps in the snow
> Wheresoever thou dost go

> Through the wintry hail and rain;
> When wilt thou return again?

Having separated away, the shadow-spectre pursues the speaker like Frankenstein's monster, while the emanation remains "within," weeping with guilt at sexual desire that is now perceived as sinful. Once again, female jealousy is blamed for ruining happiness:

> Dost thou not in pride and scorn
> Fill with tempests all my morn
> And with jealousies and fears
> Fill my pleasant nights with tears?
>
> Seven of my sweet loves thy knife
> Has bereavèd of their life.
> Their marble tombs I built with tears
> And with cold and shuddering fears.

Whether the "sweet loves" are actual affairs or just a yearning for them, the emanation has murdered them all. And the only solution seems to be to give up sexuality altogether:

> Till I turn from female love
> And root up the infernal grove
> I shall never worthy be
> To step into Eternity. . . .
>
> Let us agree to give up love
> And root up the infernal grove.
> Then shall we return and see
> The worlds of happy Eternity.
>
> And throughout all Eternity
> I forgive you you forgive me,
> As our dear Redeemer said,
> This the wine and this the bread.

Here are the bread and wine of communion again, which were so horribly defiled by the serpent in *I saw a chapel all of gold.* As for sex in the usual sense, it is an "infernal grove" that must be uprooted and left behind.[14]

The original working title of *The Four Zoas,* as has been mentioned, was *Vala,* the emanation of the emotional and sexual Luvah. Vala is a nature goddess like Tirzah; her name should probably be pronounced like "veil," a term that is regularly associated with her. At various times her veil represents the repressive moral law, the veil of the temple in Jerusalem, the mortal body, and even the ordinary empirical world that we mistake for the real one. If we can break through that veil we will continue to see the same world, but transformed, more immediate, more alive.

Collectively, Vala and Tirzah represent a force that Blake insists on calling the Female Will, and he gives them an ally in still another version of Mother Nature, Rahab, who is associated with the five senses. (In the Book of Joshua, Rahab is a harlot who conceals Joshua's spies from their enemies; Blake must have chosen the name for its associations with harlotry, not for that helpful service to the Israelites.)

Throughout the permutations of Blake's myth, the emanations tend to divide into two distinct camps. Enion and Ahania, counterparts of Tharmas and Urizen, are passive and sad, but essentially positive. It is Enion to whom Blake gives the heartbreaking song of experience previously quoted — "What is the price of experience? do men buy it for a song, / Or wisdom for a dance in the street?"[15] — but most of the time she and Ahania are dim and shadowy. Far otherwise are Urthona's Enitharmon and Luvah's Vala, the female aspects of imagination and sexuality.

Enitharmon, like Keats's Belle Dame sans Merci, entices but withholds and torments, and Vala presides over the tyrannous cycle of nature:

> She cries: "The human is but a worm, and thou O male: thou art
> Thyself female, a male; a breeder of seed: a son and husband; and lo,
> The human divine is woman's shadow, a vapor in the summer's heat.
> Go assume papal dignity, thou spectre, thou male harlot! Arthur
> Divide into the kings of Europe in times remote, O woman-born
> And woman-nourished and woman-educated and woman-scorned!"

By participating in procreation, the male becomes female in a peculiar negative sense, and yet resents being woman-educated and woman-scorned. Arthur is apparently mentioned as an example of a king brought down by a woman.[16]

One would think it unarguable that it is men, not women, who are responsible for war, but according to Enitharmon women are actually to blame. In this context, we encounter the secret tabernacle yet again, along with imagery of bloody sacrifices by Mayan priestesses:

> And thus the warriors cry, in the hot day of victory, in songs:
> "Look, the beautiful daughter of Albion sits naked upon the stone,
> Her panting victim beside her, her heart is drunk with blood
> Though her brain is not drunk with wine: she goes forth from Albion
> In pride of beauty: in cruelty of holiness, in the brightness
> Of her tabernacle and her ark and secret place. . . .
> I must rush again to war, for the virgin has frowned and refused.
> Sometimes I curse and sometimes bless thy fascinating beauty.
> Once man was occupied in intellectual pleasures and energies,
> But now my soul is harrowed with grief and fear and love and desire
> And now I hate and now I love and intellect is no more:
> There is no time for any thing but the torments of love and desire."

David Fuller comments, "Vala's prohibitions act like a funnel down which the mind is dragged. The free play of intellect narrows into an obsession with the love that is denied it; love denied narrows to sexual desire; frustrated desire creates an inward chaos, a feeling which is focused and channeled outward into violence."[17] Surely the obsession here is not just the warrior's but Blake's.

One of the bizarre sketches in the *Four Zoas* manuscript traces Vala's progress from worm to serpent to dragon (figure 43). In the lines of verse that accompany it, Luvah, the Zoa who corresponds to Vala, is speaking:

> "If I indeed am Vala's king, and ye O sons of men
> The workmanship of Luvah's hands; in times of everlasting,
> When I called forth the earthworm from the cold and dark obscure,
> I nurtured her, I fed her with my rains and dews, she grew
> A scaled serpent, yet I fed her though she hated me.

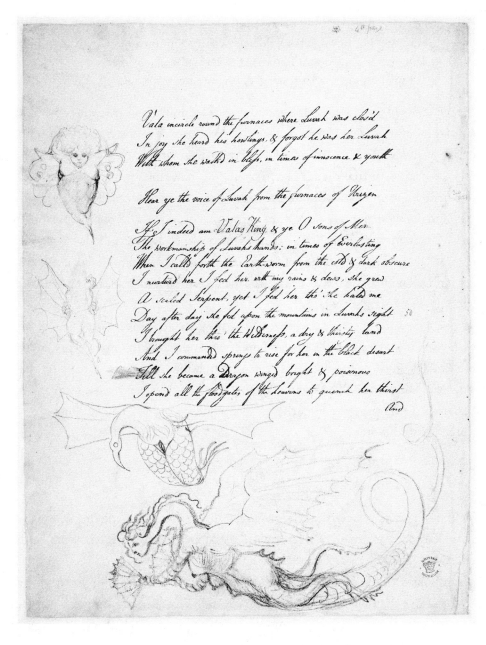

Vala incircle round the furnaces where Luvah was clos'd
In joy she heard his howlings, & forgot he was her Luvah
With whom she walkd in bliss, in times of innocence & youth

Hear ye the voice of Luvah from the furnaces of Urizen

If I indeed am Valas King & ye O sons of Men
The workmanship of Luvahs hands: in times of Everlasting
When I calld forth the Earth-worm from the cold & dark obscure
I nurturd her I fed her with my rains & dews, she grew
A scaled Serpent, yet I fed her tho' she hated me
Day after day she fed upon the mountains in Luvahs sight
I brought her thro' the Wilderness, a dry & thirsty land
And I commanded springs to rise for her in the black desart
Till she became a Dragon winged bright & poisonous
I opend all the floodgates of the heavens to quench her thirst

And

43. *Vala* manuscript, page 26

Day after day she fed upon the mountains in Luvah's sight;
I brought her through the wilderness, a dry and thirsty land,
And I commanded springs to rise for her in the black desert
Till she became a dragon winged, bright and poisonous."

This picture is like a Rorschach test, and each interpreter will have his or her own way of thinking about it. The psychoanalytic critic Brenda Webster offers a comprehensive analysis: "The first sketch of a flying woman with butterfly wings . . . suggests a voracious sexual organ: her frizzy hairdo resembles pubic hair, and Blake gives her a huge (erased) vulva. In the next figure the wings have become those of a bat, and the woman rides a penis and scrotum (complete with pubic hair). Below her is a woman with a phallically dangerous beak, scaly tail, and clearly defined vulva. . . . The final illustration is of a huge dragon with a woman's head, a serpent's neck, and bat wings. She has three breasts, the last ambiguously placed on her lower abdomen, and a long scaly tail."[18]

However one interprets these images, they are self-evidently obsessive, and no one is obliged to accept Blake's system at face value. Yet the myth also contains profound insights into the divided self, a condition that many people experience to some extent and that Blake experienced to a terrifying degree. Even if his fears and obsessions did damage the integrity of his imaginative work, he could never have created it without them.

Beatrice and Jerusalem

Although Blake reluctantly acknowledged that his prophetic poems were never likely to reach readers who could understand them, in his last years he did undertake an ambitious project for which recognition seemed possible and in which his symbolism of the female surfaced again. This was a series of illustrations for Dante's *Divine Comedy*. There are just over a hundred of them, many mere sketches but some gorgeously finished. Seven were also engraved, and he hoped to engrave them all.

Blake got so interested in the project that he began to learn Italian. He had some sympathy with Roman Catholicism, unlike most radical Protestants who saw modern Rome, like the ancient one, as the Whore of Babylon. According to Gilchrist he would assert, "rather in an opposing mode, that the Romish Church was the only one which taught the forgiveness of sins." It is true that the Calvinist tradition emphasized guilt and damnation, whereas the Catholic confessional made forgiveness seem not only possible but normal. Gilchrist understood that for Blake "forgiveness of sins was the cornerstone of Christianity." And although he hated the Catholic Church for its repressive theology and its institutional power, he admired Catholic spirituality. "He was fond of the works of St. Theresa," Samuel Palmer said, "and often quoted them with other writers on the interior life."[19]

One of the most spectacular of the Dante illustrations is *Beatrice Addressing Dante from the Car* (color plate 34). Bizarre though the imagery may appear, it comes directly from the *Purgatorio.* The episode needs to be read in full, since it shows how closely Blake followed the text even while systematically challenging it. In particular he detested Catholic veneration of the Virgin Mary. That attitude, of course, was common among many Protestants, but Blake had two reasons of his own for adopting it. One was his rejection of the idea that sex is impure and that Jesus must therefore not have been conceived in the usual way. But the other reason was his distrust of maternity itself. He thought that venerating the Virgin Mary was worshipping nature, and he associated her with his nature goddesses Tirzah and Vala. In a commentary on the Dante illustrations he declared, "Everything in Dante's *Commedia* shows that for tyrannical purposes he has made this world the foundation of all, and the goddess Nature and not the Holy Ghost."[20]

In the *Purgatorio,* four and twenty elders (representing the twenty-four books of the Old Testament) sing the praises of Beatrice, Dante's guide. And then:

> As in the sky star follows after star,
> so after these, four living Creatures came,
> each with a wreath of verdant foliage crowned.
>
> And each of them was feathered with six wings,
> their feathers full of eyes; and these were such,
> as, were they living, Argus' eyes would be. . . .

> But read thou in Ezekiel, who depicts them,
> as from the sky's cold parts he saw them move,
> accompanied by wind and clouds and fire. . . .
>
> The space extending 'tween the four contained
> a triumph-chariot moving on two wheels,
> which came along drawn by a griffin's neck.
>
> Both of his wings the latter stretched on high
> between the mid banner and the three and three,
> so that, by cleaving it, he injured none;
>
> So high they rose that they were lost to sight.
> His members were of gold as far as bird
> he was, and white the others mixed with red. . . .
>
> At its right wheel three ladies in a ring
> came dancing on; the first so red, that hardly
> would she be noticed, if in fire she were;
>
> And such the second was, as if her flesh
> and very bones were made of emerald;
> the third one looked like newly fallen snow.[21]

This is the vision of Ezekiel that meant so much to Blake—but with female figures added.

The griffin traditionally represented Christ, since a lion with the head of an eagle could suggest the union of human and divine. The chariot is the Church Triumphant, and the three ladies are the theological virtues of Faith (white), pointing to the Bible; Hope (green), described elsewhere by Dante as dancing; and Charity (red). Charity was often depicted with infants, and in Blake's picture her body is lined with them. As for Beatrice herself:

> Within and out the car, a lady, crowned
>
> with a wreath of olives o'er a pure white veil,

> appeared before me, 'neath a cloak of green,
> clothed with the color of a living flame.

At far right in Blake's picture is the pilgrim Dante, gazing up meekly at Beatrice.

Closely though he has conformed to the text, Blake makes two notable changes. One is to give Beatrice a golden crown instead of an olive wreath, and the other is to represent the chariot wheel as a dynamic swirl. Crowns almost always have negative implications in his pictures, and Beatrice appears here as Queen of Heaven, clad in a diaphanous robe that resembles the veil of Vala. Just as Blake denied the existence of a Urizenic patriarch, he had no use whatever for a heavenly matriarch.

As for the swirling wheel, which is not in Dante, we have seen it before in Blake's painting *Ezekiel's Vision*. It also suggests another Blakean symbol, the vortex, which is too arcane to describe here, and the Seven Eyes of God, a progressive intuition of the divine that will be discussed later.[22]

As Blake continued to labor at his myth, his distrust—or dread—of the female threatened to overwhelm everything else. Probably it was awareness of this tendency that impelled him to imagine a positive female counterweight to Vala, Tirzah, and Rahab. That counterweight is Jerusalem, and her name furnishes the title of the last and longest prophetic book: *Jerusalem the Emanation of the Giant Albion*. She is also, in some never-explained way, the bride of Jesus.

> Thus shall the male and female live the life of Eternity
> Because the Lamb of God creates himself a bride and wife
> That we his children evermore may live in Jerusalem
> Which now descendeth out of heaven, a city yet a woman,
> Mother of myriads redeemed and born in her spiritual palaces,
> By a new spiritual birth regenerated from death.

In the final lines of *Jerusalem* she becomes a universal emanation, in whom even inanimate substances are humanized:

> All human forms identified, even tree metal earth and stone, all
> Human forms identified, living, going forth and returning wearied
> Into the planetary lives of years months days and hours; reposing

And then awaking into his bosom in the life of immortality.
And I heard the name of their emanations: they are named Jerusalem.[23]

"I heard" sets the vision in the past, but the verbs express ongoing activity—living, going forth, returning, reposing, awakening.

Two pictures in *Jerusalem* illustrate this rehabilitation of the female. One is the title page (color plate 35), remarkable for its brilliant coloring. Hoping to sell this copy of the poem at a high price, Blake made it as opulent as he could, and some of the lettering was done with actual gold leaf. Jerusalem appears at the bottom as one of several figures whom Essick aptly describes as hovering "between the human and the lepidopterous."[24]

Jerusalem is asleep here, just as Albion will sleep through much of the poem. She has three sets of wings. Those at the left contain a sun and earth, and the middle ones contain a waxing and waning moon, suggestive of the cycle of mortality. The lowest pair of wings seems to represent a union of sky and earth: between branching rootlike structures, stars shine through. Folded, these lowest wings are reminiscent of the infant cocoon in *For Children*. All of these associations evoke the maternal role of the female; as for the sexual, Jerusalem's limply hanging head and arm recall Fuseli's *Nightmare*. The other female figures, probably Jerusalem's daughters, are evidently mourning her deathlike sleep. No one has satisfactorily explained the weird creature hovering at the top; Erdman calls it a fairy but doesn't say why.[25]

Unexpectedly, eighty-six plates further along in this enormous poem, the images on the title page are explicitly described:

I see thy form O lovely mild Jerusalem, winged with six wings
In the opacous bosom of the sleeper, lovely threefold
In head and heart and reins, three universes of love and beauty.
Thy forehead bright; holiness to the Lord with gates of pearl
Reflects Eternity; beneath thy azure wings of feathery down
Ribbed delicate and clothed with feathered gold and azure and purple
From thy white shoulders shadowing, purity in holiness!
Thence feathered with soft crimson of the ruby bright as fire
Spreading into the azure wings which like a canopy
Bends over thy immortal head in which Eternity dwells.[26]

So the butterfly of immortality will ultimately prevail. On the title page, however, Jerusalem is sound asleep in the death-in-life of Generation. It will be the labor of this long poem to wake her and Albion up.

In a plate near the middle of the poem (figure 44) Jerusalem stands at the center, resisting the attempt of Vala to lure her into the church of Babylon, which has a dome and cross like Saint Paul's Cathedral. Blake preferred Gothic form to classical, and the church at right resembles Westminster Abbey. Jerusalem seems to be locking eyes with Vala; Erdman describes her as "almost mesmerized." Alarmed, her three daughters urge her to break away, and the one who is already soaring into the air points upward. Blake's androgynous ideal is apparent too. When his women are naked they are almost as muscular as the men; as Connolly says, "they come from the body-building school."[27] He had seen more than enough limp, debile women in the art of his day.

Nobody seems to have noticed a visual allusion that is surely relevant here. Jerusalem's posture and her flowing hair resemble those of Venus rising from the sea in Botticelli's *Birth of Venus*. And the waves at the bottom of the picture, which Erdman identifies as the Thames, look more like ocean surf. In the Botticelli painting Venus is tender and lovely, waiting while an airborne male and female—the wind Zephyr and the breeze Aura—prepare to waft her ashore. At the right-hand side of the picture, the goddess of the seasons waits with a flowery robe to cover Venus's nakedness. But in classical mythology Venus is not just the goddess of love; she is also the force of reproduction in the natural world. And that, of course, Blake deeply distrusts. So in his picture the flowery cloak is replaced by the veil of Vala, who stands ominously at the "sinister" left-hand side.

Against Natural Supernaturalism

With the Sussex countryside and the sea as inspiration, Blake filled *Milton* with imagery from the natural world (far fewer natural images appear in *Jerusalem*). Since nature is a major theme in Romantic poetry, it might seem obvious that in doing so he was performing as a Romantic poet. But his conception of

44. *Jerusalem*, copy E, plate 32

nature was very different from that of Wordsworth, whom he frequently criticized, and of Coleridge and Keats, whom he never mentioned. What Blake deplored in Wordsworth was natural supernaturalism, as M. H. Abrams has defined it: the attempt to locate in nature the ultimate values that religion traditionally provided. "Nature never did betray the heart that loves her," Wordsworth declares in *Tintern Abbey,* as if "she" were a maternal deity. In his *Excursion* Wordsworth declares that the mind is "fitted" to the external world, and in the same way "the external world is fitted to the mind." In the margin of his copy of the poem Blake retorted, "You shall not bring me down to believe such fitting and fitted; I know better and please your Lordship." Blake thought that nature as described by Wordsworth doesn't deserve love and will certainly betray us. Blake did admire one of Wordsworth's poems, the Platonically inspired *Ode: Intimations of Immortality,* in which children trail clouds of glory as they enter this world from eternity. "It was remarkable," Crabb Robinson said, "that the parts of Wordsworth's ode which he most enjoyed were the most obscure and those I the least like and comprehend."[28]

Coleridge occasionally seems closer to Blake than Wordsworth does. The incantatory *Kubla Khan* is a visionary poem—literally a vision, if it's true that it originated in an opium dream. But Coleridge's usual style is meditative blank verse, with close attention to physical details in a very un-Blakean manner. In *Frost at Midnight* he watches his infant son sleeping by the fireside:

> Therefore all seasons shall be sweet to thee,
> Whether the summer clothe the general earth
> With greenness, or the redbreast sit and sing
> Betwixt the tufts of snow on the bare branch
> Of mossy apple-tree, while the nigh thatch
> Smokes in the sun-thaw; whether the eave-drops fall
> Heard only in the trances of the blast,
> Or if the secret ministry of frost
> Shall hang them up in silent icicles,
> Quietly shining to the quiet moon.

"Secret ministry" is an expression that might make one think of Blake, but we never find Coleridge's kind of leisurely, loving detail in his poems. It's not that he isn't observant of nature, but in Blake observation always expands immediately into symbolic meaning:

> There is the nettle that stings with soft down, and there
> The indignant thistle whose bitterness is bred in his milk.[29]

It would never occur to Coleridge or Wordsworth to call a thistle "indignant."

It needs to be emphasized that what Blake attacks in "nature" is never the actual world of fields and rivers and living things. Those he loved, and he celebrated them from *Songs of Innocence* right on until the end. In *Milton,* for example,

> First e'er the morning breaks, joy opens in the flowery bosoms,
> Joy even to tears, which the sun rising dries; first the wild thyme
> And meadow-sweet, downy and soft waving among the reeds,
> Light springing on the air lead the sweet dance. They wake
> The honeysuckle sleeping on the oak: the flaunting beauty
> Revels along upon the wind; the white-thorn, lovely May,
> Opens her many lovely eyes. Listening the rose still sleeps,
> None dare to wake her; soon she bursts her crimson curtained bed
> And comes forth in the majesty of beauty. Every flower:
> The pink, the jessamine, the wall-flower, the carnation,
> The jonquil, the mild lily opes her heavens! every tree
> And flower and herb soon fill the air with an innumerable dance,
> Yet all in order sweet and lovely, men are sick with love!
> Such is a vision of the lamentation of Beulah over Ololon.[30]

This is a heartfelt appreciation, yet the final line is crucial. As in the imagery in *A Sunshine Holiday,* Beulah is a place of refuge but not a final home. From the perspective of Eternity, this celebration of nature is a *lamentation.*

A case can be made that when Blake seems to criticize nature, his real target is often mistaken human constructions of nature. That is certainly what happens in *Mock on Mock on Voltaire Rousseau.* But Blake also insists that nature, as we normally understand it, is radically inadequate unless animated by the divine imagination. The passage just quoted from *Milton* evokes the odors of flowers as a joyous dance, and a related passage in the preceding plate does the same kind of thing with sounds:

Thou hearest the nightingale begin the song of spring;
The lark sitting upon his earthy bed, just as the morn
Appears, listens silent; then springing from the waving cornfield! loud
He leads the choir of day! trill, trill, trill, trill,
Mounting upon the wings of light into the great expanse,
Re-echoing against the lovely blue and shining heavenly shell.
His little throat labours with inspiration; every feather
On throat and breast and wings vibrates with the effluence divine.
All nature listens silent to him, and the awful sun
Stands still upon the mountain looking on this little bird
With eyes of soft humility, and wonder, love and awe.

Keats's nightingale—we don't know whether Blake ever read the great *Ode to a Nightingale*, which was written years after this passage in *Milton*—represents the collective immortality of nature, by contrast with the "sole self" of the poet. Blake's nightingale and lark represent nature spiritually transformed, and they sing with such inspiration that the sun itself stands still to listen.[31]

In this lovely passage, Blake was surely remembering Shakespeare:

> And then my state,
> Like to the lark at break of day arising
> From sullen earth, sings hymns at heaven's gate.

Nature in its ordinary "Romantic" sense was for Blake sullen earth, and that was his quarrel with mainstream Romanticism. Wordsworth urged acceptance of

> . . . the very world which is the world
> Of all of us—the place in which, in the end,
> We find our happiness, or not at all.[32]

As Catherine Blake commented, her husband preferred to live in Eternity.

Some lines by a modern heir to the Romantics, Wallace Stevens, likewise bring out the contrast with Blake:

> The imperfect is our paradise.
> Note that, in this bitterness, delight,
> Since the imperfect is so hot in us,
> Lies in flawed words and stubborn sounds.[33]

Blake knew all about the stubborn structure of language, but he could never make peace with the imperfect—or with Mother Nature. No wonder, then, that despite his loathing of institutional religion, he was profoundly religious in a way that few of his contemporaries were. Only a full, living incarnation of the divine within the everyday could render it bearable. Yet that divine spirit must also be wholly human. Trying to understand and articulate this paradoxical ideal became Blake's lifelong quest.

14. WRESTLING WITH GOD

All Religions Are One

RELIGION was profoundly important to Blake, in a questing and questioning way that is thought-provoking even for readers and viewers who are not religious at all. One of his first experiments in relief etching was a little pamphlet entitled *All Religions Are One,* which asserts that however much religions may differ in detail, they have a common origin. "The religions of all nations are derived from each nation's different reception of the poetic genius, which is everywhere called the spirit of prophecy. . . . As all men are alike (though infinitely various) so all religions; and as all similars, have one source. The true Man is the source, he being the poetic genius."[1]

That sounds definite, but what, really, *is* "the true Man"? Answering that question was a lifelong challenge for Blake. He always denied the existence of an omnipotent patriarch in heaven, and he would sometimes insist that the divine was simply a spiritual dimension that all human beings share. Thus, in *The Marriage of Heaven and Hell:* "All deities reside in the human breast." And the notebook verses known as *The Everlasting Gospel* include this unequivocal statement:

> Thou art a man God is no more
> Thy own humanity learn to adore.

But as Blake labored long and hard on *The Four Zoas,* and afterward on the prophecies *Milton* and *Jerusalem,* the figure of Jesus took on an increasingly crucial role. Concerned as he was with the breakdown of the self, he needed help from an agency beyond the self; without intervention by "the Saviour even Jesus," the fall into formlessness would have no end. If Jesus were simply what is best in humanity, what would be the point in calling him "the Saviour" at all?[2]

The function of religion, in Blake's view, is to ask ultimate questions about existence, and the questions are more important than the answers. He did declare once, "The Old and New Testaments are the great code of art," but that doesn't mean that the Bible has a monopoly on truth. Rather, the Bible is the particular set of symbols that are embedded in the Western imagination, inspiring Blake as it inspired Michelangelo and Raphael before him. But he always read the Bible, as Erdman puts it, counterclockwise, in explicit contrast to orthodox interpretation. As Blake says in *The Everlasting Gospel,*

> Both read the Bible day and night
> But thou read'st black where I read white.[3]

Blake explicitly rejected a great deal in the New Testament, including the doctrine of the virgin birth and the Pauline emphasis on sin. He liked the Old Testament even less, apart from the visionary prophets. The stony tablets of the Ten Commandments are a negative symbol throughout his work, as is the institution of priesthood with its repressive Law: "As the caterpillar chooses the fairest leaves to lay her eggs on, so the priest lays his curse on the fairest joys." Blake was especially revolted by biblical military history. Reading an Anglican bishop's claim that it must have been God's will "to exterminate so wicked a people" as the Canaanites, he retorted, "To me who believe the Bible and profess myself a Christian, a defence of the wickedness of the Israelites in murdering so many thousands under pretence of a command from God is altogether abominable and blasphemous."[4]

The Ancient of Days

One of Blake's most brilliant reimaginings of the biblical God is the great print known as *The Ancient of Days* (color plate 36), which is a name for God in the Book of Daniel: "I beheld till the thrones were cast down, and the Ancient of Days did sit, whose garment was white as snow, and the hair of his head like the pure wool: his throne was like the fiery flame, and his wheels as burning fire." Blake made a number of versions of this image—the one reproduced here is the frontispiece to his poem *Europe*—and he was working on yet another in the last days of his life. An early biographer wrote that "he always bestowed more time and enjoyed greater pleasure when colouring [this] print than anything he ever produced.[5]

The image derives from the Book of Proverbs, in which Wisdom declares, "When he prepared the heavens, I was there, when he set a compass upon the face of the depth." Milton expanded on the idea:

> In his hand
> He took the golden compasses, prepared
> In God's eternal store, to circumscribe
> This universe and all created things.
> One foot he centered, and the other turned
> Round through the vast profundity obscure,
> And said, "Thus far extend, thus far thy bounds;
> This be thy just circumference, O world!"[6]

In Blake's thought, however, there was never an original creation out of nothingness. On the contrary, the creation that is described in Genesis must represent a belated attempt to repair the damage that occurred when the integrated life of Eternity collapsed into fragments. So the creation in Genesis was already a fall. In *The Book of Urizen:*

> He formed a line and a plummet
> To divide the abyss beneath.
> He formed a dividing rule;
> He formed scales to weigh;
> He formed massy weights;

> He formed a brazen quadrant;
> He formed golden compasses
> And began to explore the abyss,
> And he planted a garden of fruits.[7]

In contrast to Milton's elaborately structured language, Blake's is jerky and short of breath, suggesting dogged repetition rather than effortless mastery. And the "garden of fruits" is the Garden of Eden, where according to orthodox belief—but not according to Blake—one of those fruits was inexplicably forbidden, with fatal consequences.

The most striking thing about the figure in *The Ancient of Days* is his contorted posture. This God is crouching within the orb of the sun, which he has probably just traced with his compasses—crouching, because the sun is not large enough for him to do otherwise. His left knee is jammed against his shoulder in a posture that is all but impossible anatomically, and he holds the compasses with his "sinister" left arm, which presses awkwardly against his head. An epigram in Blake's notebook entitled *To God* is relevant here:

> If you have formed a circle to go into,
> Go into it yourself and see how you would do.[8]

In *Paradise Lost* the compasses create form out of chaos; in Blake's picture they represent a vain attempt to circumscribe the infinite.

Are we mistaken, then, when we perceive grandeur in *The Ancient of Days?* By no means. Blake despised agnostics like Voltaire, who commented sarcastically in *Candide* that "Milton has the Messiah take a big pair of compasses out of a heavenly cupboard to trace out his work."[9] Blake's Ancient of Days is arrestingly grand in a way that Voltaire could never have understood. Grand—but he is not the omnipotent creator of Genesis, for grander still is the blaze of energy that pours out from *behind* his newly outlined sun. The windblown hair and beard likewise suggest powerful energy, flowing through an infinite universe far greater than the one the Ancient of Days has just finished making. He participates in that creative energy, but he is not its cause.

Translating ideas into graphic images, Blake often exploited the technical possibilities of his media, and Robert Essick comments that there is a striking embodiment of doubleness in this great picture. "Relief lines define the figure's body and arm, but the compasses reaching into the void below are executed as white lines — or, more accurately, white areas — against a black relief background. It is as though Blake were combining positive and negative photographic images to make a single design." The cross-hatching in the clouds may suggest a constricting net of Urizenic control.[10]

Visitors to Rockefeller Center in New York may not be aware that Lee Lawrie's 1933 art deco image of "Wisdom" (figure 45), over the main entrance of the GE Building, is a tribute to *The Ancient of Days* — with, of course, the ambiguity left out. Beneath it is inscribed a very different biblical text from the one in Proverbs: "Wisdom And Knowledge Shall Be The Stability Of Thy Times."[11]

The Gloomy Patriarch

When Blake published *The Book of Urizen* in 1794, his myth of the Zoas was only partly developed, but he was already certain that the patriarch in the sky was a mere human invention, nobody's daddy, as he called him in a couple of sarcastic poems:

> Then old Nobodaddy aloft
> Farted and belched and coughed
> And said I love hanging and drawing and quartering
> Every bit as well as war and slaughtering.

In this relatively early work, Blake may not yet have thought of Urizen as one of the four Zoas, but he certainly represents, as he would continue to do, a union of abstract reason with moral repression. In the title page (figure 46), a squatting Urizen is inscribing two books or tablets at the same time, a quill pen in his right hand and an etching needle or paintbrush in his left. He is apparently copying from a book on the ground, tracing its text with his foot, but his eyes are closed; perhaps he is falling asleep. Since the book is sinking roots into the ground, it is probably the book of nature. Behind him are the tablets of the Law, looking like gravestones. Urizen's

WISDOM AND ✳ KNOWLEDGE
✳ SHALL BE THE ✳
STABILITY OF THY TIMES

45. *Wisdom*, by Lee Lawrie

46. *The Book of Urizen*, copy G, title page

✧   ✧   ✧

world is oppressively heavy. In Morris Eaves's interpretation, "The force of the Law has tugged the trees into earthbound arches, and the arches are deathly, like everything else in the design. . . . Urizen, who has sunk to the bottom of the design like a stone, is depicted as a man unable to stand erect in a universe of his own creating."[12]

In the copy of the plate that is reproduced here, Blake has masked out one word in the title, which in other copies appears as *The First Book of Urizen*. That was probably an allusion to a common description of Genesis as "the first book of Moses," and he may have realized that "first" seemed to imply a forthcoming *Second Book of Urizen* that was never intended. After deleting the word in this copy he extended a branch to fill the gap.

In Genesis, after each day of creation, "God saw that it was good," and after finishing the job, "Behold, it was very good." With Urizen it is just the opposite. Fearing energy and disorder, he labors in vain to establish rigid stability:

> I have sought for a joy without pain,
> For a solid without fluctuation.

All that he is able to achieve, however, is "a wide world of solid obstruction," and at the cost of pain without joy.[13]

A full-page image (color plate 37) shows a melancholy Urizen immersed in the sea of materiality. He may be floating, since his beard extends horizontally, or treading water, or even drifting downward. Gilchrist thought it was the latter, describing him as "an old, amphibious-looking giant, with rueful visage, letting himself sink slowly through the waters like a frog." Then again, he might even be struggling to rise up. In copy B, at the Morgan Library, there is an inscription on the reverse side of this picture. Though not in Blake's hand, it may reproduce a caption of his that had been trimmed away:

> I labour upwards into
> futurity

If Urizen could return to Eternity he would live in an "eternal Now" and would no longer need to anticipate the future.[14]

It is at this point in *The Book of Urizen* that Urizen appropriates the role of the biblical God.

> Here alone I in books formed of metals
> Have written the secrets of wisdom. . . .
> Lo! I unfold my darkness, and on
> This rock, place with strong hand the book
> Of eternal brass, written in my solitude:
> Laws of peace, of love, of unity;
> Of pity, compassion, forgiveness.
> Let each choose one habitation,
> His ancient infinite mansion;
> One command, one joy, one desire,
> One curse, one weight, one measure
> One king, one God, one Law.

Urizen's proclamation recalls Paul's Epistle to the Ephesians: "There is one body, and one Spirit, even as you are called in one hope of your calling; one Lord, one faith, one baptism, one God and Father of all, who is above all, and through all, and in you all." Blake did believe that a divine principle unites all of humanity in "one spirit," but he would have regarded "laws" of love and compassion as oxymoronic, and he never accepted the authority of a deity above all. It is in another epistle that he finds the proper solution: "Christ hath redeemed us from the curse of the law" — the rigidly negative commandments that Moses brought down from Mount Sinai on tablets of stone. And Urizen's "book of eternal brass" is surely an ironic reminiscence of a hymn by Isaac Watts:

> His hand has writ the sacred Word
> With an immortal pen;
> Engraved as in eternal brass
> The mighty Promise shines.[15]

Another full-page picture (figure 47) shows Urizen shackled, weeping in despair at the hopelessness of his project of patriarchal control.

47. *The Book of Urizen,* copy G, plate 11

His soul sickened! he cursed
Both sons and daughters, for he saw
That no flesh nor spirit could keep
His iron laws one moment,
For he saw that life lived upon death.

"Tears of pious and conventional pity," Jean Hagstrum comments, "ooze from his compressed lids and drop into his ropy frozen beard."[16]

It needs always to be emphasized that Blake's attack is not just on doctrine as abstract theology, but on doctrine as a mechanism for ratifying injustice. A bitter Song of Experience begins, "Pity would be no more / If we did not make somebody poor," and in *The Four Zoas* the thought is repeated when Urizen reads out his policy from his book of brass:

Compel the poor to live upon a crust of bread by soft mild arts,
Smile when they frown, frown when they smile, and when a man looks
    pale
With labour and abstinence, say he looks healthy and happy,
And when his children sicken let them die, there are enough
Born, even too many, and our earth will be overrun.

No doubt Blake was remembering Thomas Robert Malthus's 1798 *Essay on the Principle of Population,* as well as a specific issue, a parliamentary debate in 1800 over a bread bill that would have taken action against monopolists who were driving up prices. William Pitt, the prime minister, declared that to interfere with the market in that way would "strike against the freedom of trade" and urged that measures be taken instead "to diminish the consumption." More largely, this is the hypocrisy of a society that believes it is being generous to—as the cliché has it—"those less fortunate than ourselves."[17]

Jehovah and the Elohim

In pondering the symbolism of the divine, Blake made effective use of what contemporary scholars were just beginning to recognize, that the Bible is an amalgam of multiple texts stitched together over many centuries. Groundbreaking scholarship in Germany was being reported in England by a Roman Catholic priest, Alexander Geddes, who argued that the Bible should be analyzed in exactly the same way as other ancient texts, such as the Homeric poems. It would then be obvious that there are two entirely different creation stories in the Book of Genesis. In chapter 1, "God said, Let there be light"; in chapters 2 and 3 a much more human deity creates Adam and Eve, places them in the Garden of Eden, and walks with them there in the cool of the evening. In the first story God is called the Elohim (the noun is plural), and in the second Yahweh or Jehovah. The two versions have therefore become known as the E and J texts.[18]

A bemused Crabb Robinson recorded this conversation: "'Whoever believes in Nature,' said Blake, 'disbelieves in God—for Nature is the work of the Devil.' On my obtaining from him the declaration that the Bible was the work of God, I referred to the commencement of Genesis—'In the beginning God created the heaven and the earth'—but I gained nothing by this, for I was triumphantly told that this God was not Jehovah but the Elohim."[19] That creator is the demiurge, whom the early Gnostic heretics condemned as an antagonist of the true God. But Blake's system differs from the various Gnostic versions, since for him both Jehovah and Elohim play imaginative roles as progressive avatars of the divine.

It is in this context that Blake developed his symbolism of the Seven Eyes of God, recalling the mysterious "eyes" in Ezekiel's vision and also a text in Zechariah, "They are the eyes of the Lord, which run to and fro through the whole earth." These are not just alternative names for the divine, but sequential stages in purging it from superstitious reverence and fear. Jehovah and Elohim are two of the seven Eyes, and the final Eye is Jesus, the only one willing to sacrifice himself.[20]

Elohim (or the Elohim) is the subject of Blake's great color print *Elohim Creating Adam* (color plate 38). Hovering on massive wings, he is forming Adam out of clay, pressing the head down with one hand and reaching for more clay with the other as an earthworm of mortality wraps around the just-created body. The expression of this creator is staring and distressed—"a haunted and haunting old man," Hagstrum calls him.[21] In Genesis God created man in his own image. In this picture, Adam's face is indeed similar to Elohim's, but for Blake the analogy runs in the opposite direction. It is man who has created an alarming deity in his own image, and now feels it pressing down on him like an incubus.

Christopher Heppner comments accurately that Elohim's wings "are attached in a totally non-functional way." But Blake didn't invent them; they are imitated from a representation of Boreas, the north wind, on the Tower of the Winds in Athens that had been engraved by his old master James Basire (figure 48). A biblical conception thus merges with a weird and alien pagan one.[22]

Heppner also observes that this act of creation is very different from the one Michelangelo painted on the Sistine Chapel ceiling, with which Blake was certainly familiar, if only in black and white prints. E. H. Gombrich's eloquent description of Michelangelo's version highlights just how great the difference is from Blake's: "God the Father is wrapped in a wide and majestic mantle blown out by the wind like a sail, suggesting the ease and speed with which he floats through the void. As he stretches out his hand, not even touching Adam's finger, we almost see the first man waking, as from a profound sleep, and gazing into the fatherly face of his Maker." Gombrich notes "the ease and power of this gesture of creation." In Blake's version it is more like a desperate struggle.[23]

Like the Ancient of Days, Blake's Elohim has genuine grandeur. His desire for order is not contemptible, and form is always better than formlessness. The world this demiurge creates is unquestionably preferable to chaos, and in *Milton* Elohim and Los join together in a positive context:

> Such is the world of Los, the labour of six thousand years.
> Thus Nature is a vision of the science of the Elohim.

"Science" still had the general meaning that Samuel Johnson defines: "Any art or species of knowledge."[24] That is knowledge in its full imaginative depth, as contrasted with reductive empiricist reasoning. But it is still provisional and limited. The Golgonooza that Los creates is a stopgap defense against chaos, and the Nature created by the Elohim, though likewise far better than chaos, is still the entrapping world of Generation.

48. Boreas, from *The Antiquities of Athens*

The God of This World

In a set of resolutions that Blake signed in 1789, during his brief attendance at a Swedenborgian congregation—the only church he ever belonged to—fully one-quarter of the Bible was repudiated as not divinely inspired. Long afterward, Blake's own list of inspired scriptural books in *Jerusalem* still included only the ones that were approved in 1789. It is easy to understand why the Book of Job is not among them. It begins by describing a supremely admirable person: "There was a man in the land of Uz, whose name was Job; and that man was perfect and upright, and one that feared God, and eschewed evil." Next we find God in conversation with Satan, who suggests that if Job were to lose everything he has, "he will curse thee to thy face." God accepts the challenge and replies, "Behold, all that he hath is in thy power." Job's family and flocks are thereupon destroyed, he is afflicted with plague, and he does indeed curse, shocking his so-called comforters. God then rebukes him from a whirlwind, pointing out that he was not present at the creation of the world and warning that he has no right to complain. Somehow convinced by this response to stop asking questions, Job repents in dust and ashes and is duly rewarded: "The Lord blessed the latter end of Job more than his beginning." He gets a new family, fourteen thousand sheep, and six thousand camels.[25]

In the Hebrew Bible, Satan plays a minor role and is not the mighty antagonist of God that Christian theology turned him into. In the Book of Job he acts as an authorized accuser, rather like a courtroom prosecutor. Blake was familiar with this concept, and he incorporated it in a set of watercolors illustrating the Book of Job that he made for Thomas Butts around 1805. Twenty years later the painter John Linnell commissioned him to turn the Job images into engravings, which were duly published in a magnificent edition. More than three hundred copies were printed, making this late masterpiece the least rare of Blake's works.

In an advertisement Linnell noted, "These plates are engraved entirely by Mr. Blake with the graver only (that is without the aid of aqua fortis)." That is to say, he no longer employed the etching technique of using acid, but incised the lines with a burin after an initial drawing was transferred to the plate. The finely traced lines are reminiscent of the work of a predecessor Blake greatly admired, Albrecht Dürer, and an art historian calls these engravings "the best that have been done in England."[26]

An exceptionally powerful image is plate 11, *Job's Evil Dreams* (figure 49). Job is lying on a bed that looks extremely uncomfortable, viewing with terror three devils in hellfire below. Two of them are grasping his legs firmly (the hands on his right leg must belong to unseen devils on the other side) while another prepares to bind him with a heavy chain. Above, an angry God presses down as Elohim did upon Adam, pointing at the flames with his left (sinister) hand and at a pair of stone tablets with his right. These represent the Ten Commandments, and in the earlier watercolor version Hebrew letters can be made out: "Thou shalt not kill; Thou shalt not commit adultery."[27] Jagged lightning of divine wrath lights up the sky.

49. *Job's Evil Dreams*

An indication of how little Blake's work was understood by his contemporaries is Alan Cunningham's obtuse comment, "The Scripture overawed his imagination, and he was too devout to attempt aught beyond a literal embodying of the majestic scene."[28] In this picture in particular, Cunningham evidently failed to notice two obvious clues. The first is that the serpent of temptation is shown winding around Elohim; in Blake's view any God who could authorize the torment of a good man must be satanic himself. And the second is that Elohim has a cloven hoof instead of a foot. He is himself the accuser.

A text near the bottom, curving around and finishing vertically, departs from the original in two ways. Blake's text is: "Oh that my words were printed in a Book that they were graven with an iron pen & lead in the rock for ever For I know that my Redeemer liveth and that he shall stand in the latter days upon the Earth and after my skin destroy thou This body yet in my flesh shall I see God whom I shall see for Myself and mine eyes shall behold & not Another tho consumed be my wrought Image." The King James Version reads: "And though after my skin worms destroy this body, yet in my flesh shall I see God."[29] Blake has kept the skin but left out the worms. Just as in his emblem book *For Children,* the spiritual body is invulnerable to the worms of mortality. "I know that my Redeemer liveth" was traditionally interpreted as a prophecy of Christ.

The other change is more significant. The original text reads, "Mine eyes shall behold and not another, though my reins be consumed within me." "Reins" were literally the kidneys and metaphorically the emotions. Blake omits them and substitutes "tho consumed be my wrought Image." The punitive God of the nightmare has indeed been wrought in Job's own image, which is why they have the same face. This unreal God is a projection of Job's guilt.[30]

"Thou only art holy," the Book of Revelation says of God. "Every thing that lives is holy," says Blake, in four places. Rudolf Otto, in his classic work *The Idea of the Holy,* describes God as "wholly other," the *mysterium tremendum* "whose kind and character are incommensurable with our own, and before which we therefore recoil in a wonder that strikes us chill and numb." From Blake's point of view this is exactly wrong, a formulation that reflects worship not of the true God but of the false demiurge who is mentioned in the Epistle to the Ephesians. Blake quotes from that epistle, in Greek, at the beginning of *The Four Zoas*. In English the text reads: "For we wrestle not against flesh and blood, but against principalities, against powers, against the rulers of the darkness of this world, against spiritual wickedness in high places."[31]

The emblem series *For Children* had a simple message. That message was that the cycle from birth to death, generation after generation, may seem like an endless loop. But it is not endless, for when the mortal body dies, the spirit is liberated into Eternity. When Blake reissued the emblems with the new title *For the Sexes*, he added a gnomic concluding poem that complicates the message. Entitled *To the Accuser Who Is the God of This World*, it accuses conventional religion of complicity with the merely natural world, and with the satanic force that seeks to imprison us there.

> Truly my Satan thou art but a dunce,
> And dost not know the garment from the man.
> Every harlot was a virgin once,
> Nor canst thou ever change Kate into Nan.
>
> Though thou art worshipped by the names divine
> Of Jesus and Jehovah, thou art still
> The son of morn in weary night's decline,
> The lost traveler's dream under the hill.

The "son of morn" is the fallen archangel Lucifer, whose name means "light-bearer," as in Isaiah: "How art thou fallen from heaven, O Lucifer, son of the morning!"[32] The "lost traveler" alludes to folktales in which fairy enchantment sends a person into helpless sleep. As Blake imagines it, this is the nightmare of Albion, haunted by delusions that will vanish when he awakes.

By the "Accuser," Blake does not mean the prosecutorial figure in the Book of Job but rather a projection of human anxiety and guilt. Orthodox religion identifies him as a real being and calls him Satan, a cruel antagonist whom God mysteriously allows to go on tormenting us. But just as the God in *Job's Evil Dreams* is actually diabolical, so this vengeful Satan is identical to the false deity worshipped by the churches—the judgmental Jehovah and the Jesus who dies to shield us from deserved punishment for our sins. This illusory Accuser may believe that we are his slaves, but that only means that *we* believe it; he will evaporate as soon as we see him for what he is.

Meanwhile, the only power the Accuser has is over our mortal body, and in the later poems Blake regularly calls that body a temporary covering to be left behind. The expression "dost not know the garment from the man" means that the physical body is mistaken for the entirety of a human being. But as early as *The Marriage of Heaven and Hell* Blake had asserted, "Man has no body distinct from his soul, for that called body is a portion of soul discerned by the five senses, the chief inlets of soul in this age." In the later poems the body is not even a portion of soul, but rather an entrapping cloak woven on the looms of Vala, Rahab, and Tirzah. At death that garment will be discarded, as Milton divests himself when purged of his selfhood (color plate 20).[33]

There is a further blind spot in the Accuser's understanding. Just as Oothoon, in *Visions of the Daughters of Albion,* denied that she was defiled after being raped, so in this poem Innocence remains undefiled at the core of the self: "every harlot was a virgin once." Cruel experience provokes the harlots in the lyric *London* to curse bitterly, and they have every right to curse. What they have *not* become is sinful and wicked, and their true individuality remains unchanged—"Nor canst thou ever change Kate into Nan." It may be relevant that Blake's nickname for Catherine was Kate.

The first line of *To the Accuser* is an ironic adaptation of a conventional statement in Edward Young's long poem *Night Thoughts:* "Thy master, Satan, I dare call a dunce." Young's meaning was that after rebelling against the Almighty, the fallen angel Satan was a fool to imagine he had any power except what God, for mysterious reasons, chose to permit. Blake's meaning is that the Prince of Darkness has no real existence at all. In conversation he referred superbly to Satan's empire as "the empire of nothing."[34]

In the picture that accompanies *To the Accuser* (figure 50), the lost traveler is so sound asleep that a spider has had time to spin a web on his walking stick. As he dreams, a bat-winged Satan emerges from his body—no real being at all, but just a figment in a dream. Startlingly, Satan's foot doubles as the traveler's penis. The

To The Accuser who is

The God of This World

Truly My Satan thou art but a Dunce
And dost not know the Garment from the Man
Every Harlot was a Virgin once
Nor canst thou ever change Kate into Nan

Tho thou art Worshipd by the Names Divine
Of Jesus & Jehovah: thou art still
The Son of Morn in weary Nights decline
The lost Travellers Dream under the Hill

50. *For the Sexes: The Gates of Paradise*, copy D, plate 21

dream is evidently a nocturnal emission, an expression of the genital sexuality that will no longer be needed in Eternity. Satan's wings contain a sun, moon, and stars, but a real sunrise is bursting from behind the hill, compelling the spectral god of this world to take flight.[35]

Jesus

After the *Songs of Innocence,* Jesus all but disappeared from Blake's poems for nearly a decade, reappearing at last during revision of *The Four Zoas.* He probably disappeared because Blake saw him as coopted by organized religion, and he probably returned when Blake realized he needed a power greater than ourselves, able to rescue us from our troubled condition. That was when he wrote to Butts, "I am again emerged into the light of day. I still and shall to eternity embrace Christianity, and adore him who is the express image of God."[36]

It seems clear that Blake regarded the historical Jesus as a great prophet but not as the unique incarnation of God on earth. Jesus was perhaps endowed with exceptional divine inspiration, but if so he differed from the rest of us in degree, not kind. A rather shocked Crabb Robinson reported: "On my asking in what light he viewed the great question concerning the divinity of Jesus Christ, he said, 'He is the only God;' but then he added, 'And so am I and so are you.'" Strikingly, Robinson adds, "Now he had just before (and that occasioned my question) been speaking of the errors of Jesus Christ."[37]

According to orthodox theology, God could not forgive our sins until the innocent Christ permitted himself to be executed on our behalf. "That is a horrible doctrine," Blake told Robinson; "if another man pay your debt I do not forgive it." To glorify the Crucifixion, therefore, struck Blake as altogether blasphemous, since he saw it not as a divine sacrifice but as a judicial murder of the historical Jesus. In the "Keys of the Gates" appended to *For the Sexes* he challenges believers to justify their use of the crucifix:

> O Christians Christians! tell me why
> You rear it on your altars high![38]

A full-page image of the Crucifixion appears in *Jerusalem*, symbolizing temporary bondage to the natural world (color plate 39). Jesus hangs not from a cross but from a tree that resembles a massive oak, recalling the nature worship of the despised Druids. Yet there are apples hanging from it. Evidently this is no botanically recognizable tree, but a conflation of all the mythic forms of human sacrifice. In Blake's terms, what Jesus has really done is sacrifice his own selfhood, not in order to propitiate a vengeful God but to purge away the merely "natural" in all of us. Albion (whose name is visible in several copies of this plate) stands adoring Jesus, from whose head pours a radiance far brighter than that of the merely natural sun on the horizon. Albion's outstretched arms mirror the cruciform pose, and his posture recalls the "dance of death" in the print *Albion Rose* (color plate 11).[39] Jesus is the only God—but so is Albion, and so are we all.

Reconciliation with the Father

From *Songs of Experience* onward, it is obvious that Blake had a problem with fathers, though it is never clear why. All the same, his symbolism would be crippled if it dismissed fatherhood altogether. Just as Urizen must be reintegrated with the other Zoas, so Jehovah must recover a positive role. "I see the face of my Heavenly Father," Blake wrote to Butts near the end of the time at Felpham; "he lays his hand upon my head and gives a blessing to all my works." In *Jerusalem* we hear of "the universal Father."[40]

The next to last plate of *Jerusalem* (color plate 40) is a scene of reconciliation, but strange and hard to interpret. A bearded old man, with rays of light springing from his head, leans forward to embrace an androgynous figure with long hair who may be Jerusalem or possibly humanity as a whole. The colors are so dark that an art historian complains, "The black-red Blakean oven is peculiarly grim and smothering." Morton Paley, on the other hand, says that "the variation of darks in the flames creates a truly apocalyptic effect" and notes the striking use of blue sky as a halo.[41]

Is the bearded figure a return, at last, of the Father? The younger figure seems to be falling gratefully into his arms, gazing up into his face. But why is the old man gazing off to the side? Is he looking at us? And why does he grasp the young figure's buttocks? Commentators have understandably seen the embrace as sexual, but is it? One interpreter sees the younger figure as "a terror-stricken androgyne"; another sees no terror but rather "the rapturous moment just before erotic consummation; Jerusalem and Albion are rising within the earth in heavenly flames, and 'the time of love' with its orgasmic 'holy raptures of adoration' is spreading forgiveness and life within and throughout the earth."[42] As so often, it's hard to know if intense sexual feelings are actually implied in the picture or are just imagined by Blake's commentators.

A different interpretation is suggested by Anthony Blunt, who notes the similarity of the embrace in this image to that of the Prodigal Son and his father in an engraving by Martin de Vos. We know that Blake found that parable especially moving. Samuel Palmer told Gilchrist, "I can yet recall it when, on one occasion, dwelling upon the exquisite beauty of the parable of the Prodigal, he began to repeat a part of it; but at the words, 'When he was yet a great way off, his father saw him,' could go no further. His voice faltered, and he was in tears." Here is what Blake was unable to finish:

> But when he was yet a great way off, his father saw him, and had compassion, and ran, and fell on his neck, and kissed him. And the son said unto him, Father, I have sinned against heaven, and in thy sight, and am no more worthy to be called thy son. But the father said to his servants, Bring forth the best robe, and put it on him; and put a ring on his hand, and shoes on his feet: and bring hither the fatted calf, and kill it; and let us eat, and be merry: for this my son was dead, and is alive again; he was lost, and is found.[43]

15. THE TRAVELER IN THE EVENING

Poverty Lane

AFTER returning to London from Felpham in 1803, the Blakes rented a small apartment at 17 South Molton Street, within sight of Hyde Park and bounded by an aptly named Poverty Lane (figure 51). This is the only one of their London residences that still exists; a beauty salon now occupies its ground floor. A catalog of the Blakes' other residences makes melancholy reading. Number 28 Broad Street, William's birthplace, "no longer survives; the street has been renamed Broadwick Street, and on the site is now a block of high-rise apartments." Number 28 Poland Street, where he briefly kept a print shop with James Parker, "was rebuilt in the late nineteenth century." Number 31 Great Queen Street, where he served his seven-year apprenticeship with James Basire, "was unfortunately demolished in the late nineteenth century." Henry Pars's drawing school in the Strand "was demolished in Regency times," and Fountain Court, the Blakes' final residence, "no longer exists, but was just situated behind the Coal Hole Tavern on the Strand which still stands, albeit rebuilt." We have already noted that 23 Hercules Road, in Lambeth, was torn down in 1918.[1]

In early 1804 Blake had to return to Sussex for his sedition trial, at which he was acquitted. It was the last remarkable outward event in his life. By now he seems to have realized that his suspicion of William Hayley had been irrational, and he sent

BLAKE'S HOUSE
SOUTH MOULTON ST
F.A.

51. 17 South Molton Street

him warm thanks from London, telling him optimistically, "I have indeed fought through a Hell of terrors and horrors (which none could know but myself) in a divided existence. Now no longer divided nor at war with myself, I shall travel on in the strength of the Lord God, as poor Pilgrim says." Three years later, however, a laconic notebook entry reads: "Tuesday Jan. 20, 1807 between two and seven in the evening—despair."[2]

Commercial jobs dried up, and the only income came from a few generous patrons, particularly Thomas Butts, whom Blake had met in 1800 or thereabouts and who was one of the only people who understood his religious ideas. Though not wealthy, Butts had a comfortable income as a clerk in the War Office, and whenever Blake was out of cash he knew that he had a standing order from Butts for paintings on biblical and Miltonic subjects.

As mentioned earlier, Blake's one attempt at a public exhibition, held in his brother James's haberdashery shop, was a complete failure, and elicited a contemptuous review from Robert Hunt in the widely read *Examiner*. In *Jerusalem*, Hunt makes an appearance under the name of Hand (the image of a pointing hand identified his contributions in the publication), along with Blake's Felpham accuser, the drunken soldier Schofield:

> Go thou to Skofield: ask him if he is Bath or if he is Canterbury;
> Tell him to be no more dubious: demand explicit words.
> Tell him I will dash him into shivers, where and at what time
> I please; tell Hand and Skofield they are my ministers of evil
> To those I hate: for I can hate also as well as they![3]

Hunt and Schofield, of course, never had the slightest inkling of this threat.

Given the absence of any audience for *Milton* and *Jerusalem*, it is impressive that Blake continued to work steadily on those exceptionally ambitious poems. Three copies of the fifty-plate *Milton* were printed in 1811, and one more in 1818; five copies of the massive *Jerusalem*, in a hundred plates, were printed in 1820 and 1821. Only one copy of *Jerusalem* was colored. During that late period Blake also made copies of some of his older illuminated books, brilliantly colored to appeal to collectors who had little or no interest in the texts.

The increasing obscurity of Blake's poems was due not only to the complexity of his thinking but also to the extreme isolation in which he worked. There is a poignant aptness in George Cumberland's description of the now-lost *Last Judgment* painting: "We called upon Blake yesterday evening, found him and his wife drinking tea, dirtier than ever [that is, with paint and ink]; however he received us well and showed his large drawing in water colors of the Last Judgment. He has been labouring at it till it is nearly as black as your hat."[4]

Blake's gloom at his lack of readers is strikingly evident in some strange gaps that invade the address "To the Public" with which *Jerusalem* begins (figure 52). At several points, words and phrases have been savagely gouged out of the metal plate, and after the words "the Author hopes" several whole lines have been entirely deleted. A little later we read:

> Therefore   Reader   what you do not approve, &
> me for this energetic exertion of my talent.

Working from a proof sheet that has survived, Erdman has been able to restore the missing words: "Therefore *Dear* Reader, *forgive* what you do not approve, and *love* me for this energetic exertion of my talent." Not only did Blake remove the hopeful appeal to the reader, but he deliberately left these yawning gaps in the text, even though when he printed new copies from the plate he could easily have inked in new words. "Blake's attack upon plate 3," Morton Paley suggests, "was expressive of terrible rage. The gaps were like wounds that could never heal."[5] Perhaps it is up to each reader to fill in the blanks. If we want to forgive and love Blake, that will be our choice; he's not counting on it.

In 1821 the Blakes moved for the last time, to a second-floor apartment in a dark, narrow lane known as Fountain Court, just off the busy Strand and close to the drawing school where William had gone to study when he was ten years old. The house was owned by Catherine's brother-in-law. Despite lack of money, this final period was happy on the whole. The nearby Thames could be glimpsed from a window, and Blake said it sometimes looked "like a bar of gold." The apartment itself was unprepossessing, but he didn't mind: "I live in a hole here, but God has a beautiful mansion for me elsewhere."[6]

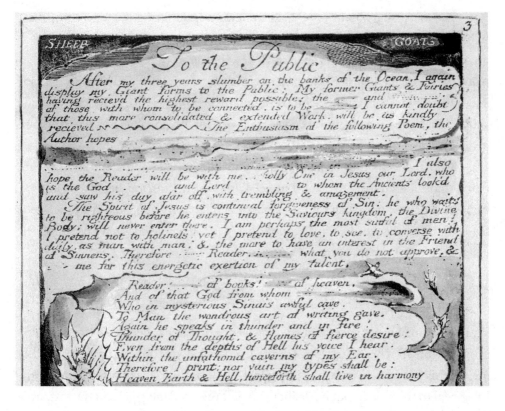

52. *Jerusalem,* copy E, plate 3 (detail)

There are a number of striking images of Blake from these last years. In 1823, when he was sixty-six, a phrenologist named James Deville made a cast of his head "as representative of the imaginative faculty." The result is haunting (figure 53). The solemn expression, however, was uncharacteristic, having been caused by the uncomfortable process Blake had to undergo. As his friend George Richmond explained,

> That is not like dear Blake's mouth. Such a look of severity was foreign to him, an expression of sweetness and sensibility being habitual; but Blake experienced a good deal of pain when the cast was taken, as the plaster pulled out a quantity of his hair. Mrs. Blake did not like the mask, perhaps the rea-

53. Life mask of William Blake

son being that she was familiar with varying expressions of her husband's fine face from daily observation. Indeed it was difficult to please her with any portrait—she never liked Phillips's portrait; but Blake's friends liked the mask.[7]

More engaging is a sketch made on Hampstead Heath by John Linnell, who lived there with his family (figure 54). Blake often visited them on foot, five miles each way, and it was there that he met Coleridge. Samuel Palmer, in his late teens at the time, sometimes accompanied him. Palmer's son remembered hearing that "as the two friends neared the farm, a merry troop hurried out to meet them, led by a little fair-haired girl of some six years old. To this day she remembers cold winter nights when Blake was wrapped up in an old shawl by Mrs. Linnell, and sent his homeward way with the servant, lantern in hand, lighting him across the heath to the main road." When the Linnells' daughter grew up she married Palmer and would tell their son how Blake used to recite *The Chimney Sweeper* and *The Tyger* while she sat at his knee.[8]

Palmer and Richmond, who was just fifteen when he met Blake in 1824, were members of a group of young disciples who referred to themselves playfully as the Ancients. They called No. 3 Fountain Court the House of the Interpreter, after an episode in *Pilgrim's Progress*. As Palmer remembered Blake, "He was a man without a mask; his aim single, his path straightforward, and his wants few; so he was free, noble, and happy. . . . He was one of the few to be met with in our passage through life who are not, in some way or other, 'double minded' and inconsistent with themselves." Consistent he may have been, but not untroubled. Another Ancient, Frederick Tatham, said that he was "a subject of much temptation and mental suffering, and required sometimes much soothing."[9]

During these years Blake endured chronic illness. In 1825 he told Crabb Robinson that reading Wordsworth's *Excursion* "caused him a bowel complaint which nearly killed him." The sarcasm is amusing, but not the complaint. It seems likely that he suffered for years from inflammatory bowel disease, and probably also cirrhosis of the liver and cholangitis, an inflammation of the bile duct. His letters are full of references to fevers, chills, and sweating, and also to intense stomach pain

54. William Blake, by John Linnell

and dysentery, all of which would be due to these causes. There is a strong probability that it was his art that made him sick—years of inhaling copper dust, as well as fumes from nitric acid biting into copper. Toward the end he described himself as "only bones and sinews, all strings and bobbins like a weaver's loom."[10]

Old friends were passing away: Henry Fuseli in 1825, John Flaxman in 1826, his brother James Blake in 1827. When Robinson told Blake that Flaxman had died, "His first observation was with a smile: 'I thought I should have gone first.' He then said, 'I cannot consider death as anything but a removing from one room to another.'" In April 1827 he wrote to Cumberland, "I have been very near the gates of death, and have returned very weak and an old man feeble and tottering, but not in spirit and life, not in the real man, the imagination which liveth for ever. In that I am stronger and stronger as this foolish body decays." In a way, Blake felt that he had already removed to another room. He wrote in a friend's autograph album, "WILLIAM BLAKE one who is very much delighted with being in good company," and added, "Born 28 Novr 1757 in London & has died several times since."[11]

An engraving made many years before, in the emblem book *For Children* (figure 55), anticipates Blake's mood as the end approached. It is captioned "The Traveller hasteth in the Evening," and when the emblems were reissued as *For the Sexes* these lines were added:

> But when once I did descry
> The immortal man that cannot die,
> Through evening shades I haste away
> To close the labours of my day.[12]

Wearing a Blakean broad-brimmed hat, the traveler strides confidently forward.

In *For Children* there was also a picture of "Deaths Door," in which an aged man on a crutch enters a massive stone tomb. But it was always Blake's belief that the spirit lives on in Eternity, though not identical to the mortal self. In 1805, for a projected edition of Robert Blair's poem *The Grave*, he reconceived the death's door motif in a new way (figure 56). The old man and the tomb are still there, but above them is a naked youthful figure who had appeared first in *The Marriage of Heaven and Hell* and again in *America: A Prophecy* (see figure 25, page 109, above, and color

55. *For Children: The Gates of Paradise,* copy D, plate 16

✧ ✧ ✧

plate 13). The publisher of *The Grave,* Robert Cromek, added a comment: "The door opening seems to make utter darkness visible; age, on crutches, is hurried by a tempest into it. Above is the renovated man seated in light and glory."[13] Remarkably, Walt Whitman had his own tomb in Camden, New Jersey, modeled on this image. He had become friendly with Anne Gilchrist, widow of the biographer Alexander Gilchrist, who showed him some of Blake's pictures.

The Grave was supposed to have been a lucrative commission, but Blake's bold white-line style struck Cromek as commercially unpromising, and the job was reassigned to Louis Schiavonetti, who executed the designs in a more fashionable style and was paid the enormous sum of £549, which Blake had expected to receive himself. As it turned out, this disappointment marked just about the end of his employment as a commercial engraver. In his notebook he dubbed Cromek and Schiavonetti "Screwmuch" and "Assassinetti."[14]

According to Frederick Tatham, Blake was working on a copy of *The Ancient of Days* shortly before he died, setting it aside only to sketch his wife: "Kate, I will draw

56. *Deaths Door*

your portrait; you have been a good wife to me." He died on August 12, 1727, aged sixty-nine, and Richmond closed his eyes "to keep the vision in." Shortly afterward Richmond wrote to Palmer, who was out of town at the time: "He said he was going to that country he had all his life wished to see, and expressed himself happy, hoping for salvation through Jesus Christ. Just before he died his countenance became fair, his eyes brightened, and he burst out in singing of the things he saw in heaven. In truth he died like a saint." If that did happen it probably wasn't at the very end, since in all likelihood Blake's illness would have rendered him comatose.[15]

Catherine lived another four years, looked after by Linnell and Tatham, who sold copies of her husband's works for her when they could. According to an anonymous but well-informed writer in a magazine,

> His widow, an estimable woman, saw Blake frequently after his decease: he used to come and sit with her two or three hours every day. These hallowed visitations were her only comforts. He took his chair and talked to her, just as he would have done had he been alive; he advised with her as to the best mode of selling his engravings. She knew that he was in the grave, but she felt satisfied that his spirit visited, condoled, and directed her. When he had been dead a twelvemonth, the devoted and affectionate relict would acquiesce in nothing "until she had had an opportunity of consulting Mr. Blake."[16]

After Catherine's death in 1831, Tatham high-handedly appropriated all of the remaining Blake materials, much to the indignation of Linnell, who had long been the Blakes' chief source of support. Still worse, Tatham became convinced that many of the papers were morally objectionable and burned a large number. Preparing her late husband's biography for publication, Anne Gilchrist mentioned "the holocaust of Blake manuscripts." A contemporary art collector underlined this passage and commented, "Why not tell the truth! F. T. burnt hundreds of them at the desire of Edward Irving, who said 'they were done under the instigation of the Devil.' This I know for I saw it done." Irving was a friend of Coleridge and Thomas Carlyle but also a prophet, faith healer, and founder of the short-lived Irvingite or Holy Catholic Apostolic Church. In time Tatham grew disenchanted with Irving and regretted what he had done. We must hope that what the prophets told Blake in *The Marriage of Heaven and Hell* would also apply here: "I asked Isaiah to favour the world with his lost works; he said none of equal value was lost. Ezekiel said the same of his."[17]

William and Catherine were both buried in a Dissenting cemetery, the Bunhill Fields Burial Ground, but the exact location is unknown. As Gilchrist noted, they were interred in inexpensive "common graves" that would be reused for later occupants.[18]

Blake's Greatness

Blake's questing imagination has never ceased to startle and inspire. The novelist Joyce Cary made his character Gulley Jimson say, "I took Blake's Job drawings out of somebody's bookshelf and peeped into them and shut them up again. Like a chap who's fallen down the cellar steps and knocked his skull in and opens a window too quick, on something too big." A character in Samuel Beckett's *Endgame* says, "The old questions, the old answers—there's nothing like them!" Blake criticized the old answers unsparingly, but he never stopped asking the old questions. What is remarkable in him, T. S. Eliot said, "is a peculiar honesty, which, in a world too frightened to be honest, is peculiarly terrifying."[19]

To speak personally, after half a century of living with Blake, I am still in awe of the depth and range of his genius. He honors the simplicity of childhood without ever condescending. He exposes hypocrisy and exploitation with challenging severity. He movingly dramatizes the turbulent dynamics of the psyche. He celebrates a spiritual connection with the world that is utterly without false piety or sentimentality. And he achieves all of this not in a single art but in two.

Like the Zen masters, Blake urges us to put aside preoccupation with self and to learn to *be*. If we could experience each moment in all its fullness, we would indeed perceive eternity in an hour. That there is a world in each grain of sand is a truth both spiritual and scientific. "As William Blake recognized," a geologist writes, "every sand grain has a story to tell, of the present and the past."[20]

Blake sought universal constants, but he insisted also on the primacy of each individual within those larger forms.

How do we distinguish the oak from the beech, the horse from the ox, but by the bounding outline? How do we distinguish one face or countenance from another, but by the bounding line and its infinite inflexions and movements? What is it that builds a house and plants a garden, but the definite and determinate?

Above all Blake teaches us, with his words and images, to *see* — "through the eye and not with it." The birds that chirp and flutter at the periphery of our ordinary consciousness are just generic birds. Not so for Blake, and not so for us if we will open our imaginations to his:

> How do you know but ev'ry bird that cuts the airy way
> Is an immense world of delight, closed by your senses five?[21]

CHRONOLOGY

1757   born in London, November 28, at 28 Broad Street, Carnaby Market

1762   birth of Robert Blake

1768   enters Henry Pars's drawing school in the Strand

1772   begins seven-year apprenticeship with James Basire, Great Queen Street

1779   briefly attends Royal Academy Schools, forms friendships with John Flaxman and George Cumberland

1780   begins commercial engraving for the bookseller Joseph Johnson; caught up in the Gordon Riots

1782   marries Catherine Boucher (b. 1762)

1783   *Poetical Sketches* privately printed, not offered for sale

1784   briefly in business as print seller with James Parker; acquires rolling press

1785   manuscript satire *An Island in the Moon*

1787   death of Robert Blake; meets Henry Fuseli

1788   first experiments in illuminated printing

1789   attends first General Conference of the Swedenborgian New Jerusalem Church; publishes *Songs of Innocence* and *The Book of Thel*; writes *Tiriel* but doesn't engrave or publish it

1790   moves to 13 Hercules Buildings, Lambeth; begins *The Marriage of Heaven and Hell* (date of publication uncertain, possibly as late as 1792)

1791   conventionally printed proof sheets for the first book of a projected poem *The French Revolution*, never continued or published; engraves illustrations for John Stedman's antislavery memoir

1793   *Visions of the Daughters of Albion; America: A Prophecy; For Children: The Gates of Paradise; Albion Rose*

1794   *Europe: A Prophecy; The [First] Book of Urizen; Songs of Experience* (usually sold in the combined volume *Songs of Innocence and of Experience*)

1795   *The Song of Los; The Book of Los; The Book of Ahania;* twelve large color prints, including *Newton* and *Elohim Creating Adam;* stops issuing illuminated books until 1802

1797   new edition of Edward Young's *Night-Thoughts,* with illustrations designed and engraved by Blake; watercolor illustrations for the poems of Thomas Gray; begins work on the manuscript of *Vala,* later retitled *The Four Zoas*

1798   begins annotating Sir Joshua Reynolds's *Discourses*

1799   paints fifty Bible illustrations for Thomas Butts, exhibits two of them at the Royal Academy

1800   moves to Felpham, Sussex, does various artistic jobs for William Hayley and his friends

1803   encounter with the soldier Schofield, indicted for sedition; returns to London; settles at 17 South Molton Street

1804   tried for seditious utterance, and acquitted; begins work on *Milton*

1805   designs illustrations for Robert Blair's *The Grave,* but the publisher, Robert Cromek, gives the commission instead to Louis Schiavonetti

1807   first of a series of paintings of the *Last Judgment;* watercolor series on *Paradise Lost;* painting of *The Canterbury Pilgrims*

1808   exhibits two watercolors at the Royal Academy; possible beginning of work on *Jerusalem*

1809   completes a set of illustrations for Milton's *Paradise Lost;* has small exhibition of paintings at his brother James's shop, 28 Broad Street; the exhibition and its accompanying *Descriptive Catalogue* are savagely reviewed by Robert Hunt in the *Examiner*

1810   *Public Address;* publishes engraving of *The Canterbury Pilgrims*

1811   first three copies of *Milton* (first publication of a new work since 1795)

1815   engravings of china designs for Josiah Wedgwood's catalog

1816   watercolor illustrations for Milton's *L'Allegro* and *Il Penseroso*

1818   fourth and final copy of *Milton; For the Sexes: The Gates of Paradise;* watercolor *Book of Job* illustrations for Butts; meets John Linnell

1819   begins drawing "visionary heads" for John Varley

1820   first three copies of *Jerusalem*

1821   final two copies of *Jerusalem,* including the only colored one; moves to 3 Fountain Court, the Strand

1824   watercolor illustrations for *Pilgrim's Progress;* meets Samuel Palmer and the other "Ancients"

1825   begins Dante illustrations for Linnell; conversations with Crabb Robinson

1826   *Illustrations of the Book of Job,* commissioned by Linnell; engraving of the *Laocoön* statue surrounded by aphoristic texts

1827   dies, August 12, probably of gallbladder and liver failure; buried in Bunhill Fields, the Dissenters' cemetery

1831   death of Catherine Blake; buried next to her husband

SHORT TITLES

Blake Records	G. E. Bentley Jr., *Blake Records,* 2nd ed. (New Haven: Yale University Press, 2004)
Blake Trust	David Bindman, gen. ed., *The Illuminated Books of William Blake,* 6 vols. (Princeton, NJ: The William Blake Trust and Princeton University Press, 1991–95): vol. 1: *Jerusalem: The Emanation of the Giant Albion;* vol. 2: *Songs of Innocence and of Experience;* vol. 3: *The Early Illuminated Books;* vol. 4: *The Continental Prophecies;* vol. 5: *Milton, A Poem;* vol. 6: *The Urizen Books*
E	David V. Erdman, ed., *The Complete Poetry and Prose of William Blake,* with commentary by Harold Bloom, 2nd ed. (Berkeley: University of California Press, 1982)
Gilchrist	Alexander Gilchrist, *The Life of William Blake,* ed. W. Graham Robertson (London: John Lane, The Bodley Head, 1907)
Illuminated Blake	David V. Erdman, *The Illuminated Blake* (New York: Anchor, 1974)
Marriage	*The Marriage of Heaven and Hell*
Urizen	*The Book of Urizen*
Visions	*Visions of the Daughters of Albion*

NOTES

INTRODUCTION

1. Arthur Schopenhauer, *The World as Will and Representation* (1819), ch. 31.
2. *Jerusalem* 3, E145.
3. G. E. Bentley Jr., *The Stranger from Paradise: A Biography of William Blake* (New Haven: Yale University Press, 2001), 381; *Blake Records,* 68.
4. Algernon Charles Swinburne, *William Blake: A Critical Essay,* ed. Hugh J. Luke (Lincoln: University of Nebraska Press, 1970), 276.
5. Blake to the Rev. Dr. Trusler, Aug. 23, 1799, E702; *Vision of the Last Judgment,* E560.
6. *Eternity,* E470.
7. Peter Ackroyd, *Blake* (New York: Alfred A. Knopf, 1996); Bentley, *Stranger from Paradise.* Ackroyd is excellent on London life in Blake's time and on his career as an artist; he is not very deeply grounded in Blake scholarship and has been rightly criticized for a number of errors. Bentley is the doyen of Blake scholarship and incomparably learned on every detail of Blake's life and works, but Ackroyd's biography may be more appealing to the general reader.
8. *Marriage* 14, E39; Plotinus' "last words to us" are quoted by William R. Inge, *The Philosophy of Plotinus,* vol. 1 (London: Longmans, Green, 1918), 10.
9. W. J. T. Mitchell, "Visible Language: Blake's Wond'rous Art of Writing," in *Romanticism and Contemporary Criticism,* ed. Morris Eaves and Michael Fischer (Ithaca, NY: Cornell University Press, 1986), 83.
10. Joseph Viscomi, *Blake and the Idea of the Book* (Princeton, NJ: Princeton University Press, 1993). On pages 375–81, Viscomi presents his chronology of all known copies, established from watermarks in the paper and other clues.
11. Michael Phillips, *William Blake: The Creation of the Songs from Manuscript to Illuminated Printing* (Princeton, NJ: Princeton University Press, 2000), 31.

12. Tristanne J. Connolly, *William Blake and the Body* (London: Palgrave Macmillan, 2002), 19.

13. David Fuller, *William Blake: Selected Poetry and Prose* (London: Pearson Longman, 2008), 21.

14. *Jerusalem* 13.21, E157; G. E. Bentley Jr., ed., *William Blake's Writings* (Oxford: Clarendon, 1978). An example of "and" instead of an ampersand is at *Urizen* 10.16, E75.

15. References are to the revised edition: David V. Erdman, ed., *The Complete Poetry and Prose of William Blake,* with commentary by Harold Bloom (Berkeley: University of California Press, 1982).

16. Alicia Ostriker, ed., *William Blake: The Complete Poems* (London: Penguin, 2004); W. H. Stevenson, ed., *Blake: The Complete Poems* (London: Pearson Longman, 2007). Once standard, but now superseded, is Geoffrey Keynes, ed., *Blake: Complete Writings* (Oxford: Oxford University Press, 1966).

CHAPTER 1: THE WORKING ARTIST

1. Details about the Blake family and their shop are drawn from G. E. Bentley Jr., *The Stranger from Paradise: A Biography of William Blake* (New Haven: Yale University Press, 2001), ch. 1.

2. John Blake is mentioned as "the evil one" in an 1802 poem (E721). It is not certain that he died abroad, but because he was not buried with the rest of the family, that seems most likely.

3. Gilchrist, 97; *Blake Records,* 663–64.

4. Notebook verses, E510; Morton D. Paley, *Energy and the Imagination: A Study in the Development of Blake's Thought* (Oxford: Clarendon, 1970), 206.

5. Blake to John Flaxman, Sept. 12, 1800, E707.

6. The evidence for the Moravian connection—suggestive but not conclusive—is summarized by John Beer, *William Blake: A Literary Life* (London: Palgrave Macmillan, 2005), 5–6.

7. *Blake Records,* 10–11, 699. Aileen Ward suggests that a degree of skepticism is appropriate for tales about Blake's childhood: "William Blake and the Hagiographers," in *Biography and Source Studies,* ed. Frederick R. Karl (New York: AMS, 1994), 13–14.

8. Bentley, *Stranger from Paradise,* 22; where not otherwise noted, biographical details are from this source. On Pars's school, see also Martin Myrone, *The Blake Book* (London: Tate, 2007), 15.

9. *Blake Records,* 16.

10. Robert N. Essick, *William Blake, Printmaker* (Princeton, NJ: Princeton University Press, 1980), 20.

11. *Public Address,* E582; Blake to William Hayley, Mar. 12, 1804, E743. On Blake's eyeglasses, see Joyce H. Townsend, ed., *William Blake: The Painter at Work* (London: Tate, 2003), 24.

12. Blake to George Cumberland, Dec. 6, 1795, E699; Blake to the Rev. John Trusler, Aug. 23, 1799, E703.

13. See D. W. Dörrbecker, "Innovative Reproduction: Painters and Engravers at the Royal Academy of Arts," in *Historicizing Blake,* ed. Steve Clark and David Worrall (London: St. Martin's, 1994), 125–46 (the quoted passage is at 130–31).

14. Blake to John Flaxman, Sept. 12, 1800, E707; Mrs. A. E. Bray, *Life of Thomas Stothard,* in *Blake Records,* 19–20; Bentley, *Stranger from Paradise,* 60.

15. Essick, *Blake, Printmaker,* 28.

16. Johann Caspar Lavater, *Essays on Physiognomy, Designed to Promote the Knowledge and the Love of Mankind,* 3 vols. in 5 (London, 1789–98), 1:159–60.

17. A melodramatic piece called *The Fall of Rosamond,* for instance, is executed in a delicate stipple technique that was fashionable among society ladies, and colored in pastel shades; see Myrone, *Blake Book,* 30–31.

18. Edward Young, "Conjectures on Original Composition," in *Eighteenth-Century English Literature,* ed. Geoffrey Tillotson et al. (New York: Harcourt Brace, 1969), 877.

19. *Blake Records,* 71.

20. This suggestion is made by Milton Klonsky, *William Blake: The Seer and His Visions* (New York: Harmony Books, 1977), 96.

21. Allan Cunningham, *Blake Records,* 638. John Mee comments on the differences between the watercolor and the engraving: "'As Portentous as the Written Wall': Blake's Illustrations to *Night Thoughts,*" in *Prophetic Character: Essays on William Blake in Honor of John E. Grant,* ed. Alexander S. Gourlay (West Cornwall, CT: Locust Hill, 2002), 178.

22. *Blake Records,* 632; Gilchrist, 117. *Blake Records,* 632. Henry Fuseli, a close friend of Blake's, said that Catherine had been a maidservant: *Blake Records,* 71.

23. *Blake Records,* 672; Shakespeare, *Othello* 1.3.171–72; Peter Ackroyd, *Blake* (New York: Alfred A. Knopf, 1996), 306–7.

24. Gilchrist, 334–35.

25. Robert N. Essick, "A (Self?) Portrait of William Blake," *Blake: An Illustrated Quarterly* 39, no. 3 (Winter 2005–6), 126–39; Bentley, *Stranger from Paradise,* pl. 88 caption.

26. *Blake Records,* 392, 684.

27. Gilchrist, 333. See Anne K. Mellor, "Physiognomy, Phrenology, and Blake's Visionary Heads," in *Blake in His Time,* ed. Robert N. Essick and Donald Pearce (Bloomington: Indiana University Press, 1978), 63–67.

28. See William M. Ivins Jr., *How Prints Look: Photographs with Commentary,* ed. Marjorie B. Cohn, rev. ed. (Boston: Beacon, 1987), 46.

29. *Public Address,* E574; Joseph Viscomi, *Blake and the Idea of the Book* (Princeton, NJ: Princeton University Press, 1993), 32.

30. *Blake Records,* 690.

31. *Marriage* 14, 27, E39, 45.

32. See Essick, *Blake, Printmaker,* 92; Michael Phillips, "The Printing of Blake's *America a Prophecy,*" *Print Quarterly* 21 (2004), 18–38; and Phillips's edition of *The Marriage of Heaven and Hell* (Oxford: Bodleian Library, 2011), 28–30.

33. E. H. Gombrich, *The Story of Art,* 16th ed. (London: Phaidon, 1995), 165.

34. *America* 3.15, E52.

35. See Viscomi, *Blake and the Idea of the Book*, 93, and Michael Phillips, "No. 13 Hercules Buildings, Lambeth," *British Art Journal* 5 (2004), 13–21.

36. On the printing process, see Essick, *Blake, Printmaker*, 25.

37. *Blake Records*, 690; Viscomi, *Blake and the Idea of the Book*, 129. On Blake's inks, see Viscomi, *Blake and the Idea of the Book*, 98; and on the watercolor paints that were used at the time, see Townsend, *Blake: The Painter at Work*, 42.

38. Phillips, "Printing of Blake's *America a Prophecy*."

39. Charles Babbage, *On the Economy of Machinery and Manufactures* (1832), 48, quoted by Saree Makdisi, *William Blake and the Impossible History of the 1790s* (Chicago: University of Chicago Press, 2003), 146.

40. Ivins, *How Prints Look*, 158.

41. On total sales, see G. E. Bentley Jr., "What Is the Price of Experience? William Blake and the Economics of Illuminated Printing," *University of Toronto Quarterly* 68 (1999), 617–41.

42. *Descriptive Catalogue*, E546–47; Morris Eaves, *William Blake's Theory of Art* (Princeton, NJ: Princeton University Press, 1982), 29.

43. On romantic classicism, see Anne K. Mellor, *Blake's Human Form Divine* (Berkeley: University of California Press, 1974), ch. 4, "Romantic Classicism and Blake's Art." On Flaxman and Blake, see Robert Rosenblum, *Transformations in Late Eighteenth Century Art* (Princeton, NJ: Princeton University Press, 1967), 183, 172.

44. *Descriptive Catalogue*, E550; on outline as moral, see Eaves, *William Blake's Theory of Art*, 5. Cumberland is quoted by David Bindman, *Blake as an Artist* (Oxford: Phaidon, 1977), 103.

45. Ralph Wornum, *Lectures on Painting* (1848), quoted by Morris Eaves, *The Counter-Arts Conspiracy: Art and Industry in the Age of Blake* (Ithaca, NY: Cornell University Press, 1992), 254; *Descriptive Catalogue*, E548; annotations to Reynolds, E655; Gombrich, *Story of Art*, 303.

46. *Descriptive Catalogue*, E538.

47. *Jerusalem* 38.23, E185 (the phrase "minute particulars" is repeated in eight other places in *Jerusalem*); *Vision of the Last Judgment*, E560. See Jenijoy La Belle, "Blake's Visions and Revisions of Michelangelo," in Essick and Pearce, *Blake in His Time*, 13–22, and Christopher Heppner, *Reading Blake's Designs* (Cambridge: Cambridge University Press, 1995), ch. 1.

48. Notebook puns, E510; *Public Address*, E580; annotations to Reynolds, E636, 641. See Eaves, *Counter-Arts Conspiracy*, 159–68.

49. Annotations to Reynolds, E641.

50. Sir Joshua Reynolds, "Discourse 3," in *Discourses on Art*, ed. Robert R. Wark (New Haven: Yale University Press, 1975), 44–45.

51. Annotations to Reynolds, E648, 656.

52. Annotations to Reynolds, E639. I discuss the problems in Reynolds's position in "Generality and Particularity," in *The Cambridge History of Literary Criticism*, vol. 4, *The Eighteenth Century*, ed. H. B. Nisbet and Claude Rawson (Cambridge: Cambridge University Press, 1997), 381–93.

53. *Descriptive Catalogue,* E541; Gilchrist, 94; annotations to Reynolds, E655; John Flaxman to William Hayley, *Blake Records,* 208.

54. Gilchrist, 247; Kingsley Amis, *The Alteration* (New York: Viking, 1976), 1–2.

55. *Examiner,* Sept. 17, 1809; *Blake Records,* 282–83.

56. David Fuller, *Blake's Heroic Argument* (London: Croom Helm, 1988), 19–20.

CHAPTER 2: HOW SHOULD WE UNDERSTAND BLAKE'S SYMBOLS?

1. *Descriptive Catalogue,* E541; *Vision of the Last Judgment,* E565–66. In a translation of Plato that Blake knew, "It is more proper to consider the eyes and ears as things through which, rather than as things by which, we perceive": *Theaetetus* 184c, in the 1804 translation of Thomas Taylor; see Kathleen Raine, *Blake and Tradition,* 2 vols. (Princeton, NJ: Princeton University Press, 1968), 2:120.

2. Blake to John Trusler, Aug. 23, 1799, E702; Trusler is quoted in a letter from Blake to George Cumberland, Aug. 26, 1799, E704. See also G. E. Bentley Jr., *The Stranger from Paradise: A Biography of William Blake* (New Haven: Yale University Press, 2001), 181–82.

3. William Butler Yeats, "William Blake and His Illustrations to *The Divine Comedy,*" in *Essays and Introductions* (New York: Macmillan, 1968), 119.

4. Thomas Gray, *Ode on . . . Eton College,* lines 21–30.

5. Samuel Johnson, "The Life of Gray," in *Lives of the English Poets,* ed. G. B. Hill (Oxford: Clarendon, 1905), 434–35; William Wordsworth, *Ode: Intimations of Immortality,* lines 200–203.

6. *Macbeth* 1.8; Cleanth Brooks, *The Well-Wrought Urn* (New York: Harcourt, Brace and World, 1947), 29.

7. Christopher Heppner suggests possible alternative titles: "Reading Blake's Designs: *Pity* and *Hecate,*" *Bulletin of Research in the Humanities* 84 (1981), 339. See also David L. Clark, "How to Do Things with Shakespeare: Illustrative Theory and Practice in Blake's *Pity,*" in *Blake 2.0: William Blake in Twentieth-Century Art, Music and Culture,* ed. Steve Clark, Tristanne Connally, and Jason Whittaker (London: Palgrave Macmillan, 2012), 106–33.

8. Gilchrist, "Supplement," 407.

9. Christopher Heppner, *Reading Blake's Designs* (Cambridge: Cambridge University Press, 1995), 114. Heppner's extended commentary on this picture is especially valuable.

10. John Milton, *L'Allegro,* lines 73–74, 91–98; Blake's descriptions of his illustrations to *L'Allegro* and *Il Penseroso,* E683.

11. See Heppner, *Reading Blake's Designs,* 268.

12. See John E. Grant, "Blake's Designs for *L'Allegro* and *Il Penseroso,*" in *The Visionary Hand: Essays for the Study of William Blake's Art and Aesthetics,* ed. Robert N. Essick (Los Angeles: Hennessey and Ingalls, 1973), 430.

13. *Four Zoas* 70.12–17, E346; the "man of sorrows" in Isaiah 53:3 was taken to be an anticipation of Christ.

14. David Hume, *The Natural History of Religion,* ed. H. E. Root (Stanford, CA: Stanford University Press, 1957), 29.

15. *Marriage* 11, E38.

CHAPTER 3: INNOCENCE

1. Inscription in the *Four Zoas* manuscript, E697.

2. Cunningham, *Blake Records,* 637; John Harvey, "Blake's Art," *Cambridge Quarterly* 7 (1977), 133.

3. Peter Berger, "The Comic as a Signal of Transcendence," *Redeeming Laughter: The Comic Dimension of Human Experience* (New York: Walter de Gruyter, 1997), 213. On the tree of knowledge, see Andrew Lincoln in Blake Trust, 2:143.

4. Isaac Watts is quoted by John Holloway, *Blake: The Lyric Poetry* (London: Edward Arnold, 1968), 48–49, and John Wesley by E. P. Thompson, *The Making of the English Working Class* (New York: Vintage, 1963), 375.

5. These and others are cited by Zachary Leader in a survey of progressive educational theory in Blake's time: *Reading Blake's Songs* (London: Routledge and Kegan Paul, 1981), 149 and fig. 7.

6. Annotations to Reynolds, E650. The final word was accidentally cut away by a bookbinder, but "body" is the best guess (probably not "form," since that would repeat "formed").

7. *Introduction,* E7; *Marriage,* E36.

8. John Thomas Smith, *Nollekens and His Times* (1828); Alan Cunningham, *Lives of the Most Eminent British Painters, Sculptors, and Architects* (1830); both in *Blake Records,* 606, 633.

9. E16.

10. Quoted by Constantine Fitzgibbon, *The Life of Dylan Thomas* (Boston: Little, Brown, 1965), 323–24.

11. William Cowper, *The Poplar Field,* in *Poetical Works,* ed. H. S. Milford, 4th ed. (London: Oxford University Press, 1967), 362; *The Ecchoing Green,* lines 11–20, E8.

12. See Walter S. Minot, "Blake's 'Infant Joy': An Explanation of Age," *Blake: An Illustrated Quarterly* 25, no. 2 (Fall 1991), 78, and Heather Glen, *Vision and Disenchantment: Blake's Songs and Wordsworth's Lyrical Ballads* (Cambridge: Cambridge University Press, 1983), 25–26, 131–32.

13. Erasmus Darwin, *The Botanic Garden, Part II, The Loves of the Plants* (1789), 2, 26. On the anemone as the flower of Adonis, see Kathleen Raine, *Blake and Tradition,* 2 vols. (Princeton, NJ: Princeton University Press, 1968), 1:108.

14. *Visions* 6.4–5, E49; see Mary Lynn Johnson, "Feminist Approaches to Teaching *Songs,*" in *Approaches to Teaching Blake's Songs of Innocence and of Experience,* ed. Robert F. Gleckner and Mark L. Greenberg (New York: MLA, 1989), 61; Helen P. Bruder, "Blake and Gender Studies," in *Palgrave Advances in William Blake Studies,* ed. Nicolas M. Williams (London: Palgrave Mac-

millan, 2006), 137–38; and Robert N. Essick's commentary to his edition of *Songs of Innocence and of Experience* (San Marino, CA: Huntington Library, 2008), 34–35.

15. *Illuminated Blake*, 69.

16. *Illuminated Blake*, 52; Dylan Thomas, *The Force That through the Green Fuse Drives the Flower*.

17. *The Blossom*, E10; *Marriage*, E36.

18. The "clockwise" interpretation is David Wagenknecht's: *Blake's Night: William Blake and the Idea of Pastoral* (Cambridge, MA: Harvard University Press, 1973), 58–59; *Illuminated Blake*, 52. The halo-sun can be seen in copy Y in the Blake Archive, and in the Kings College, Cambridge, copy reproduced in Blake Trust 2:pl. 11.

19. G. E. Bentley Jr., "Blake's Pronunciation," *Studies in Philology* 107 (2010), 114–29.

20. E8–9.

21. *Four Zoas* 18.1–3, E310.

22. E17.

23. *Holy Thursday*, E13 (and see *The Little Black Boy*, E9); Revelation 19:6; Hebrews 13:2.

24. Stephen C. Behrendt, *Reading William Blake* (London: Macmillan, 1992), 54.

25. E10.

26. See Martin K. Nurmi, "Fact and Symbol in 'The Chimney Sweeper' of Blake's *Songs of Innocence*," in *Blake: A Collection of Critical Essays*, ed. Northrop Frye (Englewood Cliffs, NJ: Prentice-Hall, 1966), 15–22.

27. See David V. Erdman, *Blake: Prophet against Empire*, 3rd ed. (Princeton, NJ: Princeton University Press, 1977), 132.

28. Glen, *Vision and Disenchantment*, 96–101, 363.

29. Zachary Leader, *Reading Blake's Songs* (London: Routledge and Kegan Paul, 1981), 47.

30. Edward Larrissy invokes ideology in this nonjudgmental sense: *William Blake* (Oxford: Basil Blackwell, 1985), 19–20, 29.

31. Raine, *Blake and Tradition*, 1:25–26, quoting Emanuel Swedenborg, *Concerning the Earths in Our Solar System* (1758).

32. *Auguries of Innocence*, E490.

33. Noted by Alexander Gourlay, "'More on Blake's Auguries,'" *Notes and Queries* (December 2011), 523.

CHAPTER 4: EXPERIENCE

1. *Europe* 5.7, E62; see Andrew Lincoln's commentary on the *Experience* frontispiece, Blake Trust, 2:172.

2. *Marriage* 14, E39.

3. E28. See Angela Esterhammer, *Creating States: Studies in the Performative Language of John Milton and William Blake* (Toronto: University of Toronto Press, 1994), 144.

4. E29–30; Romans 7:7.

5.   E26.

6.   *Ah! Sun-Flower,* E25.

7.   Harold Bloom, *Blake's Apocalypse: A Study in Poetic Argument* (Garden City, NY: Doubleday, 1963), 135; *The Sick Rose,* E23; Stephen Cox, *Love and Logic: The Evolution of Blake's Thought* (Ann Arbor: University of Michigan Press, 1992), 109.

8.   Samuel Richardson, *Clarissa, or the History of a Young Lady,* ed. Angus Ross (London: Penguin, 1985), 892 (letter 261).

9.   Matthew Prior, *A True Maid,* in *The Literary Works of Matthew Prior,* ed. H. Bunker Wright and Monroe K. Spears, 2 vols. (Oxford: Clarendon, 1959), 1:455.

10. Susanne Langer, *Feeling and Form: A Theory of Art* (New York: Scribner, 1953), 260.

11. *Marriage* 14, E39.

12. *The Clod and the Pebble,* E19.

13. *Marriage* 7, E36; *The Everlasting Gospel,* E518. Paul is cited by Mary Lynn Johnson and John E. Grant in their edition of *Blake's Poetry and Designs* (New York: W. W. Norton, 2008), 31; on self-abnegation I follow the suggestion of David Fuller, *Blake's Heroic Argument* (London: Croom Helm, 1988), 11.

14. Bloom, *Blake's Apocalypse,* 133.

15. E24–25.

16. Alexander Welsh, *Roots of Lyric: Primitive Poetry and Modern Poetics* (Princeton, NJ: Princeton University Press, 1978), 8–9; *Paradise Lost* 1.25–26. B. H. Fairchild comments on Blake's trochees: *Such Holy Song: Music as Idea, Form, and Image in the Poetry of William Blake* (Kent, OH: Kent State University Press, 1980), 36–37.

17. *Public Address,* E576. The crossed-out lines were recovered by David V. Erdman and Donald K. Moore, *The Notebook of William Blake: A Photographic and Typographic Facsimile* (Oxford: Clarendon, 1973), 109. The 1771 *Britannica* article is quoted by John E. Grant in a masterly article to which my comments are much indebted: "This Is Not Blake's 'The Tyger,'" *Iowa Review* 19 (1989), 112–15.

18. Fuller, *Blake's Heroic Argument,* 82.

19. *Paradise Lost* 2.634–35. On the spears as beams of light, see Nelson Hilton, *Literal Imagination: Blake's Vision of Words* (Berkeley: University of California Press, 1983), 175–77.

20. *Marriage* 6, E35.

21. *Illuminated Blake,* 84; I am indebted also to Stephen C. Behrendt, "'Something in My Eye': Irritants in Blake's Illuminated Texts," in *Blake in the Nineties,* ed. Steve Clark and David Worrall (New York: St. Martin's, 1999), 88.

22. Bloom, *Blake's Apocalypse,* 137; Jean H. Hagstrum, *William Blake: Poet and Painter* (Chicago: University of Chicago Press, 1964), 86. Tigers are pictured in Erdman and Moore, *Notebook of William Blake,* Notebook p. 2.

23. *Night,* lines 33–40, E14.

24. E22–23.

25. E12–13, 27; Mark Twain, *Huckleberry Finn*, ch. 19. The mention of chimney sweeps forbidden to enter churches is from Jonas Hanway, *A Sentimental History of Chimney Sweepers in London and Westminster* (1785), quoted by Martin K. Nurmi, "Fact and Symbol in 'The Chimney Sweeper' of Blake's *Songs of Innocence*," in *Blake: A Collection of Critical Essays*, ed. Northrop Frye (Englewood Cliffs, NJ: Prentice-Hall, 1966), 18.

26. E26–27.

27. James Joyce, lecture on Blake (translated from an Italian original), in *James Joyce: The Critical Writings*, ed. Ellsworth Mason and Richard Ellmann (New York: Viking, 1959), 215. Joyce did not realize that Blake was referring to Saint James's Palace; Buckingham Palace was not yet the royal residence.

28. Ezekiel 9:4–6; there is a similar passage at Revelation 13:16.

29. George Orwell, "Charles Dickens," in *A Collection of Essays* (New York: Doubleday Anchor Books, 1954), 71; Michael Ferber, "'London' and Its Politics," *ELH* 48 (1981), 310.

30. *Jerusalem* 84.11–12, 15–16, E243.

31. Preface to *The Revolt of Islam* (1818) in *The Complete Poetical Works of Percy Bysshe Shelley*, ed. Thomas Hutchinson (London: Oxford University Press, 1943), 33; P. B. Shelley, *Julian and Maddalo: A Conversation*, 182; *Four Zoas* 71.11, E348; Steve Biko, "White Racism and Black Consciousness," in *I Write What I Like* (Chicago: University of Chicago Press, 1978).

32. *Jerusalem* 69.34–35, 57.8–10, E223, 207; T. S. Eliot, "A Dialogue on Dramatic Poetry," in *Selected Essays* (London: Faber and Faber, 1951), 47.

33. John Holloway, *Blake: The Lyric Poetry* (London: Edward Arnold, 1968), 30; Bloom, *Blake's Apocalypse*, 142. On venereal disease and tears, see G. C. Roti and D. L. Kent, "The Last Stanza of Blake's 'London,'" *Blake: An Illustrated Quarterly* 11 (1977), 19–21.

34. *Marriage* 8, E36.

35. *Auguries of Innocence*, E492; David Punter, "Blake and the Shapes of London," *Criticism* 23 (1981), 7. Gavin Edwards notes the range of Blake's indictments: "Mind-Forg'd Manacles: A Contribution to the Discussion of Blake's 'London,'" *Literature and History* 5 (1979), 88.

36. Annotations to Reynolds, E636.

37. *Blake Records*, 396.

38. G. E. Bentley Jr., *The Stranger from Paradise: A Biography of William Blake* (New Haven: Yale University Press, 2001), 286; John Thomas Smith, *Nollekens and His Times* (1828), *Blake Records*, 619.

39. *Blake Records*, 438, 312–13, 337.

40. Charles Burney in the *Monthly Review* (June 1799), 202, quoted by Heather Glen, *Vision and Disenchantment: Blake's Songs and Wordsworth's Lyrical Ballads* (Cambridge: Cambridge University Press, 1983), 2. On the ranking of poets in Blake's time, see the comments by Nicolas M. Williams and Edward Larrissy in *Palgrave Advances in William Blake Studies*, ed. Williams (London: Palgrave Macmillan, 2006), 1, 256.

41. *Four Zoas* 35:11–15, E325.

CHAPTER 5: REVOLUTION

1. Acts 17:6; Revelation 14:6.

2. E. P. Thompson wrote the classic *Making of the English Working Class* (New York: Vintage, 1963); his *Witness against the Beast: William Blake and the Moral Law* (Cambridge: Cambridge University Press, 1993) was published shortly after his death. Jon Mee gives a valuable review of what we know and don't know about Blake and the radical underground: *Dangerous Enthusiasm: William Blake and the Culture of Radicalism in the 1790s* (Oxford: Clarendon, 1992).

3. Annotations to Bishop Watson, E617; *Vision of the Last Judgment,* E560, quoting Numbers 11:19. Richard Brothers's bizarre career is described by Morton D. Paley, "William Blake, the Prince of the Hebrews, and the Woman Clothed with the Sun," in *William Blake: Essays in Honour of Sir Geoffrey Keynes,* ed. Paley and Michael Phillips (Oxford: Clarendon, 1973), 260–93.

4. Robert N. Essick gives an authoritative account of the several states of this print: *William Blake, Printmaker* (Princeton, NJ: Princeton University Press, 1980), 70–74.

5. Gilchrist, 33; *Albion Rose* inscription, E671; *There Is No Natural Religion* [b], E2.

6. Milton, *Samson Agonistes,* line 41; *Areopagitica* in *The Complete Prose Works of John Milton,* ed. Don M. Wolfe et al., vol. 2 (New Haven: Yale University Press, 1959), 557–58.

7. On "invenit" and "sculpsit," see Essick, *Blake, Printmaker,* 70, and Morris Eaves, *The Counter-Arts Conspiracy: Art and Industry in the Age of Blake* (Ithaca, NY: Cornell University Press, 1992), 110.

8. The historical context is reviewed by David V. Erdman, *Blake: Prophet against Empire,* 3rd ed. (Princeton, NJ: Princeton University Press, 1977), 7–11; Burke is quoted from the 1796 *Letter to a Noble Lord.*

9. W. J. T. Mitchell, "Style as Epistemology: Blake and the Movement toward Abstraction in Romantic Art," *Studies in Romanticism* 16 (1977), 153; the second comment is in Mitchell's *Blake's Composite Art: A Study of the Illuminated Poetry* (Princeton, NJ: Princeton University Press, 1978), 55. Tatham, *Blake Records,* 673.

10. See Essick, *Blake, Printmaker,* 182–83, and Joseph Anthony Wittreich, *Angel of Apocalypse: Blake's Idea of Milton* (Madison: University of Wisconsin Press, 1975), 56–60.

11. See Joseph Viscomi, "The Lessons of Swedenborg; or, The Origin of William Blake's *The Marriage of Heaven and Hell,*" in *Lessons of Romanticism: A Critical Companion,* ed. Thomas Pfau and Robert F. Gleckner (Durham, NC: Duke University Press, 1998), 182–84.

12. *Marriage* 3, E34.

13. Gilchrist, 90.

14. Michael Phillips reproduces an enlargement of these two figures in his edition of *The Marriage of Heaven and Hell* (Oxford: Bodleian Library, 2011), 88.

15. My comments are indebted to Blake Trust, 3:131.

16. Edmund Burke, *Reflections on the Revolution in France,* ed. Conor Cruise O'Brien (London: Penguin, 1969), 194–95; Thomas Paine, *The Rights of Man,* in *Common Sense and Other Political Writings,* ed. Nelson F. Adkins (New York: Liberal Arts Press, 1953), 77, 80; *Marriage* 7, E35.

---

17.   *Jerusalem* 45:9–12, E194.

18.   *Marriage* 7–10, E35–38. The difference between Blake's proverbs and traditional ones is explored by John Villalobos, "William Blake's *Proverbs of Hell* and the Tradition of Wisdom Literature," *Studies in Philology* 87 (1990), 246–59, and by Mike Goode, "Blakespotting," *PMLA* 121 (2006), 769–86.

19.   See Michael Phillips, "The Printing of Blake's *America a Prophecy*," *Print Quarterly* 21 (2004), 29.

20.   For helpful interpretations, see *Illuminated Blake*, 139; Blake Trust, 4:50–52; and Leslie Tannenbaum, *Biblical Tradition in Blake's Early Prophecies: The Great Code of Art* (Princeton, NJ: Princeton University Press, 1982), 135. I explore affinities between Prometheus and the crucified Christ in *Symbol and Truth in Blake's Myth* (Princeton, NJ: Princeton University Press, 1980), 107–11.

21.   *Europe* 5.6, E62; *Jerusalem* 30.57, E177; *Tiriel* 8.11, E285.

22.   *America* 2.1–7, E52; *Song of Solomon* 3:4.

23.   *America* 8.13–14, E54; on sales of *America*, see Andrew Lincoln, "From *America* to *The Four Zoas*," in *The Cambridge Companion to William Blake*, ed. Morris Eaves (Cambridge: Cambridge University Press, 2003), 210, and David Worrall, "Blake and 1790s Plebeian Radical Culture," in *Blake in the Nineties*, ed. Steve Clark and David Worrall (New York: St. Martin's, 1999), 195.

24.   *America* 14.10–19; see Erdman, *Blake: Prophet against Empire*, 57n. An important theme in Saree Makdisi's *William Blake and the Impossible History of the 1790s* (Chicago: University of Chicago Press, 2003) is Blake's emphasis on revolutionary goals far more radical than the American leaders envisioned.

25.   *Marriage* 10, E37; Christopher Z. Hobson, *Blake and Homosexuality* (New York: Palgrave, 2000), 45.

26.   *America* 6.1–15; Matthew 24:41, 27:66; John 20:17; Ezekiel 37:7–10.

27.   Makdisi, *Blake and the Impossible History*, 182–83, makes the point about activity and stasis. Some possible references for the small creatures are given in *Illuminated Blake*, 144, and in Blake Trust, 4:58.

28.   W. M. Rossetti, appendix to Gilchrist, 423; *The French Revolution* 10.189, E294; *Song of Los* 6.6, E68; *King Lear* 3.2.4; Mitchell, *Blake's Composite Art*, 59.

29.   *America* 8.1–6, E54.

30.   Essick makes this point: *Blake, Printmaker*, 144.

31.   Northrop Frye, *Fearful Symmetry: A Study of William Blake* (Princeton, NJ: Princeton University Press, 1947), 207–35; Milton O. Percival, *William Blake's Circle of Destiny* (New York: Columbia University Press, 1938), 31. Frye's "Orc cycle" is trenchantly critiqued by Christopher Z. Hobson, *The Chained Boy: Orc and Blake's Idea of Revolution* (Lewisburg, PA: Bucknell University Press, 1999), 48 ff.

32.   I originally proposed this distinction between iconic and dynamic symbols in *Symbol and Truth in Blake's Myth*, 79 ff.

33.   *Illuminated Blake*, 157; Morton D. Paley, *Energy and the Imagination: A Study of the Development of Blake's Thought* (Oxford: Clarendon, 1970), 79.

34. *Europe* 10.16–23, E63.

35. The Herculaneum image is mentioned by Milton Klonsky, *William Blake: The Seer and His Visions* (New York: Harmony Books, 1977), 51.

36. *America* 7.3–5, E53, and 6.15, E53.

37. James Hall, *Michelangelo and the Reinvention of the Human Body* (New York: Farrar, Straus and Giroux, 2005), xvi.

38. Kenneth Clark, *The Nude: A Study in Ideal Form* (New York: Pantheon, 1956), 29; *Europe* 9.8, E63. W. J. T. Mitchell suggests the visual pun on "blasts": "Style as Epistemology: Blake and the Movement toward Abstraction in Romantic Art," *Studies in Romanticism* 16 (1977), 154.

39. *America* 2.18–21, E52; the "vales of Kent" refers to the Old Kent Road in London, not to the county of that name. When Blake printed *America* again in 1807 he masked these lines so they did not appear, but they show up once more in the final copy of 1821. A Welsh bard refusing to play his harp for the conqueror is the subject of a then-famous poem by Thomas Gray, *The Bard*, which Blake would later illustrate.

40. Royal proclamation and Stationers' Company resolution quoted by Michael Phillips, "Blake and the Terror, 1792–93," *Library*, 6th ser., no. 16 (December 1994), 266, 272; see also Stephen C. Behrendt, "History When Time Stops: Blake's *America, Europe,* and *The Song of Los,*" *Papers on Language and Literature* 28 (1992), 379–97.

41. Notebook entry, E694; annotations to Watson, E611.

42. *Public Address*, E580.

43. Jacob Bronowski, *William Blake and the Age of Revolution* (New York: Harper, 1965), 3.

44. *Marriage* 3, E34.

CHAPTER 6: ATOMS AND VISIONARY INSIGHT

1. E477–78.

2. *Blake Records*, 703.

3. E. A. Burtt, *The Metaphysical Foundations of Modern Physical Science* (London: Routledge, 1950), 236–37.

4. Annotations to Lavater, E595.

5. Alexander Pope, *Epitaph Intended for Sir Isaac Newton, in Westminster Abbey;* William Wordsworth, *The Prelude* (1850 version), 3.61–63.

6. Isaac Newton, *Opticks* (New York: Dover, 1952), 400; the quotation about "sands on the shore" comes from Charles C. Gillispie, *The Edge of Objectivity: An Essay in the History of Scientific Ideas* (Princeton, NJ: Princeton University Press, 1960), 132.

7. *Auguries of Innocence*, E490; Jacob Boehme, *Mysterium Magnum; or, An Exposition of the First Book of Moses Called Genesis*, in the 1654 translation of John Sparrow, vol. 1 (London, 1965), 4; *Blake Records*, 404, 343; Robert Frost, *After Apple-Picking*, line 9.

8. Annotations to Lavater, E592; Ludwig Wittgenstein, *Tractatus Logico-Philosophicus*, trans. D. F.

Pears and B. F. McGuinness (London: Routledge and Kegan Paul, 1961), 147; *Marriage* 7, E36; *Milton* 24.72–73, E121.

9. On a source in Michelangelo, see Jenijoy La Belle, "Michelangelo's Sistine Frescoes and Blake's 1795 Color-Printed Drawings," *Blake: An Illustrated Quarterly* 14, no. 1 (Summer 1980), 81.

10. *Blake Records,* 500.

11. *Blake Records* (Frederick Tatham), 48; on Blake's printing technique, see Martin Myrone, *The Blake Book* (London: Tate, 2007), 81.

12. Mark Crosby, "'The Sculptor Silent Stands before His Forming Image': Blake and Contemporary Sculpture," in *Blake 2.0: William Blake in Twentieth-Century Art, Music and Culture,* ed. Steve Clark, Tristanne Connally, and Jason Whittaker (London: Palgrave Macmillan, 2012), 127.

CHAPTER 7: "THE GATE IS OPEN"

1. Blake to George Cumberland, Sept. 1, 1800, *Blake Records,* 97; printed with a facsimile by Robert N. Essick and Morton D. Paley, "'Dear Generous Cumberland': A Newly Discovered Letter and Poem by William Blake," *Blake: An Illustrated Quarterly* 32, no. 1 (Summer 1998), 4–13.

2. Blake to William Hayley, Dec. 18, 1804, E759; see Robert W. Rix, "Healing the Spirit: William Blake and Magnetic Religion," *Romanticism on the Net* 25 (February 2002), http://id.erudit.org /iderudit/006011ar.

3. Blake to Thomas Butts, Sept. 23, 1800, E711; Butts to Blake, undated, *Blake Records,* 101.

4. Blake to Butts, Oct. 2, 1800, E712–13; W. T. Stace, *Mysticism and Philosophy* (Philadelphia: Lippincott, 1960), 61. See also Arnold M. Ludwig, "Altered States of Consciousness," *General Psychiatry* 15 (1966), 25–34.

5. *Vision of the Last Judgment,* E565–66; Isaiah 6:3; Thomas Gray, *The Progress of Poesy,* 2.1.

6. Gilchrist, 159, 196.

7. E504, 506; *Henry IV, Part I* 3.2.25.

8. *Milton* 41.8, E142; Paul Youngquist, *Madness and Blake's Myth* (University Park: Pennsylvania State University Press, 1989), 19.

9. Blake to Cumberland, July 2, 1800, E706–7.

10. *Milton* 4.26, E98.

11. Blake to Butts, Aug. 16, 1803, E733; Matthew 25:29–30.

12. *To H——,* E506; *Fair Elenor,* line 68, in *Poetical Sketches,* E412. I have argued for the schizoid interpretation in *Symbol and Truth in Blake's Myth* (Princeton, NJ: Princeton University Press, 1980), 311–13; Robert N. Essick likewise suggests "a mild form of schizophrenia" in "*Jerusalem* and Blake's Final Works," in *The Cambridge Companion to William Blake,* ed. Morris Eaves (Cambridge: Cambridge University Press, 2003), 257.

13. Hayley to Lady Hesketh, Aug. 3, 1805, *Blake Records,* 205–6.

14. Annotations to Spurzheim, E663; R. D. Laing, *The Politics of Experience* (New York: Vintage, 1976), 67.

15. Blake to Butts, Jan. 10, 1803, E724.

16. Blake to Hayley, Oct. 23, 1804, E756; see Morton D. Paley, "The Truchsessian Gallery Revisited," *Studies in Romanticism* 16 (1977), 265–77.

17. Michelangelo quoted by James Hall, *Michelangelo and the Reinvention of the Human Body* (New York: Farrar, Straus and Giroux, 2005), 108.

CHAPTER 8: UNDERSTANDING BLAKE'S MYTH

1. Sigmund Freud, "Fragment of an Analysis of a Case of Hysteria" and "A Difficulty in the Path of Psychoanalysis," in *The Standard Edition of the Complete Psychological Works of Sigmund Freud*, ed. James Strachey, 24 vols. (London: Hogarth, 1953–74), 7:109, 17:143; *Jerusalem* 39.41–42, E187.

2. Anthony Storr, *The Dynamics of Creation* (New York: Atheneum, 1972), 196; William Hayley, *An Essay on Epic Poetry* (1782), 3.114, 5.268–70, quoted by Joseph A. Wittreich, *Angel of Apocalypse: Blake's Idea of Milton* (Madison: University of Wisconsin Press, 1975), 235–36.

3. *Jerusalem* 10.20–21, 11.5, E153–54. Nelson Hilton makes the point about "striving with" in "Blakean Zen," *Studies in Romanticism* 24 (1985), 183.

4. *Jerusalem* 5.16–22, E147.

5. Blake to Thomas Butts, Nov. 22, 1802, E722; *Milton* 30.1–3, 8–14, E129.

6. Brian Wilkie and Mary Lynn Johnson, *Blake's Four Zoas: The Design of a Dream* (Cambridge, MA: Harvard University Press, 1978), 1. Morris Eaves has said, "It takes the massive intellectual pressure of a Northrop Frye to bind Blake's formidable difficulties into an illusion of total coherence, which inevitably falls into contradictions, fragments, and dead ends as soon as the pressure lets up": "On Blakes We Want and Blakes We Don't," *Huntington Library Quarterly* 58 (1995), 415–17.

7. *Jerusalem* 77, E231; Morris Eaves, quoted by Kari Kraus, "'Once Only Imagined': An Interview with Morris Eaves, Robert N. Essick, and Joseph Viscomi," *Studies in Romanticism* 41 (2002), 161; Andrew Lincoln, "From *America* to *The Four Zoas*," in *The Cambridge Companion to William Blake*, ed. Morris Eaves (Cambridge: Cambridge University Press, 2003), 210.

8. Samuel Taylor Coleridge to H. F. Cary, Feb. 6, 1818, and to Charles Augustus Tulk; both in *Blake Records*, 336. Some commentators assume that "anacalyptic" is simply a synonym for "apocalyptic," but that seems wrong. I proposed my interpretation of this word in *Symbol and Truth in Blake's Myth* (Princeton, NJ: Princeton University Press, 1980), 74, and Nicholas M. Williams has recently concurred in the introduction to his collection *Palgrave Advances in William Blake Studies* (London: Palgrave Macmillan, 2006), 1.

9. Vincent A. De Luca, *Words of Eternity: Blake and the Poetics of the Sublime* (Princeton, NJ: Princeton University Press, 1991), 61; B. H. Fairchild, *Such Holy Song: Music as Idea, Form, and Image in the Poetry of William Blake* (Kent, OH: Kent State University Press, 1980), 85–86; Nelson Hilton, "Literal / *Tiriel* / Material," in *Critical Paths: Blake and the Argument of Method*, ed. Dan Miller, Mark Bracher, and Donald Ault (Durham, NC: Duke University Press, 1987), 99.

10. Alcuin, *Commentariorum in Apocalypsim*, quoted by Barbara Nolan, *The Gothic Visionary Perspective* (Princeton, NJ: Princeton University Press, 1977), 7.

11. *Jerusalem* 3, E145–46; *Four Zoas* 34.77, E324; Arthur Golding, *Metamorphoses* 15.984–95; *Four Zoas* 3.1–3, E300.

12. *Four Zoas* 61.24–31, E341–42; David Fuller, *Blake's Heroic Argument* (London: Croom Helm, 1988), 92. (I have altered his patterning slightly.)

13. *Milton* 1, E95–96; Numbers 11:29.

14. Isaiah 52:7.

15. 2 Kings 2:11; *Vision of the Last Judgment*, E560. On active response, see Stephen C. Behrendt, "'Something in My Eye': Irritants in Blake's Illuminated Texts," in *Blake in the Nineties*, ed. Steve Clark and David Worrall (New York: St. Martin's, 1999), 85. My comments are indebted as well to Nancy M. Goslee, "'In Englands Green & Pleasant Land': The Building of Vision in Blake's Stanzas from 'Milton,'" *Studies in Romanticism* 13 (1974), 105–25.

16. Song of the New Model Army, quoted by A. L. Morton, *The Everlasting Gospel: A Study in the Sources of William Blake* (London: Lawrence and Wishart, 1958), 59; *Jerusalem* 34.14–15, E180.

17. *Jerusalem* 65.12–24, E216; the French visitor to the Carron ironworks in Scotland in 1784 is quoted by Michael Ferber, *The Social Vision of William Blake* (Princeton, NJ: Princeton University Press, 1985), 136–37.

18. A. D. Nuttall, *The Alternative Trinity: Gnostic Heresy in Marlowe, Milton, and Blake* (Oxford: Clarendon, 1998), 226.

19. See Michael Ferber, "Blake's 'Jerusalem' as a Hymn," *Blake: An Illustrated Quarterly* 34, no. 3 (Winter 2000–2001), 82–94. Ferber offers a detailed analysis of how Parry's score brings out the force of Blake's words. David Cameron is quoted by Susan Matthews, "'And *Did* Those Feet'? Blake and the Role of the Artist in Post-War Britain," in *Blake 2.0: William Blake in Twentieth-Century Art, Music and Culture*, ed. Steve Clark, Tristanne Connally, and Jason Whittaker (London: Palgrave Macmillan, 2012), 161.

20. Jez Butterworth, *Jerusalem* (London: Nick Hern Books, 2009), 78.

21. *Blake Records*, 310; *Four Zoas* 122.16–20, E391.

22. *Jerusalem* 27.1–36, E171–72; Gilchrist, 7; details from David V. Erdman, *Blake: Prophet against Empire*, 3rd ed. (Princeton, NJ: Princeton University Press, 1977), 288–90, 472–75, and Morton D. Paley, *The Continuing City: William Blake's Jerusalem* (Oxford: Clarendon, 1983), 75. Peter Ackroyd, *Blake* (New York: Alfred A. Knopf, 1996), 32–33, traces a typical route that Blake might have followed.

23. Details from S. Foster Damon, *A Blake Dictionary: The Ideas and Symbols of William Blake* (reprint ed., Boulder, CO: Shambhala, 1979; orig. publ. Brown University Press, 1965), 246, and Anne Janowitz, *England's Ruins: Poetic Purpose and the National Landscape* (Oxford: Blackwell, 1990), 165. On executions, see Douglas Hay et al., eds., *Albion's Fatal Tree: Crime and Society in Eighteenth-Century England* (New York: Pantheon, 1975).

24. *Milton* 25.48–55, E122.

25. Michael Phillips, "No. 13 Hercules Buildings, Lambeth," *British Art Journal* 5 (2004), 13–21.

26. *Four Zoas* 95.26–28, E360–61; details from David V. Erdman, "Lambeth and Bethlehem in Blake's Jerusalem," *Modern Philology* 48 (1951), 184–92.

27. *Jerusalem* 24.25, 29–35, E169; Zechariah 11:13; *Jerusalem* 52, E201; *Four Zoas* 109.5–6, E378.

CHAPTER 9: THE ZOAS AND OURSELVES

1. Revelation 4:6.

2. *Four Zoas* 4.6, E301.

3. I adapt this formulation from Diana Hume George, *Blake and Freud* (Ithaca, NY: Cornell University Press, 1980), 79. Freud's analogy of the unruly mob is quoted from his "My Contact with Josef Popper-Lynkeus" by Philip Rieff, *Freud: The Mind of the Moralist* (New York: Anchor, 1961), 63.

4. Ezekiel 1:1, 4–6, 10–11, 16–18.

5. See David Bindman, "Blake as a Painter," in *The Cambridge Companion to William Blake,* ed. Morris Eaves (Cambridge: Cambridge University Press, 2003), 98; the Raphael painting is in the Palatine Gallery, Palazzo Pitti, Florence.

6. G. E. Bentley Jr., *The Stranger from Paradise: A Biography of William Blake* (New Haven: Yale University Press, 2001), pl. 77 caption.

7. *Jerusalem* 15.18–20, E159.

8. *Four Zoas* 3.4–6, E300–301; John 17:21, 1:14.

9. *Milton* 21.8–10, E115.

10. *Four Zoas* 44.5–45.3, E329–30; Andrew Lincoln, *Spiritual History: A Reading of William Blake's Vala, or The Four Zoas* (Oxford: Clarendon, 1995), 93.

11. Sigmund Freud, *The Interpretation of Dreams,* in *The Standard Edition of the Complete Psychological Works of Sigmund Freud,* ed. James Strachey, 24 vols. (London: Hogarth, 1953–74), 4:312. The fourteen versions of the fall are summarized by Brian Wilkie and Mary Lynn Johnson, *Blake's Four Zoas: The Design of a Dream* (Cambridge, MA: Harvard University Press, 1978), 255–60.

12. *Milton* 24.71, E121.

CHAPTER 10: THE PROPHETIC CALL

1. *Milton* 2.25, E96 ("Mark well my words" is repeated at 3.5 and 4.20); *Jerusalem* 5.16–23, E147.

2. Samuel Johnson, *Life of Milton,* in *Lives of the English Poets,* ed. G. B. Hill, 3 vols. (Oxford: Clarendon, 1905), 1:177–78.

3. Stephen C. Behrendt makes this suggestion: *Reading William Blake* (London: Macmillan, 1992), 156.

4. *Milton* 2.16–22, E96; *Paradise Lost* 7.173.

5. Harold Bloom first advanced his theory in *The Anxiety of Influence* (New York: Oxford University

Press, 1973). A case for a more positive focus in Blake's response to Milton is argued by Joseph Anthony Wittreich Jr., *Angel of Apocalypse: Blake's Idea of Milton* (Madison: University of Wisconsin Press, 1975).

6. *Paradise Lost* 1.26.

7. *Milton* 40.35–41.4, E142.

8. *Milton* 16.47–50, E110, and 1, E95.

9. Laura Quinney suggests this interpretation in *William Blake on Self and Soul* (Cambridge, MA: Harvard University Press, 2009), 134.

10. See, e.g., Peter Ackroyd, *Blake* (New York: Alfred A. Knopf, 1996), 311, and *Illuminated Blake*, 248.

11. On astral bodies, see Nelson Hilton, *Literal Imagination: Blake's Vision of Words* (Berkeley: University of California Press, 1983), 203.

12. Blake to William Hayley, May 6, 1800, E705.

13. Genesis 1:3; *Jerusalem* 16.12–15, E160.

14. Percy Bysshe Shelley, *A Defense of Poetry* (1821); *Marriage* 14, E39.

15. Ben Jonson, *To the Memory of My Beloved, the Author Mr. William Shakespeare,* lines 58–62; James Joyce, *A Portrait of the Artist as a Young Man,* ed. Seamus Deane (London: Penguin, 1992), 275–76. The Joseph Wright painting described here was executed in 1771 and is in the Derby Museum.

16. *Jerusalem* 98.24, E257.

17. *Book of Los* 4.27–36, E92.

18. *Urizen* 10.15–18, E75; *Milton* 24.72–73, E121.

19. *Book of Los* 4.19–26, E92; 5.33–34, 41–47, E94.

20. The similarity of vocabulary is noted by Paul Miner, "'The Tyger': Genesis and Evolution in the Poetry of William Blake," *Criticism* 3 (1961), 67–68. More largely, see my chapter "Los, Mulciber, and the Tyger" in *Symbol and Truth in Blake's Myth* (Princeton, NJ: Princeton University Press, 1980), 373–81.

21. *Urizen* 10.35–39, E75, and 13.20–21, E77; *Illuminated Blake,* 193; David Bindman, *Blake as an Artist* (Oxford: Phaidon, 1977), 92.

22. *Urizen* 18.1–5, E78. On the medical theory, see Hilton, *Literal Imagination,* 83. My comments are indebted as well to W. J. T. Mitchell, *Blake's Composite Art: A Study of the Illuminated Poetry* (Princeton, NJ: Princeton University Press, 1978), 156.

23. Robert N. Essick, *William Blake, Printmaker* (Princeton, NJ: Princeton University Press, 1980), 129; *Book of Los* 5.47, E94. Copy E is in the Huntington Library in Pasadena, California.

24. *Jerusalem* 45.3, E194; James Joyce, *Ulysses* (New York: Random House, 1961), 37. Mitchell suggests the printer's smock: *Blake's Composite Art,* 51.

25. *Jerusalem* 1.9, E144.

26. Isaiah 21.11–12; John 10:9, as suggested by Wittreich, *Angel of Apocalypse,* 244. Erdman mentions also the wicket gate through which Bunyan's Christian begins his journey to salvation in *Pilgrim's Progress: Illuminated Blake,* 281.

27. Blake to Thomas Butts, Nov. 22, 1802, E721 (he says the poem was written "above a twelve-month ago").

28. *Milton* 22.4–14, E116–17. Udan-Adan is a formless chaos outside the humanized world.

29. W. J. T. Mitchell, "Style and Iconography in the Illustrations of Blake's Milton," *Blake Studies* 6 (1973): 67; Christopher Heppner, *Reading Blake's Designs* (Cambridge: Cambridge University Press, 1995), 220–21; Christopher Z. Hobson, *Blake and Homosexuality* (New York: Palgrave, 2000), 135.

30. Julia Ward Howe, *The Battle Hymn of the Republic; Vision of the Last Judgment*, E562.

CHAPTER 11: BREAKTHROUGH TO APOCALYPSE

1. Northrop Frye, *Fearful Symmetry: A Study of William Blake* (Princeton, NJ: Princeton University Press, 1947), 359, 351; *Jerusalem* 75.10–17, E230–31, and 72.17–20, E226.

2. *Jerusalem* 6.2–7.8, E148–49.

3. *Jerusalem* 52, E200; on the figure of the double, see Edward J. Rose, "Blake and the Double: The Spectre as *Doppelgänger*," *Colby Library Quarterly* 2 (1977), 127–39.

4. *Jerusalem* 10.51–55, E153–54.

5. *Jerusalem* 8.21–22, 39–40, E151, and 10.17–24, E153.

6. *My Spectre around me night and day*, E475.

7. *Four Zoas* 117.7–13, E386.

8. *Four Zoas* 119.4–13, 21–23, E388, and 136.21–22, E404.

9. *Milton* 42.36–43.1, E144; Robert N. Essick, "*Jerusalem* and Blake's Final Works," in *The Cambridge Companion to William Blake*, ed. Morris Eaves (Cambridge: Cambridge University Press, 2003), 251.

10. Ronald Britton, "The Preacher, the Poet, and the Psychoanalyst," in *Acquainted with the Night: Psychoanalysis and the Poetic Imagination*, ed. Hamish Canham and Carole Satyamurti (London: Karnac, 2003), 125–26.

11. Frye, *Fearful Symmetry*, 27; Britton, "Preacher," 130. Peter Otto assembles a remarkable mini-anthology of quotations from a long series of critics who echo Frye: *Constructive Vision and Visionary Deconstruction: Los, Eternity, and the Productions of Time in the Later Poetry of William Blake* (Oxford: Clarendon, 1991), 9–11.

12. *Jerusalem* 53.15–19, E203, and 72, E227.

13. *Jerusalem* 98.28–29, E257, and 36.58–60, E183.

14. John Harvey, "Blake's Art," *Cambridge Quarterly* 7 (1977): 138. Harvey refers to this image as "Stonehenge," which it is not.

15. *Descriptive Catalogue*, E542; *Jerusalem* 27, E171, and 47.7–11, E196. See Peter F. Fisher, "Blake and the Druids," *Journal of English and Germanic Philology* 58 (1959): 569–612.

16. *Jerusalem* 66.2–9, E218; see Nelson Hilton, *Literal Imagination: Blake's Vision of Words* (Berkeley: University of California Press, 1983), 71–72.

17. My comments are indebted to *Illuminated Blake*, 379, and to Morton Paley, Blake Trust, 1:297.

18. William Stukeley, *Abury: A Temple of the British Druids, with Some Others, Described* (1743), 54; *Europe* 10.23, E63.

19. W. J. T. Mitchell, *Blake's Composite Art: A Study of the Illuminated Poetry* (Princeton, NJ: Princeton University Press, 1978), 181.

20. Otto, *Constructive Vision and Visionary Deconstruction*, 217.

CHAPTER 12: "THE TORMENTS OF LOVE AND JEALOUSY"

1. *Four Zoas* 90.36, E370; *Blake Records*, 137, 140.

2. *Blake Records*, xxvi–xxvii; Aileen Ward, "William Blake and the Hagiographers," in *Biography and Source Studies*, ed. Frederick R. Karl (New York: AMS, 1994), 16–17. "Intense! naked!" is quoted from *America* 4.8, E53.

3. Gilchrist, 60.

4. Notebook, E473–75.

5. E469, E516; *Blake Records*, 290.

6. *Visions* 8.13, E51.

7. E470.

8. *Visions* iii, E45. Recent feminist critics have suspected more explicit allusions to the clitoris, to multiple orgasm, and to lesbian sex: Anne K. Mellor, "Sex, Violence, and Slavery: Blake and Wollstonecraft," *Huntington Library Quarterly* 58 (1995): 366; Helen P. Bruder, *William Blake and the Daughters of Albion* (London: Macmillan, 1997): 75; Helen P. Bruder and Tristanne Connolly, eds., *Queer Blake* (London: Palgrave Macmillan, 2010), Introduction, 12.

9. *Visions* 1.1–13, E45–46; see David Worrall, "William Blake and Erasmus Darwin's *Botanic Garden*," *Bulletin of the New York Public Library* 78 (1975), 402.

10. *Visions* 1.16–25, E46; Mary Wollstonecraft, *A Vindication of the Rights of Woman*, ed. Carol H. Poston (New York: Norton, 1975), 167.

11. *Visions* 5.3–6, 3.16–19, 7.16, E45–50.

12. *Visions* 7.23–29, E50; *Jerusalem* 69.15–17, E223; Bruder, *William Blake and the Daughters of Albion*, 82.

13. *Visions* 2.11–20, E46.

14. Christopher Frayling, "Fuseli's *The Nightmare*: Somewhere between the Sublime and the Ridiculous," in *Gothic Nightmares: Fuseli, Blake and the Romantic Imagination*, ed. Martin Myrone (London: Tate, 2006), 13.

15. Darwin is quoted by Nelson Hilton, "An Original Story," in *Unnam'd Forms: Blake and Textuality*, ed. Hilton and Thomas A. Vogler (Berkeley: University of California Press, 1986), 74. Bruder, *William Blake and the Daughters of Albion*, 70, quotes Fuseli's aphorism.

16. *Visions* 2.35–36, E47; *Europe* 10.28–29, E64.

17. Gilchrist, 334; *Blake Records*, 447.

18.   *Four Zoas* 34.63–65, E324.

19.   *Paradise Lost* 4.698–711.

20.   *Paradise Lost* 4.505–11; Rossetti, supplement to Gilchrist, 426.

21.   My comments are indebted to David Wagenknecht, *Blake's Night: William Blake and the Idea of Pastoral* (Cambridge, MA: Harvard University Press, 1973), 310; Pamela Dunbar, *William Blake's Illustrations to the Poetry of Milton* (Oxford: Clarendon, 1980), 56–60; and Bette Charlene Werner, *Blake's Vision of the Poetry of Milton* (Lewisburg, PA: Bucknell University Press, 1986), 71–72. I also repeat some thoughts from my *Symbol and Truth in Blake's Myth* (Princeton, NJ: Princeton University Press, 1980), 223–25.

22.   *Urizen* 20.2–25, E80; François, duc de La Rochefoucauld, *Maxims*, no. 324, trans. Leonard Tancock (London: Penguin, 1959), 79.

23.   *Four Zoas* 60.6–12, 19–22, E340–41; *Paradise Lost* 6.328–30.

24.   Friedrich Nietzsche, *Beyond Good and Evil*, in *The Philosophy of Nietzsche*, trans. Helen Zimmern (New York: Modern Library, 1954), aphorism 168, p. 470; *Europe* iii.1, 5–6, E60; Proverbs 9:17. There are fourteen surviving copies of *Europe;* no one knows why the Prologue was omitted from twelve of them.

25.   E467; *Jerusalem* 96.5–6, E361.

26.   See Jacques Lacarrière, *Les Gnostiques* (Paris: Gallimard, 1973), 99–100.

27.   *Jerusalem* 44.33–37, E193–94.

28.   *Jerusalem* 69.43–44, E223. Here is one attempt to explain the "cominglings": "The senses as we conceive them drop out to be replaced by faculties, which, as separate entities, themselves drop out to be replaced by a fourfold organ of imagination, the body of Albion." Thomas Frosch, *The Awakening of Albion: The Renovation of the Body in the Poetry of William Blake* (Ithaca, NY: Cornell University Press, 1974), 29.

29.   Sigmund Freud, "The Most Prevalent Form of Degradation in the Erotic Life," in *Sexuality and the Psychology of Love,* ed. Philip Rieff (New York: Collier, 1963), 68.

CHAPTER 13: THE FEMALE WILL

1.   Jean-Jacques Rousseau, *Confessions,* book 12, in *Oeuvres complètes,* ed. Marcel Raymond et al., vol. 1 (Paris: Gallimard, Bibliothèque de la Pléiade, 1959), 644; David Hume, *A Treatise of Human Nature,* 1.4.6.

2.   See Jean H. Hagstrum, *William Blake: Poet and Painter* (Chicago: University of Chicago Press, 1964), ch. 4, "The Emblem."

3.   *For the Sexes,* E268; *Tiriel* 8.11, E285; also *Europe* 5.6, E62; *Jerusalem* 30.57, E177. The complete series of emblems is reproduced in E259–67.

4.   E268.

5.   *Jerusalem* 93.8, E253; Genesis 30:14–16; John Donne, "Go and Catch a Falling Star," line 2.

6.   E269.

7. *To Tirzah*, E30; Wordsworth, *Ode: Intimations of Immortality*, line 207; John 2:4. David Erdman thinks *To Tirzah* was added to the *Songs* in 1803 (E800), and Andrew Lincoln agrees, Blake Trust, 2:18n. Joseph Viscomi argues that it may have been as early as 1795: *Blake and the Idea of the Book* (Princeton, NJ: Princeton University Press, 1993), 238–39.

8. *Jerusalem* 96.23–28, E256.

9. *Jerusalem* 30.23–26, E176; Helen P. Bruder, *William Blake and the Daughters of Albion* (London: Macmillan, 1997), 182, 36, 3. Elsewhere Bruder surveys recent studies and shows that the ambiguity of Blake's imagery has permitted critics to detect every possible attitude, pro and con, toward sex and gender: "Blake and Gender Studies," in *Palgrave Advances in William Blake Studies*, ed. Nicolas M. Williams (London: Palgrave Macmillan, 2006), 132–66.

10. Alicia Ostriker, "Desire Gratified and Ungratified: William Blake and Sexuality," *Blake: An Illustrated Quarterly* 16, no. 3 (Winter 1982–83), 156–65; annotations to Lavater, E596; *Milton* 36.31, E137. See Susan Fox, "The Female as Metaphor in William Blake's Poetry," in *Essential Articles for the Study of William Blake, 1970–1984*, ed. Nelson Hilton (Hamden, CT: Archon Books, 1986), 15–32, and Leo Damrosch, *Symbol and Truth in Blake's Myth* (Princeton, NJ: Princeton University Press, 1980), 75–90.

11. Northrop Frye, *Fearful Symmetry: A Study of William Blake* (Princeton, NJ: Princeton University Press, 1947), 73; Tristanne J. Connolly, *William Blake and the Body* (London: Palgrave Macmillan, 2002), x.

12. Samuel Johnson, *Life of Milton*, in *Lives of the English Poets*, ed. G. B. Hill, 3 vols. (Oxford: Clarendon, 1905), 1:157.

13. Susan Fox, *Poetic Form in Blake's Milton* (Princeton, NJ: Princeton University Press, 1976), xii.

14. *My Spectre around me night and day*, E475–77. The sequence of stanzas in this poem is far from certain; I follow Erdman's version.

15. *Four Zoas* 35.11–12, E325.

16. *Jerusalem* 64.12–17, E215; I follow W. H. Stevenson's explanation of Arthur: *Blake: The Complete Poems* (London: Pearson Longman, 2007), 804. Enion's song of experience is quoted at the end of chapter 4, page 95, above.

17. *Jerusalem* 68.10–15, 63–68, E221–22; David Fuller, *Blake's Heroic Argument* (London: Croom Helm, 1988), 205.

18. *Four Zoas* 26.5–13, E317; Brenda Webster, *Blake's Prophetic Psychology* (Athens: University of Georgia Press, 1983), 213–14.

19. Gilchrist, 348; *Blake Records*, 57.

20. E689. The tradition of detecting negative implications in Blake's Dante illustrations was inaugurated by Albert Roe in *Blake's Illustrations to the Divine Comedy* (Princeton, NJ: Princeton University Press, 1953).

21. Dante, *Purgatorio*, 29:91–96, 100–102, 106–14, 121–26 in *The Divine Comedy of Dante Alighieri*, trans. Courtney Langdon (Cambridge, MA: Harvard University Press, 1920), 345–47.

22. Dante, *Purgatorio*, 30:31–33, in Langdon, *Divine Comedy*, 353. Nelson Hilton gives an illuminat-

ing interpretation of various meanings of the vortex: *Literal Imagination: Blake's Vision of Words* (Berkeley: University of California Press, 1983), ch. 10.

23. *Four Zoas* 122.15–20, E391; *Jerusalem* 99.1–5, E258–59.

24. Robert N. Essick, "Blake and the Production of Meaning," in *Blake in the Nineties,* ed. Steve Clark and David Worrall (New York: St. Martin's, 1999), 13. On Blake's use of gold and silver, see Blake Trust, 1:15–16.

25. I follow *Illuminated Blake,* 282–83, and Blake Trust, 1:131–32.

26. *Jerusalem* 86.1–10, E244.

27. *Illuminated Blake,* 325; Connolly, *William Blake and the Body,* 43. My comments are indebted also to *Illuminated Blake,* 325, and Blake Trust, 1:181.

28. *Tintern Abbey,* lines 123–24; annotations to Wordsworth, E665–67; *Blake Records,* 430. M. H. Abrams's study is *Natural Supernaturalism: Tradition and Revolution in Romantic Literature* (New York: Norton, 1971).

29. *Four Zoas* 136.35–36, E404–5.

30. *Milton* 32.50–63, E131.

31. *Milton* 31.28–38, E130–31. On "nature" as a construct, see Kevin Hutchins, *Imagining Nature: Blake's Environmental Poetics* (Montreal: McGill-Queen's University Press, 2002).

32. Shakespeare, sonnet 29; Wordsworth, *The Prelude* 10.725–27 (1805 version).

33. Wallace Stevens, *The Poems of Our Climate,* in *Collected Poems* (New York: Knopf, 1955), 194.

CHAPTER 14: WRESTLING WITH GOD

1. *All Religions Are One,* E1–2.

2. *Marriage* 11, E38; *Everlasting Gospel,* E520; *Four Zoas* 100.10, E372.

3. *Laocoön,* E274; David V. Erdman, " 'Terrible Blake in His Pride': An Essay on *The Everlasting Gospel,*" in *From Sensibility to Romanticism,* ed. Frederick W. Hilles and Harold Bloom (New York: Oxford University Press, 1965), 336; *Everlasting Gospel,* E524.

4. *Marriage,* E37; annotations to Watson, E614.

5. Daniel 7:9; J. T. Smith, *Blake Records,* 620.

6. Proverbs 8:27; *Paradise Lost* 7.224–31.

7. *Urizen* 20.33–41, E80–81.

8. E516.

9. Voltaire, *Candide* ch. 25.

10. Robert N. Essick, *William Blake, Printmaker* (Princeton, NJ: Princeton University Press, 1980), 242.

11. Isaiah 33:6.

12. "Let the brothels of Paris be opened," E499; Morris Eaves, "The Title-Page of *The Book of Urizen,*" in *William Blake: Essays in Honour of Sir Geoffrey Keynes,* ed. Morton D. Paley and Michael Phillips

(Oxford: Clarendon, 1973), 225–30. Erdman makes the suggestion about the book of nature: *Illuminated Blake*, 183.

13. Genesis 1:10–31; *Urizen* 4.10–11, 23, E71–72.

14. Gilchrist, 130–31; G. E. Bentley, *Blake Books: Annotated Catalogues of William Blake's Writings in Illuminated Printing*, rev. ed. (Oxford: Clarendon, 1977), 176. The "eternal Now" is in the Lavater annotations, E592.

15. *Urizen* 4.24–40, E72; Ephesians 4:4–6; Galatians 3:13; Isaac Watts, *The Faithfulness of God in the Promises*, quoted by John Beer, *William Blake: A Literary Life* (London: Palgrave Macmillan, 2005), 9.

16. *Urizen* 23.23–27, E81; Jean H. Hagstrum, *William Blake: Poet and Painter* (Chicago: University of Chicago Press, 1964), 106. The tears are not visible in all copies of the poem.

17. *The Human Abstract*, E27; *Four Zoas* 80.9–13, 27, E355–56. Urizen's first line is repeated in *Jerusalem* 44.30, E193; see David V. Erdman, *Blake: Prophet against Empire*, 3rd ed. (Princeton, NJ: Princeton University Press, 1977), 368–69. On the larger relevance of this passage, see Nicholas Williams, *Ideology and Utopia in the Poetry of William Blake* (Cambridge: Cambridge University Press, 1998), 20–21.

18. Blake's debt to Alexander Geddes, who was reporting the work of the Lutheran theologian Johann Gottfried Eichhorn, is traced by Jerome J. McGann, "The Idea of an Indeterminate Text: Blake's Bible of Hell and Dr. Alexander Geddes," *Studies in Romanticism* 25 (1986), 303–24. The "indeterminate" in McGann's title refers to a suggestion that Blake may have reshuffled the sequence of plates in *The Book of Urizen* so as to imitate what happens when disparate elements get recombined.

19. *Blake Records*, 701.

20. Zechariah 4:10; *Four Zoas* 115.50, E381. For details on the Seven Eyes, see S. Foster Damon, *William Blake: His Philosophy and Symbols* (Boston: Houghton Mifflin, 1927), 388–89, and individual entries in Damon's *Blake Dictionary: The Ideas and Symbols of William Blake* (reprint ed., Boulder, CO: Shambhala, 1979; orig. publ. Brown University Press, 1965). Northrop Frye also gives a helpful account: *Fearful Symmetry: A Study of William Blake* (Princeton, NJ: Princeton University Press, 1947), 128–34.

21. Hagstrum, *Blake: Poet and Painter*, 127.

22. Christopher Heppner, *Reading Blake's Designs* (Cambridge: Cambridge University Press, 1995), 49–53. On the Boreas picture, see C. H. Collins Baker, "The Sources of Blake's Pictorial Expression," in *The Visionary Hand: Essays for the Study of William Blake's Art and Aesthetics*, ed. Robert N. Essick (Los Angeles: Hennessey and Ingalls, 1973), 124–26.

23. E. H. Gombrich, *The Story of Art*, 16th ed. (London: Phaidon, 1995), 312.

24. *Milton* 29.64–65, E128; Samuel Johnson, *A Dictionary of the English Language* (1755).

25. *Blake Records*, 52n; *Jerusalem* 48.9–11, E196; Job 1:1, 11–12, 42:12.

26. *Blake Records*, 439; John Harvey, "Blake's Art," *Cambridge Quarterly* 7 (1977), 144. Full details of

the exacting process of engraving and printing are given by Michael Phillips, "The Printing of Blake's *Illustrations of the Book of Job*," *Print Quarterly* 22 (2005), 138–59.

27. On the Hebrew, see Christopher Rowland, *Blake and the Bible* (New Haven: Yale University Press, 2010), 43.

28. *Blake Records*, 652.

29. Job 19:23–27.

30. Ben F. Nelms has studied in detail "Text and Design in *Illustrations of the Book of Job*," in *Blake's Visionary Forms Dramatic* (Princeton, NJ: Princeton University Press, 1970), 336–58.

31. Revelation 15:4; *Marriage* 27, E45; *Visions* 8.10, E51; *America* 8.13, E54; *Four Zoas* 34.80, E324; Rudolf Otto, *The Idea of the Holy*, trans. John W. Harvey (Oxford: Oxford University Press, 1950), 28; *Four Zoas* 3, E300, quoting Ephesians 6:12.

32. E269; Isaiah 14:12.

33. *Marriage* 4, E34; see Morton D. Paley, "The Figure of the Garment in *The Four Zoas, Milton*, and *Jerusalem*," in *Blake's Sublime Allegory: Essays on* The Four Zoas, Milton, Jerusalem, ed. Stuart Curran and Joseph Anthony Wittreich Jr. (Madison: University of Wisconsin Press, 1973), 119–39.

34. *For the Sexes*, E269; Edward Young, *Night Thoughts* (1742–45), final line of book 8; *Blake Records*, 427.

35. My comments are indebted to Nelson Hilton, *Literal Imagination: Blake's Vision of Words* (Berkeley: University of California Press, 1983), 166, and to Morton D. Paley, *The Traveller in the Evening: The Last Works of William Blake* (Oxford: Oxford University Press, 2003), 17–18.

36. Blake to Thomas Butts, Nov. 22, 1802, E720.

37. *Blake Records*, 421.

38. *Blake Records*, 453; *Jerusalem* 35.25–26, E181; *For the Sexes*, E259.

39. *Four Zoas* 106.6, E379; "giving himself for the nations" is at E671. My comments are indebted to *Illuminated Blake*, 355; W. J. T. Mitchell, *Blake's Composite Art: A Study of the Illuminated Poetry* (Princeton, NJ: Princeton University Press, 1978), 210; John E. Grant, "Jesus and the Powers That Be in Blake's Designs for Young's *Night Thoughts*," in *Blake and His Bibles*, ed. David V. Erdman (West Cornwall, CT: Locust Hill, 1990), 105–7; and Morton D. Paley, *The Continuing City: William Blake's Jerusalem* (Oxford: Clarendon, 1983), 113–18.

40. Blake to Butts, Apr. 25, 1803, E728; *Jerusalem* 97.5–6, E256.

41. John Harvey, "Blake's Art," *Cambridge Quarterly* 7 (1977), 136; Morton Paley, Blake Trust, 1:296, 15.

42. Tom Hayes, "William Blake's Androgynous Ego-Ideal," *ELH* 71 (2004), 156; Susanne Sklar, *Blake's Jerusalem as Visionary Theatre* (Oxford: Oxford University Press, 2011), 248, quoting *Jerusalem* 69.24, 79.44, E223, 235.

43. Anthony Blunt, *The Art of William Blake* (New York: Columbia University Press, 1959), 81; *Blake Records*, 392; Luke 15:20–24.

CHAPTER 15: THE TRAVELER IN THE EVENING

1. "Blake's London," http://www.tate.org.uk/learn/online-resources/william-blake/william-bla kes-london.

2. Blake to William Hayley, Dec. 4, 1804, E758; notebook memoranda, E694.

3. *Jerusalem* 17.59-63, E162.

4. *Blake Records*, 320.

5. *Jerusalem* 3, E145; Paley, Blake Trust, 1:12. On this remarkable plate, see Joseph Viscomi, *Blake and the Idea of the Book* (Princeton, NJ: Princeton University Press, 1993), 339; Jerome J. McGann, *Towards a Literature of Knowledge* (Chicago: University of Chicago Press, 1989), 11-12, 37; and Tristanne J. Connolly, *William Blake and the Body* (London: Palgrave Macmillan, 2002), 11-12.

6. *Blake Records*, 753; on the neighborhood, see Angus Whitehead, "'Humble but Respectable': Recovering the Neighbourhood Surrounding William and Catherine Blake's Last Residence, No. 3 Fountain Court, Strand, c. 1820-27," *University of Toronto Quarterly* 80 (2011), 858-79.

7. *Blake Records*, 387.

8. *Blake Records*, 402.

9. Gilchrist, 319, 322; *Blake Records*, 405, 680.

10. *Blake Records*, 438; Blake to John Linnell, Aug. 1, 1826, E780. On the illnesses, see Aileen Ward, "William Blake and the Hagiographers," in *Biography and Source Studies,* ed. Frederick R. Karl, vol. 1 (New York: AMS, 1994), 1-24; and Lane Robson and Joseph Viscomi, "Blake's Death," *Blake: An Illustrated Quarterly* 30, no. 1 (Summer 1996), 36-49.

11. *Blake Records*, 453; Blake to George Cumberland, Apr. 12, 1827, E783; William Upcott's album, E698.

12. E269.

13. *Blake Records*, 269.

14. "And his legs carried it like a long fork," E504.

15. *Blake Records*, 682, 459, 464. On the unlikelihood that Blake sang on his deathbed, see the articles cited in n. 10, above.

16. *Blake Records*, 493.

17. *Blake Records*, 559, 731-32; *Marriage* 13, E39.

18. Gilchrist, 384-85.

19. Joyce Cary, *The Horse's Mouth* (New York: New York Review of Books, 1999), 81; Samuel Beckett, *Endgame* (New York: Grove, 1958), 38; T. S. Eliot, "Blake," in *The Sacred Wood,* 6th ed. (London: Methuen, 1948), 151, 156-58.

20. Michael Welland, *Sand: The Never-Ending Story* (Berkeley: University of California Press, 2009), xiii.

21. *Descriptive Catalogue,* E550; *Vision of the Last Judgment,* E566; *Marriage* 6-7, E35.

ILLUSTRATION CREDITS

FIGURES

Note: Plate numbers from Blake's illuminated books, as given here, are those in the particular copies being reproduced. They correspond with the "object" numbers in the Blake Archive but often differ from the sequence of plates in David Erdman's text.

Frontispiece: Map by Bill Nelson.

1. *Gravure, en taille-douce, en manière noire, etc.* (Paris, 1767). Houghton Library, Harvard University, f Typ 715.67.435.
2. Etching by Thomas Stothard. Collection of Robert N. Essick. Used with permission.
3. *Democritus.* Illustration from Johann Caspar Lavater, *Essays on Physiognomy, Designed to Promote the Knowledge and the Love of Mankind* (London, 1789). Houghton Library, Harvard University, HOU F Typ 705.89.513 (A).
4. *Sense Runs Wild.* Illustration for Edward Young, *Night-Thoughts,* page 46. Collection of Robert N. Essick. Copyright © 2014 William Blake Archive. Used with permission.
5. *Catherine Blake,* by William Blake. © Tate, London 2014.
6. *William Blake,* engraving after a painting by Thomas Phillips. Frontispiece to Robert Blair, *The Grave* (London, 1808). Houghton Library, Harvard University, HEW 1.13.5.
7. William Blake, probable self-portrait. Collection of Robert N. Essick. Used with permission.
8. *The Man Who Taught Blake Painting.* © Tate, London 2014.
9. *America: A Prophecy.* Fragment of the original copperplate for plate 3. By permission of the National Gallery of Art, Washington.

10. *America: A Prophecy*, copy E, plate 3. Lessing J. Rosenwald Collection, Library of Congress. Copyright © 2014 William Blake Archive. Used with permission.

11. A rolling press. Illustration from Abraham Bosse, *De la manière de graver à l'eau forte et au burin* (Paris, 1758). Houghton Library, Harvard University, HOU GEN Typ 715.58.230.

12. *Father Thames*. Illustration for Thomas Gray's *Ode on a Distant Prospect of Eton College*. Yale Center for British Art.

13. *Songs of Innocence and of Experience*, copy L, plate 1. Yale Center for British Art.

14. *Songs of Innocence and of Experience*, copy L, plate 24. Yale Center for British Art.

15. *Songs of Innocence and of Experience*, copy L, plate 30. Yale Center for British Art.

16. *Songs of Innocence and of Experience*, copy L, plate 29. Yale Center for British Art.

17. *Songs of Innocence and of Experience*, copy L, plate 39. Yale Center for British Art.

18. *Songs of Innocence and of Experience*, copy Z, plate 32. Lessing J. Rosenwald Collection, Library of Congress. Copyright © 2014 William Blake Archive. Used with permission.

19. Manuscript page from Blake's notebook. Copyright © The British Library Board, Add. MS 49,460, f. 56.

20. *Songs of Innocence and of Experience*, copy L, plate 41. Yale Center for British Art.

21. *Songs of Innocence and of Experience*, copy N, plate 21. Reproduced by permission of The Huntington Library, San Marino, California.

22. *Albion Rose* (Glad Day), second state. Lessing J. Rosenwald Collection, Library of Congress.

23. Paris boutique. Photo by Leo Damrosch.

24. *America: A Prophecy*, copy E, plate 4. Lessing J. Rosenwald Collection, Library of Congress. Copyright © 2014 William Blake Archive. Used with permission.

25. *America: A Prophecy*, copy E, plate 8. Lessing J. Rosenwald Collection, Library of Congress. Copyright © 2014 William Blake Archive. Used with permission.

26. *America: A Prophecy*, copy E, plate 12. Lessing J. Rosenwald Collection, Library of Congress. Copyright © 2014 William Blake Archive. Used with permission.

27. *America: A Prophecy*, copy E, plate 10. Lessing J. Rosenwald Collection, Library of Congress. Copyright © 2014 William Blake Archive. Used with permission.

28. *America: A Prophecy*, copy E, plate 13. Lessing J. Rosenwald Collection, Library of Congress. Copyright © 2014 William Blake Archive. Used with permission.

29. *Newton*. Sculpture by Eduardo Paolozzi. Photo by Leo Damrosch.

30. Blake's cottage at Felpham. By kind permission of Jackson Stops and Staff.

31. No. 23 Hercules Buildings. Etching by Frederick Adcock. From Arthur S. Adcock, *Famous Houses and Literary Shrines of London* (London: Dent, 1912).

32. *The Whirlwind: Ezekiel's Vision*. Pen and watercolor. Museum of Fine Arts, Boston.

33. *Milton*, copy C, plate 1. New York Public Library.

34. *Milton*, copy C, plate 31. New York Public Library.

35. *Milton*, copy C, plate 36. New York Public Library.

36. *Jerusalem*, copy E, plate 1. Yale Center for British Art.

37. *Jerusalem*, copy E, plate 100. Yale Center for British Art.

38. *Avebury*. Illustration from William Stukeley, *Abury, a Temple of the British Druids* (London, 1743). Houghton Library, Harvard University, F Arc 855.214.

39. Manuscript page from *Vala*, page 86. Copyright © The British Library Board, Add. MS 39764, f. 48v.

40. *For Children: The Gates of Paradise*, copy D, plate 1. Lessing J. Rosenwald Collection, Library of Congress. Copyright © 2014 William Blake Archive. Used with permission.

41. *For Children: The Gates of Paradise*, copy D, plate 3. Lessing J. Rosenwald Collection, Library of Congress. Copyright © 2014 William Blake Archive. Used with permission.

42. *For Children: The Gates of Paradise*, copy D, plate 18. Lessing J. Rosenwald Collection, Library of Congress. Copyright © 2014 William Blake Archive. Used with permission.

43. Manuscript page from *Vala*, page 26. Copyright © The British Library Board, Add. MS 39764, f. 48v.

44. *Jerusalem*, copy E, plate 32. Yale Center for British Art.

45. *Wisdom*. Sculpture by Lee Lawrie, GE Building, Rockefeller Center, New York. Photo by David Damrosch.

46. *The Book of Urizen*, copy G, plate 1. Lessing J. Rosenwald Collection, Library of Congress. Copyright © 2014 William Blake Archive. Used with permission.

47. *The Book of Urizen*, copy G, plate 11. Lessing J. Rosenwald Collection, Library of Congress. Copyright © 2014 William Blake Archive. Used with permission.

48. *Boreas*. Engraving by James Basire. Illustration from James Stuart and Nicholas Revett, *The Antiquities of Athens*, vol. 1 (London, 1762). Houghton Library, Harvard University, HOU GEN Arc705.5*.

49. *The Book of Job*, plate 11, "Job's Evil Dreams." Collection of Robert N. Essick. Copyright © 2014 William Blake Archive. Used with permission.

50. *For the Sexes: The Gates of Paradise*, copy D, plate 21. The Pierpont Morgan Library, New York. PML 63936. Photography by Graham S. Haber, 2014.

51. No. 17 South Molton Street. Etching by Frederick Adcock. From Arthur S. Adcock, *Famous Houses and Literary Shrines of London* (London: Dent, 1912).

52. *Jerusalem*, copy E, plate 3. Yale Center for British Art.

53. Life mask of William Blake. Copyright © Joanna Kane, from *The Somnambulists: Photographic Portraits from before Photography* (Stockport, England: Dewi Lewis, 2008).

54. William Blake, pencil sketch by John Linnell. © The Fitzwilliam Museum, Cambridge.

55. *For Children: The Gates of Paradise*, copy D, plate 16. Lessing J. Rosenwald Collection, Library of Congress. Copyright © 2014 William Blake Archive. Used with permission.

56. *Deaths Door* (1805). Collection of Robert N. Essick. Copyright © 2014 William Blake Archive. Used with permission.

PLATES

Note: plate numbers from Blake's illuminated books, as given here, are those in the particular copies being reproduced. They correspond with the "object" numbers in the Blake Archive but often differ from the sequence of plates in David Erdman's text.

1. *Pity.* © Tate, London 2014.

2. *A Sunshine Holiday.* Illustration for John Milton's *L'Allegro.* The Pierpont Morgan Library, New York, 1949.4:4. Purchased with the assistance of the Fellows with the special support of Mrs. Landon K. Thorne and Mr. Paul Mellon.

3. *Songs of Innocence and of Experience,* copy Z, plate 3. Lessing J. Rosenwald Collection, Library of Congress. Copyright © 2014 William Blake Archive. Used with permission.

4. *Songs of Innocence and of Experience,* copy Z, plate 25. Lessing J. Rosenwald Collection, Library of Congress. Copyright © 2014 William Blake Archive. Used with permission.

5. *Songs of Innocence and of Experience,* copy Z, plate 11. Lessing J. Rosenwald Collection, Library of Congress. Copyright © 2014 William Blake Archive. Used with permission.

6. *Songs of Innocence and of Experience,* copy Z, plate 12. Lessing J. Rosenwald Collection, Library of Congress. Copyright © 2014 William Blake Archive. Used with permission.

7. *Songs of Innocence and of Experience,* copy C, plate 2. Lessing J. Rosenwald Collection, Library of Congress. Copyright © 2014 William Blake Archive. Used with permission.

8. *Songs of Innocence and of Experience,* copy Z, plate 39. Lessing J. Rosenwald Collection, Library of Congress. Copyright © 2014 William Blake Archive. Used with permission.

9. *Songs of Innocence and of Experience,* copy F, plate 42. Yale Center for British Art.

10. *Songs of Innocence and of Experience,* copy Z, plate 42. Lessing J. Rosenwald Collection, Library of Congress. Copyright © 2014 William Blake Archive. Used with permission.

11. *Albion Rose.* Reproduced by permission of The Huntington Library, San Marino, California.

12. *The Marriage of Heaven and Hell,* copy D, plate 1. Lessing J. Rosenwald Collection, Library of Congress. Copyright © 2014 William Blake Archive. Used with permission.

13. *The Marriage of Heaven and Hell,* copy D, plate 21. Lessing J. Rosenwald Collection, Library of Congress. Copyright © 2014 William Blake Archive. Used with permission.

14. *America: A Prophecy,* copy M, plate 3. Yale Center for British Art.

15. *Europe: A Prophecy,* copy E, plate 2. Lessing J. Rosenwald Collection, Library of Congress. Copyright © 2014 William Blake Archive. Used with permission.

16. *America: A Prophecy,* copy M, plate 9. Yale Center for British Art.

17. *Europe: A Prophecy,* copy A, plate 10. Yale Center for British Art.

18. *Newton.* © Tate, London 2014.

19. *Hyperion,* illustration to Thomas Gray, *The Progress of Poesy.* Yale Center for British Art.

20. *Milton*, copy D, plate 16. Lessing J. Rosenwald Collection, Library of Congress. Copyright © 2014 William Blake Archive. Used with permission.
21. *The Book of Urizen*, copy A, plate 14. Yale Center for British Art.
22. *The Book of Urizen*, copy F, plate 17. Houghton Library, Harvard University.
23. *The Song of Los*, copy E, plate 4. Reproduced by permission of The Huntington Library, San Marino, California.
24. *Milton*, copy D, plate 47. Lessing J. Rosenwald Collection, Library of Congress. Copyright © 2014 William Blake Archive. Used with permission.
25. *Jerusalem*, copy E, plate 6. Yale Center for British Art.
26. *Jerusalem*, copy E, plate 70. Yale Center for British Art.
27. *Visions of the Daughters of Albion*, copy G, plate 3. Houghton Library, Harvard University.
28. *Visions of the Daughters of Albion*, copy G, plate 6. Houghton Library, Harvard University.
29. Henry Fuseli, *The Nightmare*, oil on canvas. Detroit Institute of Arts / Bridgeman Art Library.
30. *Visions of the Daughters of Albion*, copy G, plate 2. Houghton Library, Harvard University.
31. *Satan Watching the Caresses of Adam and Eve.* Pen and watercolor. Museum of Fine Arts, Boston.
32. *The Book of Urizen*, copy C, plate 18. Yale Center for British Art.
33. *Milton*, copy C, plate 39. New York Public Library.
34. *Beatrice Addressing Dante from the Car.* © Tate, London 2014.
35. *Jerusalem*, copy E, plate 2. Yale Center for British Art.
36. *The Ancient of Days: Europe: A Prophecy*, copy E, plate 1. Lessing J. Rosenwald Collection, Library of Congress. Copyright © 2014 William Blake Archive. Used with permission.
37. *The Book of Urizen*, copy F, plate 5. Houghton Library, Harvard University.
38. *Elohim Creating Adam.* © Tate, London 2014.
39. *Jerusalem*, copy E, plate 76. Yale Center for British Art.
40. *Jerusalem*, copy E, plate 99. Yale Center for British Art.

INDEX

Page numbers in *italic* type indicate images.